WHAT
DOES THIS
BUTTON
DO?

BRUCE DICKINSON

An Autobiography

HarperCollins*Publishers*

HarperCollins*Publishers*
1 London Bridge Street
London SE1 9GF

www.harpercollins.co.uk

First published by HarperCollins*Publishers* 2017

3 5 7 9 10 8 6 4 2

A catalogue record of this book is
available from the British Library

HB ISBN 978-0-00-817243-5
PB ISBN 978-0-00-817247-3

Printed and bound in Great Britain by
CPI Group (UK) Ltd, Croydon

To Paddy, Austin, Griffin and Kia.

If eternity should fail, you will still be there.

Contents

Foreword

I had been circling for two hours over Murmansk, but the Russians would not let us land.

'Landing permission denied,' said in the best *Star Trek* original-series Mr Chekov accent.

I didn't know if this controller was an Iron Maiden fan, but he would never have believed me anyway; a rock star moonlighting as an airline pilot – incredible. In any case, I didn't have Eddie on board and this wasn't *Ed Force One*. It was a fishing expedition.

A Boeing 757 from Astraeus Airlines with 200 empty seats and me as first officer. There were only 20 passengers from Gatwick to Murmansk: lots of men called John Smith, close personal protection, all of them armed to the teeth. Not that Lord Heseltine needed it. He was pretty good at swinging the mace around when he had to. Then there was Max Hastings, former editor of the *Daily Telegraph*. He was on board too. I wondered if the Soviet controller read any of his leader columns. I thought not.

'What sort of fish are there in Murmansk?' I had enquired of one of the John Smiths.

'Special fish,' he deadpanned.

'Big fish?' I offered.

'Very big,' he concluded as he left the cockpit.

Murmansk was the headquarters of the Soviet Northern Fleet. Lord Heseltine was a former Secretary of State for

Defence, and what Max Hastings didn't know about the world's armed forces wasn't worth printing.

The world below us was secret and obscured, submerged beneath a cotton-wool bed of low cloud. To negotiate, I had a radio and an old Nokia mobile phone. Incredibly, it got a signal halfway round each holding pattern, and I could text our airline operations who would talk to Moscow via the British Embassy. No sat phone, no GPS, no iPad, no Wi-Fi.

As James Bond says to Q at the beginning of *Skyfall*: 'A gun and a radio. Not exactly Christmas, is it?'

After two hours of going round in circles, physical and metaphorical, the rules of the game changed: 'Unless you go away, we will shoot you down.'

One day, I thought as we turned and headed towards Ivalo in Finland, I should write a book about this.

Born in '58

The events that aggregate to form a personality interact in odd and unpredictable ways. I was an only child, brought up as far as five by my grandparents. It takes a while to figure out the dynamic forces in families, and it took me a long while for the penny to drop. My upbringing, I realised, was a mixture of guilt, unrequited love and jealousy, but all overlaid with an overwhelming sense of duty, of obligation to do the very best. I now realise that there wasn't a great deal of affection going on, but there was a reasonable attention to detail. I could have done a lot worse given the circumstances.

My real mother was a young mum married in the nick of time to a slightly older soldier. His name was Bruce. My maternal grandfather had been assigned to watch over their courting activities, but he was neither mentally nor morally judgemental enough to be up to the task. I suspect his sympathies secretly lay with the young lovers. Not so my grandmother, whose only child was being stolen by a ruffian, not even a northerner, but an interloper from the flat lands and seagull-spattered desolation of the Norfolk coast. East England: the fens, marshes and bogs – a world that has for centuries been the home of the non-conforming, the anarchist, the sturdy beggar and of hard-won existence clawed from the reclaimed land.

My mother was petite, worked in a shoe shop and had won a scholarship to the Royal Ballet School, but her mother had forbidden her to go to London. Denied the chance to live her dream, she took the next dream that came along, and with that came me. I would stare at a picture of her, on pointe, probably aged about 14. It seemed impossible that this was my mother, a pixie-like starlet full of naïve joy. The picture on the mantelpiece represented all that could have been. Now, the dancing had gone out of her, and now it was all about duty – and the odd gin and tonic.

My parents were so young that it is impossible for me to say what I would have done had the roles been reversed. Life was about education and getting ahead, beyond working class, but working multiple jobs. The only sin was not trying hard.

My father was very serious about most things, and he tried very hard. One of a family of six, he was the offspring of a farm girl sold into service aged 12 and a raffish local builder and motorcycle-riding captain of the football team in Great Yarmouth. The great love of my father's life was machinery and the world of mechanisms, timing, design and draughtsmanship. He loved cars, and loved to drive, although the laws relating to speed he deemed inapplicable to himself, along with seatbelts and driving drunk. After losing his driving licence, he volunteered for the army. Volunteers got paid better than conscripted men and the army didn't seem picky about who drove their jeeps.

Driving licence (military) instantly restored, his engineering talents and tidy hand led to a job drawing up the plans for the end of the world. Around a table in Düsseldorf he would carefully draw the circles of megadeaths expected in the anticipated Cold War apocalypse. The rest of his time was spent drinking whisky to drown the boredom and the hopelessness of it all, one imagines. While still enlisted, this beefy Norfolk swimming champion – butterfly, no less – swept my waif-like ballerina mum off her feet.

As the unwanted offspring of the man who stole her only daughter, I represented the spawn of Satan for my grandmother

Lily, but for my grandfather Austin I was the closest he would ever have to a son of his own. For the first five years of my life, they were de facto *in loco parentis*. As early childhood goes, it was pretty decent. There were long walks in the woods, rabbit holes, haunting flatland winter sunsets and sparkling frost, shimmering under purple skies.

My real parents had been travelling and working in a succession of nightclubs with their performing-dog act – as in poodles, hoops and leotards. Go figure.

The number 52 on the house at Manton Crescent was painted white. It was a standard, brick-built, semi-detached council house. Manton Colliery was a deep coal mine, and it was where my grandfather worked.

My grandfather had been a miner since the age of 13. Too small to be legal, he cunningly and barefacedly lied about his age and his height, which, like mine, was not very much. To get round the regulation that said you were tall enough to go 'down the pit if your lantern did not trail on the ground by its lanyard while suspended from the belt' he simply put a couple of knots in it. He came close to going to war, but got as far as the garden gate. He was in the Territorial Army, a part-time volunteer, but as coal mining was a reserved occupation he didn't have to fight.

So he stood in his uniform, ready, as his platoon marched off to fight in France. It was one of these *Back to the Future* moments, when opening that garden gate and going to war along with his mates would have prevented a lot of things happening, including me. My grandmother stood defiant, hands on hips in the front doorway. 'If you bloody go I won't be here when you get back,' she said. He stayed. Most of his regiment never came back.

With a miner for a grandfather, we got the council home and free coal delivered, and the art of making the coal fire that heated the house has turned me into a lifelong pyromaniac. We did not possess a telephone, a refrigerator, central heating, a car or an inside toilet. We borrowed other people's fridges and had a small larder, dank and cold, which I avoided like the plague. Cooking was two electric hobs and a coal-fired oven, although electricity was seen as a luxury to be avoided at all costs. We had a vacuum cleaner and my favourite device, a mangle – two rollers that squeezed the water from washed clothing. A giant handle turned the machine over as sheets, shirts and trousers flopped out into a bucket after being squeezed through its rollers.

There was a plastic portable bath for me, as my grandfather would arrive home clean from the pit washrooms. On occasions he would come back from the pub, stinking of beer and onions, and crawl into bed next to me, snoring loudly. In the light from the moon through the wafer-thin curtains, I could see the blue scars that adorned his back: souvenirs of a life underground.

We had a shed in which bits of wood would be hammered and banged, to what end I have no idea, but for me it was a place to hide. It became a spaceship or a castle or a submarine. Two old railway sleepers in our small yard served as a sailing boat, and I fished repeatedly from the side catching sharks that lived in the crevices of the concrete. There was an allotment and some short-lived chrysanthemums that went up in smoke one bonfire night after a rocket went astray.

We had no pets, save a goldfish called Peter who lived for a suspiciously long time.

But one thing we did have was ... a television. The presence of this television refocused the whole of my early existence. Through the lens of the TV screen – seven or eight inches across, black and white and grainy – came the wide world. Valve-driven, it took minutes to warm up, and there was a long, slow dying of the light to a singularity when it was switched off, which became a watchable event in its own right.

We hosted visitors who came to look at it, caress it and not even watch it – it had such mystique. On the front were occult buttons and dials that turned like great combination locks to select the only two channels available.

The outside world, that is to say anywhere outside Worksop, was accessed primarily by gossip – or the *Daily Mirror*. The newspaper was always used to make the fire and I usually saw the news two days late, shortly before it was consigned to the inferno. When Yuri Gagarin became the first man to go into space I remember staring at the picture and thinking, *How can we burn that?* I folded it up and kept it.

If gossip or old newspaper wouldn't do, the world outside might require a phone call. The big red phone box served as a cough, cold, flu, bubonic plague, 'you name it you'll catch it' distribution centre for the neighbourhood. There was always a queue at peak hours, and a hellish combination of buttons to press and rotary dials in order to make a call, with large buckets of change required for long conversations.

It was like a very inconvenient version of Twitter, with words rationed by money and the vengeful stares of the other 20 people waiting in line to inhale the smoke-and-spit-infused mouthpiece and press the hair-oiled and sweat-coated Bakelite earpiece to the side of their head.

There were certain codes of conduct and regimes to obey in Worksop, although etiquette around the streets was very relaxed. There was little crime and virtually no traffic. Both my grandparents walked everywhere, or caught the bus. Walking five or ten miles each way across fields to go to work was just something they were brought up to do, and so I did it too.

The whole neighbourhood was in a permanent state of shift work. Upstairs curtains closed in daytime meant 'Tiptoe past – coal miner asleep'. Front room curtains closed: 'Hurry past – dead person laid out for inspection'. This ghoulish practice was quite popular, if my grandmother was to be believed. I would sit in our front room – permanently freezing, deathly quiet, bedecked with horse brasses and candlesticks that constantly required polishing – and imagine where the body might lie.

During the evening the atmosphere changed, and home turned into a living Gary Larson cartoon. Folding wooden chairs turned the place into a pop-up hair salon, with blue as the only colour and beehive the only game in town. Women with vast knees and polythene bags over their heads sat slowly evaporating under heat lamps as my grandmother roasted, curled and produced that awful smell of dank hair and industrial shampoo.

My escape committee was my uncle John. He forms quite an important part of what button to push next.

First of all, he wasn't my uncle. He was my godfather – my grandfather's best mate – and he was in the Royal Air Force and had fought in the war. As a bright working-class boy he was hoovered up by an expanding RAF, which required a whole host of technological skills that were in short supply, as one of Trenchard's apprentices. An electrical engineer during the Siege of Malta, Flight Sergeant John Booker survived some of the most nail-biting bombardments of the war on an island Hitler was determined to crush at all costs.

I have his medals and a copy of his service Bible, annotated accordingly with verses to give support at a time when things must have been unimaginably grim. And there are pictures, one with him in full flying gear, about to stow away on a night-flying operation, which, as ground crew, was utterly unnecessary – done just for the hell of it.

While I sat on his knee he regaled me with aircraft stories and I touched his silvered Spitfire apprentice model, and a brass four-engined Liberator, with plexiglass propeller disc melted from a downed Spitfire and a green felt pad under its wooden plinth, the material cut from a shattered snooker table in a bombed-out Maltese club. He spoke of airships, of the history of engineering in Britain, of jet engines, Vulcan bombers, naval battles and test pilots. Inspired, I would sit for hours making model aircraft like many a boy of my generation, fiddling with transfers – later upgraded to decals, which sounded so much cleverer. It was a miracle any of my plastic pilots ever survived combat at all, given the fact that their entire bodies were encased in glue and their canopies covered in opaque fingerprints. The model shop in Worksop where I built my plastic air force was, amazingly, still there the last time I looked, on the occasion of my grandmother's funeral.

Because Uncle John was a technical sort of chap, he had a self-built pond the size of the Möhne Dam, full of red goldfish and cunningly protected by chicken wire, and he drove a rather splendid Ford Consul, which was immaculate, of course. It was this car that transported me to my first airshow in the early sixties, when health and safety was for chickens and the term 'noise abatement' had not even entered the vocabulary.

Earthquaking jets like the Vulcan would shatter roofs performing vertical rolls with their giant delta wings while the English Electric Lightning, basically a supersonic firework with a man perched astride it, would streak past inverted, with the tail nearly scoring the runway. Powerful stuff.

Uncle John introduced me to the world of machinery and mechanisms, but I was equally as drawn to the steam trains that still plied their trade through Worksop station. The footbridge and the station today are virtually unchanged to those of my childhood. I swear that the same timbers I stood on as a boy still exist. The smoke, steam and ash clouds which enveloped me mingled with the tarry breath of bitumen to sting my nostrils. I walked to and from the station recently. I thought it was a bloody long way, but as a child it felt like nothing. The smell still lingers.

In short order, I would have settled for steam-train driver, then maybe fighter pilot ... and if I got bored with that, astronaut was always a possibility, at least in my dreams. Nothing in childhood is ever wasted.

Somewhere, the fun has to stop, and so I went to school. Manton Primary was the local school for coalminers' kids. Before it was closed, it achieved a level of notoriety with *Daily Mail* readers as the school where five-year-olds beat up the teachers. Well, I don't recollect beating up any teachers, but I was given the gift of wings and also boxing lessons, after a fracas over who should play the role of Angel in the nativity play. I was lusting after those wings but instead got a good kicking in the melee that continued outside the school gates. The outcome was far from satisfactory. When I returned from school, dishevelled and clothes ripped, my grandfather sat me down and opened my hands, which were soft and pudgy. His hands were rough, like sandpaper, with bits of calloused skin stuck like coconut flakes to the deep lines that opened up as he spread his palms in front of me. I remember the glint in his eye.

'Now, make a fist, lad,' he said.

So I did.

'Not like that – you'll break your thumb. Like this.'

So he showed me.

'Like this?' I said.

'Aye. Now hit my hand.'

Not exactly *The Karate Kid* – no standing on one leg on the end of a boat, no 'wax on, wax off' Hollywood moment. But after a week or so he took me to one side, and very gently, but with a steely determination in his voice, said, 'Now go and find the lad that did it. And sort him out.'

So I did.

I think it was about 20 minutes before I was dragged away by the teacher and frogmarched home with a very firm grip.

My boxing lessons had been rather too effective, and my judgement, at the age of four or five, rather less than discerning.

The ratatat-tat of the letterbox elicited an impassive grandfather: slippers, white singlet and baggy trousers. I don't remember what the teacher said. All I remember was what my grandfather said: 'I'll take care of it.'

And with that, I was released.

What I got was not a beating, or a telling-off, but quiet disapproval and a lecture on the morality of fisticuffs and the rules of the game, which were basically don't bully people, stick up for yourself and never strike a woman. A gentle, forgiving and thoroughly decent man, he never failed to protect what mattered to him.

Not bad for 1962.

In the midst of all this, my real parents, Sonia and Bruce, were back from the dog-show circuit and living in Sheffield. They would visit on Sunday lunchtimes. I still have the cream-and-brown Bakelite radio set that was on at these occasions. They were always rather strained affairs, leaving me with a lifelong horror of sit-down meals, as well as gin and lipstick. I would push food around the plate and be lectured about not leaving my Brussels sprouts and the perils of not eating food when it was rationed, which of course it wasn't anymore, but no one could comprehend that reality. The same post-war hangover restricted you to three inches of bathwater, anxiety over the use of electricity and a morbid fear of psychological dissipation caused by speaking on the telephone excessively.

Conversations were peppered with local disasters. So and so had a stroke ... auntie somebody had fallen downstairs ... teenage pregnancy was rife ... and some poor lad had sunk through the crust of one of the many slag heaps that surrounded the pit, only to find red-hot embers beneath, leaving the most horrific burns.

It was following one particular Sunday lunch, when I'd eaten the Brussels sprouts and the chicken formerly wandering about in the garden allotment, that it was time to move on and in with my parents. With my uncle John, I always rode in the front seat, but now I was in the back, staring through the rear window as the first five years of my life shrank away into the distance – then around the corner.

I finally faced forward, into an uncertain future. I could fight a bit, had caught several nasty bugs, commanded my own air force and was pretty close to defying gravity. Living with parents – how hard could it be?

Life on Mars

I have never smoked tobacco, except in the odd joint when I was aged 19 to 21, which we'll address a bit later on. I say this because, in fact, I probably smoked a pack a day just by being around my parents. My God, could they puff away. Aged 16, they tried to enlist me in the filthy weed society, but it was my greatest act of rebellion to evade their yellow-stained clutches.

Drink was frequent, and frequently reckless. My father was violently anti-seatbelts on the grounds that they might strangle you, and I lost count of the number of times he drove home blind drunk.

Nothing in childhood is ever wasted, except occasionally parents.

So now I really don't recommend drinking anything alcoholic at all and then driving, not even one. Of course, youth and indestructibility means I am guilty of hypocrisy of the first order, but fortunately I grew up a little bit before I killed myself, or, more importantly, killed an innocent somebody else.

But we have fast-forwarded way too far in our time machine. The button to push for the cassette recorder did not even exist as I joined my new school in what was supposedly a rough area of Sheffield, Manor Top.

Actually, I thought it was okay. I learnt to extrude mashed potato, fish and peas (it was Friday, after all) through pursed lips, forming a crinkly curtain with which you could compete with your fellow diners for longevity before it fell from your mouth.

I think Gary Larson must have attended this school too, because the scary horn-rimmed glasses on the female staff gave them that designer concentration-camp-guard look beloved of seventies sexploitation films. Better still were the Hannibal Lecter types who administered the punishment beatings. Abusing mashed potato and peas was a beatable offence, and a stick was laid heavily into your outstretched palm. To be quite honest I don't even remember if it hurt that much. It just seemed a bizarre thing to do, witnessed and solemnly entered in the punishment book. I felt as though I should have been wearing striped pyjamas on Devil's Island.

I didn't stay at that school for long because we moved. Moving was to become a feature of my life forever, but as a family our stock in trade was moving house, mainly to make money. My new abode was a basement, which I shared with my new sister, Helena, who was by now a sentient being capable of actual words.

There was a window the size of an iPad, which opened into a gutter full of dead leaves. There was a refrigerator with an enjoyable electrical fault. I would hang on to it with a damp cloth and see how much electricity I could take before my teeth started rattling. Up the stone steps was the rest of humanity. And oh ... what humanity. I was living in a hotel. A guest house. My parents ran it. My father had bought it. He sold second-hand cars from the front of it.

Dramatically, the house next door was purchased. Suddenly, the empire struck back and built an extension linking the two properties. Dad rolled out his blueprints, which he'd drawn and designed himself. I found a piece of wallpaper and tried to design a spaceship with life-support systems to go to Mars.

Builders appeared and they seemed to be working for him as well. As for me, I gained useful, if poorly paid employment.

I didn't put up buildings but it was bloody good fun knocking them down. Demolishing toilets was my speciality. When I was at university later on I could never take seriously the exhortation to 'smash the system'; I knew much more about smashing cisterns than they ever would. It was all very impressive.

Next, the hotel, the Lindrick, had a bar constructed to Dad's own design. As far as I could tell, the Lindrick never really closed at weekends, especially with Dad behind the bar. I would hear the tales on Monday from Lily.

'Ooh, that Mr So and So headbutted Mr Rigby ... and then that other fellow was dancing on the table and fell over. Ooh, he broke the table in half, you know. It was teak as well. I think it was his head what did it ...'

It was all bed-hopping among the travelling salesmen, and some of the people who stayed were just plain odd. One creepy individual stayed for two weeks and gave me a card and whispered, 'Ay up, I practise Karma Yoga.' He would then leave at 7 p.m. and walk the streets till dawn. And no, he didn't have a dog to walk.

Other people came, and some never left. A few dropped dead in bed. If it was a horrible death, everyone was kept informed by Grandma Lily: 'She were burnt to death in her car ...'

One evening, two gentlemen surprised each other in the dark, each of them assuming they had been fondling a female guest. That took quite some sorting out in the morning. It was like living in a permanent state of farce.

More bits were being added to the hotel all the time, and more of the family moved up to Sheffield. My paternal grandparents, Ethel and Morris, sold up their seaside boarding house and moved in down the road. Grandad Dickinson was a dead ringer for rascally actor Wilfrid Hyde-White, only with a broadish Norfolk accent. A roll-up behind one ear, a pencil behind the other and the racing paper in hand, he set about what would now be called 'repurposing' buildings. In practice that meant knocking them down, but using the dressed stone to put them up somewhere else.

Grandma Dickinson was a formidable woman. Six foot tall, with intense, black curly hair and a gaze that would fell a tree at 20 paces, she'd worked as a servant girl, and had been purchased from the railway carriage where she lived with 18 other girls on the land. She was fleet of foot and might have had an athletic career, but she couldn't afford shoes: 200 metres barefoot was no match for the opposition in spikes. She never forgot that humiliation till the day she died.

While Ethel baked cakes, Morris would emerge from the toilet with a half-smoked roll-up and lots of boxes ticked for the horses. 'Here you are, sonny – don't let on,' he'd say, and he would slip me half a crown from his hand, clawed from years of laying bricks and handling trowels.

At a family summit spent drinking all afternoon in our hotel bar, my uncle Rod did me several favours, one of which was to persuade me never to have a tattoo. Uncle Rod (who was actually my uncle – my dad's brother) was charismatic to say the least, and frankly looked a bit like one of these roguish gangsters who might be surrounded by women of easy virtue. Right now, though, I sat on his knee aged 10 as he explained the British film-certification system to me: 'Now, yer 'ave yer X films and, basically, yer have your sex X and yer horror X ...'

Whatever he said next faded into the background as I stared at the scars on the back of both of his hands. Uncle Rod had a habit in his youth of misplacing other people's motorcars. Despite the family's best efforts, he was so prolific that he was sent to a horrific young offender's institution known as borstal. Self-tattooing with brick dust and ink was the thing in borstal, and it marked you for life as a product of that institution. Uncle Rod had spent what then would have been a considerable amount of money to get them removed. It was early skin-graft surgery, and these days it would qualify as a special effect in a low-budget horror movie. I just thought, *I think I'll stick with what I've got. That really doesn't look like much fun.*

Then Uncle Rod reverted to talking about war films. I had seen loads of them with Grandfather Austin: *633 Squadron*, *The Dam Busters*, *Battle of Britain*, *The Charge of the Light Brigade*.

'And what about *Ice Station Zebra*?' I piped up.

''Aven't seen that one,' he grunted, and he went back to his pint.

Ice Station Zebra was the movie that introduced me to my first rock 'n' roll band. Yes, with a truck, electric guitars and gigs. The band were called the Casuals. They'd had a hit with a track called 'Jesamine' and were now playing residencies at clubs for a week or so at a time. They stayed in the hotel, and during the daytime – which for them, being creatures of the night, didn't start till midday – they would surface, bleary-eyed and longhaired, in stack-heeled boots and white trousers, for a late breakfast of tea and toast provided by Lily, who was all of a twitter.

I am sure I must have appeared precocious with my questions about rockets and submarines, and it was probably a way of levelling the playing field that the guitarist brought down his electric guitar. I held it. It was surprisingly heavy. He explained carefully how it worked, and I just stared at the round steel discs under the strings and tried to imagine how sound really worked, produced from such tiny fragments with the tinniest-sounding twanging strings.

Like most bands, they were bored silly during the day, and they decided to go to the cinema. *Ice Station Zebra* was on at the Sheffield Gaumont. Popcorn in hand, aged 10, sitting in a cinema with a rock 'n' roll band watching a war movie about nuclear submarines and rockets: I thought, *This is living.*

Dad expanded his empire and purchased a bankrupt petrol station. It was a huge property, an old tram garage with four ancient petrol pumps, no canopy, and workshops full of caked oil and dirt half an inch thick adhering to 50-year-old bricks. The motor trade started to dominate our lives. I pumped petrol in between falling off scaffolding (repurposing buildings), and polished cars and scrubbed wheels with wire wool until my fingers turned blue in winter. I washed windscreens, checked tyres and watched the growing number of cars coming and going as sales picked up.

Dad was an encyclopaedia of motor-car components. He was a natural engineer and would go straight to the heart of the problem. His diagnosis was seldom wrong. He could recount the provenance of the exhaust system of the Fiat whatever-it-was, and why it was superior to the gizmo of the Ford, but anyway, both of them were actually designed by an unknown Hungarian genius. That sort of thing. Get him started, it could go on for hours.

We sold up the hotel as he acquired the dealership for Lancia motor cars, and did rather well until they produced one that rusted faster than you could drive it. I expect money must have been made on the house transactions because there was a property boom, and a house was still an achievable objective for a working family. At one point we made the mistake of selling before we had anywhere else to live. It must have been a very good deal.

In the end we moved back into a terraced house only a hundred yards up from the hotel we'd vacated a year or so earlier. Some people are addicted to crack. We were addicted to moving house.

If You Want Skool, You Got It

In the midst of all this I was relocated to a hothouse environment. I was being spirited away from the evil influence of mashed potato, spit and being straight-armed by the locals.

I was on my way to a private school: Birkdale preparatory school, alma mater of, among others, Michael Palin of Monty Python fame. It was one of the strangest, most eccentric educational institutions I have ever encountered and actually, in the end, I quite enjoyed it. I say in the end because in the beginning the bullying was fairly intense. I use the term 'fairly intense' only in comparison with what came later, at boarding school.

Bullying happens because weak people need to prop up their ego by beating up or humiliating others. Of course, if you are a new arrival, or just different, you become a prime target. I ticked all the boxes. Break time was the worst, up against the dustbins with 12 kids hitting you, watched over by a female teacher, whom I assume must have got some kind of power trip from not stopping it. In remembrance of both grandfathers I always refused to submit. The odds were ridiculous, but I still fought back. I wasn't going away.

After a year or so it calmed down, and a year after that it was as if nothing had happened and my very own self was assimilated into the group mind – or so they thought.

I took refuge in books, the library, writing and drama. The angelic wings of yore came back to haunt me, and I got my first namecheck in a review of a school play in the *Sheffield Star*, no less.

'Mole, besmudged of face, played by Paul Dickinson.' (Bruce, of course, is my middle name, but then you knew that.)

I was a bit disappointed that they omitted to mention that I got a good, proper laugh from the audience. Early lessons in comic timing during our school production of *The Wind in the Willows* also included dropping my wooden sword during a pregnant pause, which corpsed the stalls, and delivering the correct line 'I say Ratty, this chicken is delicious' while clearly eating a lemon tart.

Further productions followed and I was sold on the stage, though, truthfully, actors seemed to take it awfully seriously.

Lessons proceeded normally. In other words, I don't remember a thing, except that the Merino sheep has a spectacular coat, and a rather splendid view of Tolkien from my history teacher, Mr Quiney: 'One bloody feast after another, a long dreary walk, a battle and some rubbish songs.' I read *The Hobbit* and *The Lord of the Rings* when I was 12. Entertaining, but he had a point.

For those wishing to learn French there was Mr White. But Mr White was only interested in playing with his vast train set, which occupied half of the top floor. French lessons consisted of watching the OO-gauge *Flying Scotsman* whizzing round for 20 minutes.

Classes were streamed in sets A, B, C or D, from the most brilliant to the severely challenged or just plain bored. I yo-yoed from one set to another. I was always just plain bored, but was bribed to do well by the promise of a bike with racing handlebars should I leap up the pecking order.

Towards the end of my time I found myself in a class with only eight people, and we didn't have lessons as such. We sat around, talked, argued, discussed, wrote things because we wanted to, and played practical jokes that tried to be interesting rather than just cruel. Teachers came and we spoke as equals. It was extraordinary. It felt like my brain was popping with ideas, like popcorn in a pan. Delightful.

Of course, there was a reason. The aim of this whole process was to take a fairly stiff set of exams that took a whole week in order to get into the highly competitive boarding-school system from age 12 or 13 to 18.

Big boys' stuff.

School wasn't the only place to get an education, however. I learnt to ride a bike, and hurtled around the neighbourhood. I had a chemistry set, which stubbornly refused to make anything of any entertainment value, and my dad taught me to play chess. We played frequently, until one day I beat him, and then we stopped.

On holidays in Great Yarmouth I spent my time surrounded by zinc buckets full of pennies. The expression 'bucketloads of money' was simply work in progress for an amusement arcade on the sea front. It was owned by my cousin Russell's parents.

Every trip to Great Yarmouth ended up in the flat above the amusement arcade. It was furnished with questionable coffee tables supported by Nubian-slave statues, and a carpet that was more like a white hairy sea of synthetic tendrils that looked like it would eat you if it didn't like your shoes. There was small talk, and then I was presented with the cast-offs from my cousins: hideous suede-fronted cardigans and other monstrosities designed to make a 10-year-old look like 50 years old.

Buoyancy was a family trait. In order to learn not to drown, my father had simply been thrown in the Norfolk Broads. I learnt to swim under his supervision, but in not quite as abusive a fashion. Somewhere, lurking in the bottom of a mouldy suitcase, is my certificate from Heeley Baths, Sheffield, listing that I, on that day, swam 10 yards in approved style. After ingesting enough chlorine to blind a First World War battalion, I squinted pink-eyed from the sunlight, relieved that the ordeal was over. My dad swam like a fish. He would swim three miles in the ocean as a boy. I, on the other hand, have always regarded swimming as thoroughly hazardous. It is merely preventative drowning. I am one of nature's sinkers. 'Relax,' cry the floaters, but sadly my feet go the way of gravity and the rest follows suit.

Before we venture through the hallowed portals of an English public school, there are a few more pieces of the jigsaw to throw on the table.

I was reasonably solitary. I wasn't interested in sport. I spent long afternoons at the weekend in the public library, browsing and daydreaming. I had discovered wargaming, and my evenings were spent researching the accuracy of the Brown Bess musket and the tactics of the infantry square, and painting my white-metal Scots Highlanders, shortly to be unleashed on an unsuspecting Napoleon.

My uncle Stewart, a teacher, had been a county table-tennis champion, so, for Christmas, a rather fine table-tennis table appeared. Dad and his brothers batted away and argued over who had won, then went off to the pub. I immediately organised the Battle of Waterloo to be refought on it the next day. It was green and it was flat – perfect. It was one of many small events that caused my father to regard me somewhat strangely, as if subverting a table-tennis table was somehow unmanly.

I had developed a wonderful set of spots as I approached the day I would leave home and take up residence for the next four years at Oundle School in Northamptonshire. Not great, but seeing as there were no girls anywhere on the horizon, not a showstopper. What made them break out into suppurating sores was the application of engine oil, burnt rubber and grime-encrusted fingernails. Just before semi-leaving home, I'd been introduced to motor racing.

Tim, a friend at school, and his elder brother Nick had a very enthusiastic father. He drove a massive Cadillac and had a huge trailer, in which was a miniature racing team for his sons. As far as I could gather, he owned a nightclub and drank a great deal of barley wine.

The karts were 100cc rotary valve, and they were very fast. I had never even turned a wheel before, but I just got in the seat, got my bump start and hurtled off towards the first corner down the long straight at Lindholme, the former RAF base.

I turned the wheel, did a 360-degree spin and stalled the engine. I did the same thing at just about every corner round the circuit before I got back to the trailer, followed by two very sweaty brothers gasping their last after chasing me round the circuit and restarting me half-a-dozen times.

We debriefed. Clearly I needed more information as to what was going on.

By the end of the day I thought I was flying: foot flat to the floor, down the straight, braking as hard and as late as I dared, the adrenalin shooting through my hands and heart. The truth is, I probably just about made it round without spinning off, but bugger that, steam engine driver, fighter pilot and astronaut – add racing-car driver to the list.

Angelic Upstart

Before we go to boarding school, with all that entails, can I just have a word about religion? Something I experienced, and experimented with and had experimented upon me at four, too early an age. The outcome, though, was totally unexpected, and if God ever moved in a mysterious way, here was proof positive.

I don't recall my baptism, but apparently I somehow managed to ingest quite a quantity of holy water. I could have drowned in the font. I am not sure that swallowing God's special sauce caused any sort of aura to appear, but it might have been an influence on my early interest in angel wings.

School had the usual harvest festival and a bit of dreary carol singing, but it was only when I arrived at Birkdale that I was exposed to evangelical religion, bible black and fighting Satan on all fronts.

There was a cabal of zealous teachers and, by chance or design, they were the same teachers that ran school expeditions, including one to Fort William in Scotland. It consisted of 10 days' camping, playing robust semi-military games, climbing mountains, bridging rivers, leaping from tree to tree ('The Lumberjack Song', anyone?) and religious brainwashing. Think Bear Grylls with no possibility of escape.

There were prayers and lectures, and every evening there was a group assembly in which 10-year-olds were encouraged to stand up and identify sins, and would be rewarded for their folly by rapturous praise, hugs and applause. I stood up and identified a fly on the wall, which was clearly a servant of Satan, because it had been distracting me from the balderdash being spouted by the part-time messiahs and full-time school teachers.

With no sense of irony at the age of 10, I was welcomed into the fold, and told that I was now evangelised. My purpose in life was to go and convert people to Christ.

Well, being a mission-oriented sort of chap, I sallied forth into the town and set about converting a couple of Highland girls by handing them a leaflet and inviting them to the campsite for a fun evangelical evening of happy-clappy hymns accompanied by bad guitar-playing and Aran sweaters.

'Fuck off, you twat,' was the robust response.

At home in Sheffield I was enrolled in the Christian Union, where I wore a little badge and was encouraged to read *The Screwtape Letters* and lots of other rather less inventive tracts, some of which covered subjects like masturbation and marriage. Confused, I thought, *Did they go hand in hand?*

My parents were a bit bemused, having seldom been near a church since I half-swallowed one when I was nine months old. However, they tolerated it on the basis that it seemed harmless enough and gave me something to do on Sunday mornings.

Not too long after this, hormones kicked in, and I began to look at girls in a rather different light. I no longer wanted only to convert them; there was something more that you could diddle about with. I just couldn't put my finger on it.

My school friend Tim was discussing the subject of exactly where to put fingers. Incredibly, it was the only time anybody had spoken about sex thus far, other than being told it was, by and large, sinful, except for making babies. Further in-depth enquiries about what this fairly sexually advanced chap got up to revealed that he did something on his own time involving a sock and his pyjamas.

'Then what happens?' I asked, trying to picture the scene.

So he told me.

'Really?' This was all news to me. Well, God hates a coward, as the expression goes, and my monastic existence turned into an onanistic one. As for Sunday school, given a choice between wanking yourself silly and Christian Union, there was a clear winner. It was masturbation and libraries that saved my soul from the narrow-minded proselytising and a stifling, evangelical straitjacket, and thank God for that.

But I never got around to telling you the good bit about God and his mysterious ways.

The official custodian of our spiritual health at Birkdale was the Reverend B.S. Sharp, at the time the vicar of Gleadless at the splendidly dark Victorian Millstone Grit church. Unlike the part-time evangelical types, 'Batty', as his nickname suggested, was more than a little eccentric, and he was stone deaf. As reverends go, he was regarded as being harmless.

Batty would conduct hymn practice, and the entire school would traipse into his church and commence singing while he walked up and down the aisle waving his arms about, seemingly oblivious to the out-of-time, out-of-tune and smirking schoolboys (no girls, of course). As he passed me – I was standing at the end of a pew – singing, or rather mumbling, he paused; he cocked his head, rather like a parrot, and peered round at me. I suspect he was positioning his good ear.

'Sing up, lad,' he said.

So I sang a bit louder. He brought his entire face close to my mouth. I realised he was missing a lot of teeth and I tried hard not to laugh.

'Sing up, lad.'

Well, I like a challenge, so I yelled at the top of my lungs, and once I started I didn't stop. The embarrassment left me and I carried on to the end of whatever verse it was in whatever hymn. I confess that it felt wonderful – not that I would admit it at the time.

He stood up and waved his arms about a bit more, then leaned back over to me.

'You have a very fine voice, boy,' he said. And then he strode off down the aisle and I never saw him again.

Like I say, nothing in childhood is ever wasted, and if there is a God, he or she is full of mischief.

Sadly, the choirmaster at Oundle didn't share Batty's enthusiasm for my dulcet tones. It became clear that singing, as in singing in church, was very undesirable, although to describe the school chapel as a church would be to do it an injustice.

Oundle's chapel had pretensions of being a cathedral at the very least. It had a choir and the usual, and possibly verifiable, rumours about choirboys and choirmasters. The school choir dressed in frocks and had their free time spirited away from them in fruitless praising of the ineffable one until their voices broke.

There was a singing test, which was compulsory. I was very proud to say that I failed in spectacular fashion. Every note that was white on a keyboard was black when I returned the favour. I was given a chit – a piece of paper – to deliver to my housemaster. On it was written: 'Dickinson – Sidney House, NON-SINGER'.

The Kipper's Revenge

I was never too sure why I ended up in boarding school. My parents kept asking me if I wanted to go, and my immediate instinct was, *Anything to get out of this place*. So I smiled and passed the crazy exams, and sat the IQ test and did the interview. The only part I remotely enjoyed was the IQ test because it was interesting and there was nothing you had to remember by rote. You only had to do your best. In early summer the letter arrived. I had passed: here are the uniform restrictions and please pay lots of money.

Oundle was, and still is, a small market town near Peterborough in the rolling countryside of Northamptonshire. Nestled in a bend of the sleepy but often disobedient River Nene, it sits on a mound above the flood plain. Fotheringhay Castle is a couple of miles down the road, along with its associated church, and the whole area is steeped in English, as opposed to British, history.

Half the town was occupied by the school. Most of the old buildings were either school rooms or accommodation, and the Worshipful Company of Grocers of the City of London founded the whole enterprise in the sixteenth century. The hub of it all was a faux-Oxbridge quadrangle with pillars and porticos, grand marble balustrades and architecture to remind you of your place. That is to say, small, ignorant and insignificant.

Hundreds of alumni hung on boards at every turn in the quadrangle. Rugby, fives, athletics, Classics, mathematics and all those boys whose names never got written down until they came back in body bags as dead heroes from two world wars. There were quite a few of those.

I still didn't know why I was here. It got me out of the house was my best guess, and I must have proved something by passing all the wretched exams. One reason, though, could have been that my aunt was the cook. There was no clear logic to this, and even I was confused as to the relationship between school dinners and academic excellence, but there was some suggestion that life might be easier for me if people knew that my aunt cooked the school meals.

No one in my family, from any branch of it, had ever been to a private school. My father had been denied a place at university after getting into grammar school because Ethel could only afford to send one son out of four to higher education. Stewart was the eldest, so he received the college education.

Dad never forgot that.

My sister was to go down an entirely different path, leaving school with few academic qualifications and taking a long, hard road, virtually self-taught, to becoming one of the world's leading show jumpers. When I was dragging my 19-year-old arse around East London playing pubs to three people, my 14-year-old sister was debuting a horse she'd trained herself in the Horse of the Year Show at Wembley Arena.

So, at the age of 13, having left Sheffield, I began a process of disengagement from family, and involuntary alienation from the human race, at least for a couple of years. It is hard to say, even in hindsight, whether there was a net gain or loss as a human being.

Academically, there is no question that the hothouse environment pushed up the less able and enabled the truly talented to excel – with the odd possible exception. I remember myself being stolidly average, but memorable for a variety of other reasons.

All boys were assigned to a house, around 50 or 60 strong, and this served as their tribe. Everything about the place was competitive. There were inter-school competitions, inter-house competitions and intra-house competitions. No stone was left unturned in the search for winners. If you weren't a winner on the sports field, you might be a winner as an academic. If not as an academic, well, things got a little stickier – perhaps Oundle was not for you.

My house was called Sidney, and it had a grand mock-Georgian façade with a sweeping gravel drive. It backed onto acres of rugby and cricket pitches, and was miles away from the school classrooms. To this day I walk at breakneck pace everywhere in mortal terror of being late for English Lit. I covered, I guess, about five miles before lunch with an armful of textbooks. Nowadays, it's probably hoverboards and iPads doing the hard work.

One of the first things to strike me, before the whips, chains and blunt instruments (more of that later), was a most-illuminating bout of salmonella poisoning. Along with red lipstick and beehive hairdos, you can add fish pie to the chamber of horrors that haunts me to this very day.

My auntie Dee attempted to kill me, along with 20 of my house mates, and a sharp piece of microbial detective work traced the offending pathogen back to a serving spoon. Those unlucky enough to take the left-hand path (fun though it might seem for witches) in the serving line were struck down by Pasteur's revenge. Those in the right-hand queue suffered no ill effects. The stomach cramps began three hours after ingestion of the emetic fish pie. Shortly afterwards I was admitted to a ward to join my similarly stricken schoolmates. For three days stuff erupted from every available orifice. The lyric 'And I filled them – their living corpses with my bile' from 'If Eternity Should Fail' didn't require all that much imagination.

We were kept rather busy with sport. Being no good at it meant being designated 'pathetic'. Being good at it meant you walked on a small cloud and were infallible.

The school had innumerable rugby teams, and had a boathouse with eights, fours and sculls, plus cricket teams, shooting teams, tennis, squash and the somewhat obscure but popular game of fives.

Before being allowed to go in a boat of any description, children underwent the 'boat test'. In the Middle Ages witches underwent a similar ordeal. It involved being dressed in army boots, jeans and a thick wool army sweater, and then being chucked in the river.

A road bridge over the River Nene served as the vantage point to observe the drowning of the adolescent witches. Victims were picked up and tossed into the freezing water, and had to swim 25 yards or so without drowning. Imagine how much I enjoyed that. I was regarded as being a possible rower, so I had a discreet second attempt, and a third. I think they would have just carried on until I drowned, so I gave up breathing, thought of my baptism and swallowed a lot of water before finally being fished out by a boat hook. The practice was discontinued shortly thereafter, when dead cows were found, infected with some horrendous bug, floating bloated upstream.

I was, of course, bullied, and as before in my previous school I didn't back down, change my opinion or shut up. So, two years later, a bit of a fuss blew up, parents were called in, pupils were suspended and then it all petered out. But for those two years life was average-to-middling hellish.

We slept in dormitories, army-barrack style: cold giant windows with no curtains, and two lines of iron beds; a thin mattress on a chipboard base, a couple of blankets and cotton sheets. There was no privacy, no locks on drawers, and it was communal baths and washrooms. Things got interesting after lights out. After the teacher had left, the senior boy would wake me up. Half an hour later, a crowd would gather round. He was around 18, a big lad. He had a pillow wrapped into a tight ball.

'Time for your lesson, Dickinson. Defend yourself,' he'd say.

Not exactly Queensberry rules, and not much you could do about it, except build a reservoir of rage and anger. Often, my bed was pre-soaked or covered in eggs, or my personal kit was covered in washing-up liquid, or any number of petty infractions of personal space.

By year two I was pretty fucking angry. Rugby didn't even touch the beginning of my rage, and I quite enjoyed rugby. Believe it or not, I was a prop, and as others got bigger but I did not, I was variously a hooker (not enjoyable), scrum half (not very good) and I finally settled down as a flanker, or wing forward as it was in rugby pre-history.

My sidestep was the Army Cadet Force. Sure, there was a hierarchy, but oddly the regime wasn't directed mindlessly against me. It was the same bullshit for everyone. We had 400 in our cadet force, and I progressed rapidly through the various ranks, until one day I found myself being promoted to the exalted rank of under officer.

There were only two of us, and the other was one of my few close friends at Oundle, Ian, who went on to be a lieutenant colonel in the Highland Regiment and served in some pretty hairy locations. The last time we met, after 25 years, was in a grubby hotel in Jeddah. I was a captain flying a Boeing 757 chartered by Saudi Airlines during the Hajj and he was in charge of the Saudi National Guard. Go figure.

At Oundle we found ourselves with unexpected privileges. There were enough guns and ammunition in the school armoury to start a *coup d'état* in a small African nation. All of it was Second World War vintage. There were 100 or so 303 Lee–Enfield rifles, half-a-dozen Bren guns, thunderflashes, two-inch mortars, smoke grenades, and live and blank ammunition. Both of us had attended the UKLF leadership course, where we were equipped with all the latest army kit and spent two weeks in Thetford being chucked out of helicopters, doing 24-, 36- and 48-hour exercises, and getting a lot of blisters.

My platoon supervisor had been in the SAS, and he told me I was above average in teamwork, but average everywhere else. I spent summers on attachment with the Royal Anglian Regiment and the Royal Green Jackets, and dangled off lots of ropes at Lympstone with the Royal Marines. I was pretty serious about joining the army.

Ian and I hatched a plan to make our Wednesday afternoons more interesting and productive. Incredibly, as 16-year-olds, we had the authority to sign for and withdraw rifles and automatic weapons, high explosives and blank ammunition. So every Wednesday, that's what happened. We would come up with scenarios then wander off armed to the teeth into a local wood and shoot the crap out of each other.

I should set the scene at Oundle School. Before 1914, the British Empire was demanding technocrats. The traditional public schools churned out the Greek-and-Latin educated civil servants to be, but the dark days of the future demanded leaders who understood metalwork, mechanical engineering and electronics.

Oundle established what was essentially an industrial estate. It had an aluminium foundry, composite and fibreglass workshops, lathes, milling machines, and woodworking, blacksmithing and metalworking shops. Every term, I spent one week dressed in overalls learning to chop and assemble bits of wood, metal and plastic.

The aim of all this activity was to build a vice. The halves were cast from wooden moulds in the foundry. The sand moulds you made yourself, and there were various ways of sabotaging them to make life less dreary.

Excessive moisture and too much tamping of the sand in the mould would cause it to explode. Even better was to leave a hole in the bottom of the mould so that molten aluminium dripped onto the shoes of the pourer – the taciturn master in charge, Mr Moynihan. I suspect he quite enjoyed having his shoes set on fire. To this end he came equipped with multi-layered steel-capped boots, asbestos helmet and gloves, plus a rich choice of language, which meant that no one would skip the foundry lesson.

'Faacking 'ell ... 'Oo faacking set fire to my faacking feet?'

Mr Moynihan was a good sport and he taught me never to panic, even when you are on fire.

In woodwork I was an abject failure, although I designed and built the world's most useless and uncomfortable chair and the most incompetent set of bookshelves yet devised. Even M.C. Escher would have been confused as to where to position his books.

In the machine shop I broke windows with the chuck key, using the rotary action of the lathe as a catapult. Finally, by an act of sheer mechanical stupidity, I destroyed a vertical milling machine. Had I been parachuted in to a Nazi factory, I could not have done a better job at sabotage. I wish I could say it was deliberate. As the machine ripped itself in half, the drive shaft stripping its thread, I stood and watched as it vibrated itself to pieces. It was the master in charge I felt sorry for. He was actually crying as he switched it off.

'Oh, no,' he sighed. 'You have broken the machine.'

The only bit about the electronics shop I liked was the smell of the circuit board. I carried it around in a plastic case with various resistors rattling around. I don't recall what the point of it was, possibly an oscillator.

Disinterested, disgraced and dangerous, I entered the last iteration of my workshop sojourn at Oundle, and unexpectedly hit the jackpot when I discovered an inspirational teacher who knew a bit about metal.

John Worsley was calm and tidy, and wore such a large pair of glasses that it seemed impossible to imagine that he wasn't interested in you. The moment he picked up a piece of metal, I noticed his fingers. They were thin and nimble, and they floated across the surface of the billet of steel as if he was imbuing it with some otherworldly quality. John would always turn up to classes on his bicycle – racing handlebars, cycle clips on the bottom of his trousers. He had a curious gait, as if one side of him was a sailor and the other had been employed in a previous incarnation as one leg of a tarantula. One of his favourite words was 'plangent', and it was an odd, almost archaic-sounding expression. John Worsley was like a hybrid between a bicycle repairman and Gandalf.

Metalworking covered wrought iron, forging, silversmithing and jewellery, plus welding and associated skills. Our project was to make a nickel-silver bracelet, which I quite enjoyed and was rather proud of. When I brought it home, Dad regarded it with deep suspicion.

John Worsley had a plan to get our attention. He thrust a shaft of steel into a glowing brazier and sparks showered forth. He pulled it out, still red hot, placed it on an anvil and started to beat out the shape of what I immediately realised was a sword. He quenched the metal with a satisfying hiss in a bucket of water, and thrust it back in the fire. Without saying a word, he produced a leather blanket and dramatically unfurled it to reveal a replica of Excalibur. The crossbar of the hilt was leather-covered, but the blade, broad and gleaming, was what entranced me.

'I could teach you all to make this, if you want,' he stated, rolling the weapon over and over in his palm. He paused for effect. 'And I could teach you how to use it, of course.'

'Sir? What, you mean ... sword fighting?'

The reason John Worsley walked funny was because he had been a fencing teacher for most of his life. On arrival at a posh public school, as a working-class northerner, he seized his chance. My hand was up right away. I signed up. I would learn how to fence. It would change my life.

My drama teacher also had a profound effect on me. John Campbell was one of those rare but essential teachers who give you permission to dream.

Drama, as opposed to music, was another line of escape, and I was in several productions: *Macbeth*, *Hadrian VII*, *The Royal Hunt of the Sun* and some local inhouse plays that were usually awful West End farces.

In *Macbeth* I was a witch, murderer and various messengers, spending much of my time under a gigantic polystyrene skull encased in toilet paper. Downgraded to acolyte in *Hadrian VII*, I stepped up a gear as the mercenary in *The Royal Hunt of the Sun* and oily manservant in *According to the Evidence*, a play so silly I was amazed that Samuel French kept it in stock.

Nevertheless, the roar of the greasepaint and the smell of the crowd were taking their toll on my subconscious. The germ of a philosophy started to take root. The idea that it didn't matter what it was that you engaged in, as long as you respected its nature and attempted some measure of harmony with the universe.

An Unexpected Journey

It wasn't just the senior boys who kicked you around. You could be legally beaten up by teachers. Corporal punishment was common. It ranged from slippers across the backside by individual teachers to more formal floggings with a cane or birch. Opinions varied about the efficacy of a beating. The event was usually administered during the evening, with the unfortunate recipient in his pyjamas, after lights out. This was to ensure maximum psychological anxiety and maximum physical discomfort, as six strokes through cotton pyjamas was almost certain to draw blood. The now thankfully meaningless expression 'books down the trousers' was intended to convey a situation where, in anticipation of physical sanction, a geography notebook might shield the buttocks from damage.

There was general agreement that fives or squash players were the most devastating floggers on account of their fearsome backhand. Golfers came a close second. A great deal of discussion in dorm rooms revolved around angles, velocity and acceleration. After a beating, the victim usually stood on top of a chest of drawers and dropped his pants to invite comments by flashlight.

'Not bad grouping.'

'Ooh, stroke number four a bit low.'

'He doesn't like you much, does he?'

My housemaster had a variety of implements, ranging in length, flexibility and thickness according to the severity of the transgression. Four to six strokes were delivered, and his favourite armchair became the flogging stool, with the cushion removed and the boy exhorted to bend over and touch the bottom of the chair. There was a fetishistic streak to all this. Many of his beatings were administered while he was dressed in his rowing kit.

There are possibly people who still regard this sort of thing as character building. I am not one of them.

I began to think of school as a prison camp, and my duty was to disrupt, subvert and/or escape. But, of course, there was no escape. I felt I should make some kind of statement. I decided to deliver two tons of horseshit to my housemaster. Just one of those spur-of-the-moment ideas that comes with no logic in tow, but a great deal of emotional momentum.

I was wandering through town, considering the colour scheme for my squadron of Hannibal war elephants, which required painting before being blooded during the wargames society Roman stand-off. Pottering past the post office, I saw a postcard in the window, which read fatefully: 'Manure delivered to your door.'

I went to the phone box and dialled.

'Hello, do you deliver? Excellent. I'd like two tons, please ... Yes, drop it in front of my house ... The address? Sidney House, Oundle School. Thank you so much.'

That evening, the house gathered for supper. The housemaster stood up, sucking air through his teeth in lieu of the pipe he perennially puffed away at.

'This afternoon,' he said, 'some wag thought it amusing to deliver two tons of shit onto my front doorstep. Unless the person owns up there will be no electricity for kettles or stereos in the house.'

Standard tactics for a low-grade despot. The stereo was an essential part of student existence. There were no CDs, and cassette recorders were in their infancy. Chronic audiophiles with rich daddies had reel-to-reel studio recorders and busily spliced tapes together to make compilations from their vinyl collections. It was only in your third year at Oundle that you were allocated to a study, a room not quite of your own but which you shared with one or two others. Decoration was possible and, inevitably, a music system was essential. By strolling past open study doors on a Sunday afternoon it was possible to sample most of the premier rock bands of the sixties and seventies. To cut off this lifeline to sanity and escape from the Oundlian Alcatraz, if only in spirit, was a dark and cruel punishment.

After supper, I knocked on the housemaster's door.

'Come!'

Seldom was the word 'in' ever used. I entered. He looked around from where he was seated at his desk, yellow pipe clenched in his teeth.

'Ah, Dickinson. I thought it might be you.'

Actually, I was quite pleased. 'Very amusing,' he said. An unexpected compliment. He looked down. 'Of course, I'll thrash you for it.' I heard the clack of his teeth on the pipe stem. Was he salivating? He looked up, startled. I just continued to stare. He dismissed me with an imperious wave.

On the dot at 9 p.m. I heard the squeak, squeak, squeak of rubber soles, and then the knock at the door.

'I'll see you now,' the housemaster said.

He had changed into his rowing kit: shorts, chunky V-neck sweater and tennis shoes. His legs were ridiculously skinny and covered with a childlike coating of thin red hair. With every step I respected him less. He was using an extra-long cane, so he needed space for a good swing, and he was an amateur golfer, which did not bode well for the next 30 seconds or so. Really, these people should have been locked up.

Thankfully, among these sadistic floggers and the failed Oxbridge dons existed a small core of decent eccentrics. In this perverse society of dystopian hypocrisy, with its own internal politics and rigid hierarchy, the brown, smoky common room inhabited by the staff had a secret cabal of visionaries who made our lives worth living, and gave us hope. As well as Mr Campbell and Mr Worsley, we had an art teacher who somehow managed to promote rock concerts in Oundle's Great Hall.

It's probably time to come clean about music and how I ended up singing. Music, not singing, came first, and it is one of the peculiar schizophrenic traits of my academic boot camp that it introduced me to rock 'n' roll more close-up than you could possibly imagine.

The first band I ever saw was called Wild Turkey. Then Van der Graaf Generator and, in similar prog-rock vein, we had String Driven Thing and a prog-folk band, Comus. Queen almost played, but they cancelled when they became massive overnight in America. The big story was that Genesis had played, the year before I arrived, complete with Peter Gabriel wearing a box on his head.

Wild Turkey had ex-Jethro Tull bass player Glenn Cornick in their lineup, and their first album, *Battle Hymn*, stands the test of time to this very day. Out of my mind on Fanta and Mars bars, raging with hormones, I was on a high for days. Every square inch of me was drenched in sweat as I staggered back to my dormitory across the forbidding lawns topped with dark shadows from academic spires. My heart was thumping, my ears were ringing and it seemed like my head was full of bells, with a madman tugging at ropes to ring the changes and pulling at the back of my eyeballs as if to say, 'Listen to this feeling and never forget.' Wild Turkey actually name-checked the gig in an interview as 'one of the craziest reactions we've ever had'. That was me, with my head stuffed in the bass bin.

Afterwards, a long succession of prog bands took over; all very cerebral, but with the exception of Peter Hammill and

Van der Graaf, not nearly so visceral. Nevertheless, when wandering the corridors with music drifting out from the individual studies in Sidney House, I was stopped in my tracks. What the fuck was that? I knocked tentatively. The senior boy looked at me scathingly: 'What do you want?'

'Er, what is that track?'

'Oh, that. Deep Purple, "Speed King", *Deep Purple in Rock*.' He rolled his eyes and shut the door. My insides continued to churn. I wanted music.

My first record was a sampler called *Fill Your Head with Rock*, comprising mainly West Coast American CBS Records acts, and although I played it to death, it was barely satisfactory. I wanted a straight shot of adrenalin. A second-hand *Deep Purple in Rock*, scratched to bits, cost 50 pence in an auction of albums because someone needed to pay their tuck-shop bill. Now, my friends, we were cooking on gas.

A family trip to Jersey – that's the Channel Islands, not New Jersey, folks – netted brand-new gatefold editions of Van der Graaf Generator classics *H to He* and *Pawn Hearts*. (The latter was such a manically depressive record that you could actually empty a room with it after a couple of minutes. On the other hand, I could listen to it for hours on end in solitary confinement, probably because I am not a manic depressive.) I took the two albums out of their brown paper bag. The gatefolds had some rather splendid surrealistic artwork by Paul Whitehead. I showed it to my father, who was an amateur oil painter.

'What do you think?' I offered.

'Degenerate,' he replied scathingly. We spent the rest of the day in silence. I decided that given a choice between being beaten at waterboarding school or being looked at as if I had two heads, I would take my chances back at school. I was determined to spend as much time as possible away from home, and set about signing up for school trips, army placements and whatever I could lay my hands on.

During summer holidays I moped around town, hanging around record shops and pressing my nose up against the glass of guitar and amplifier stores, lusting after speaker cabinets and hardware. My exposure to bands, albums and the stage had grown into a fantastic dream world. I had a transistor radio with a small earplug, and I would listen to pirate station Radio Caroline, the scratchy sound fading in and out, under the bed sheets at night.

I had memorised Deep Purple's *Made in Japan* note for note. Every drumbeat, every thud of Ian Paice's bass-drum beater, I had tried to replicate. Ditto the first Black Sabbath album, *Aqualung* by Jethro Tull, plus my eccentric collection of Van der Graaf Generator albums and treasured copy of Wild Turkey's first offering.

Back home in Sheffield, I still had some friends from prep school. Seeing as we'd all been packed off to boarding schools, holidays were the only time we ever met up. Paul Bray was one of them. Paul had a drum kit in his garage, a real one: actual cymbals, the whole shebang. He was in a band and his guitarist came to visit. I sat in awe as he rattled off 'Layla' and half-a-dozen Cream standards. He may well have ended up as a chartered accountant. Paul is actually quite a successful solicitor these days. Life's like that.

Back then I was spotty, wore an anorak, had flared blue jeans with 'Purple' and 'Sabbath' biro-engraved on the thighs, and rode an ear-splittingly uncool moped. Oh yes, and I wanted to be a drummer. My parents would have been horrified. It was my guilty secret. I had a pair of drumsticks, which I kept hidden, and a practice pad. Their intention was that I should be a doctor, vet, accountant, solicitor or some other 'professional' occupation.

I returned to school and set about forming a band. When deprived of something essential, the human mind is capable of surprising and often perverse adaptability. The Marquis de

Sade, denied paper and sexual contact, solved both problems by writing down his increasingly feverish fantasies on toilet paper, recently retranslated by an academic at the university where I would shortly end up, but now we really are overreaching ourselves. So let's presently deal with the past.

The bands I listened to were not the bands I would ever see in their heyday, stuck as I was in boarding school at the time, so my imagination filled the gaps. I overlaid their on-stage antics in my mind's eye with some operatic stage setting, plus the energy from the improv drama I had engaged in. It was all very fevered, very intense, and I wanted to recreate it as a drummer. It was simply a question of activity, and drumming was frenzied. It was the thrashing around at the front of the stage; it was the sweat and the focus, but also the possibility of being a Keith Moon, an eccentric, a showman. The drummer, it seemed to me, was in the driving seat.

However, I possessed neither a driving seat nor a drum kit. Amusingly, a drummer's chair or stool is technically termed a 'throne', and while I admired the sentiment, the delusion of grandeur was of no practical help. I conscripted several volumes of *The Cambridge Medieval History*. My drumsticks were strips of plywood, and I arranged the leather-bound volumes like tom-toms around my small rickety desk in my study. With the speaker close to my ear, I battered them in hopeful symphony. Eventually, I snuck into the music room and purloined a pair of bongos.

There were kids at boarding school in possession of real drum kits, amplifiers and electric guitars. They rehearsed in commandeered classrooms on a Saturday or Sunday afternoon. I gatecrashed one of their rehearsals. It was disorganised and it was all about how cool they looked. It was about fashion, about posing – about nothing. I was disgusted, though slightly jealous about their equipment. I was searching for the holy grail of innocence and experience. My vision was cloudy, but my purpose was crystal clear. Entertainment, yes, but truth above all things.

Four of us formed a band, at least for five minutes. The bass player, an Australian called Mike Jordan, had made his own bass in the woodwork and electric workshops. He was also my partner in crime when it came to running the school wargames society. He had failed to evade the curse of the school choir and had a classically trained bass voice. Two acoustic guitars completed the ensemble, and we attempted to play one Saturday afternoon. The only song we could agree on was 'Let It Be' by the Beatles, so we gave it a go. Hideously out of time, and with my hands beaten raw on the bongos, we staggered towards the chorus, at which point Mike realised that classical bass voices did not really suit extended Liverpudlian baritones.

'Let it be …' dissolved into a strangled yelp, while I carried on beating the song into submission on the two available skins.

We stopped. I was disappointed, as my enthusiasm was overcoming any pretence of accuracy. Mike could not handle the vocal high notes. He cleared his throat and, sounding terribly grown up, said, 'Perhaps we might change the key?'

I didn't know what he was talking about, but I chimed in with: 'How does it go?'

I opened my mouth and let rip, and the guitarists carried on to the end of the song. My head was spinning with the vibrations from the resonance of my voice. There was a surprised silence when we ran out of talent at the end.

'You can put those fucking bongos away.'

Mike, our bass player admitted defeat: 'I think you are our vocalist, dear boy.'

Our future in the music business thus secured, we broke for tea, margarine, jam and toast. It was 6 p.m., after all.

* * *

My acting endeavours had continued to flourish, and I had started writing and even directing, after a fashion. *The Dark Tower* was a radio play by Louis MacNeice, which I adapted for the stage, playing the oily butler myself as well as directing and producing it, all with the encouragement of my mentor, Mr Campbell.

My fencing classes had turned into a full-time 'official' school sport. Having won the school fencing championship, I was declared 'school captain of fencing', and I had my picture taken looking pompous with prominent sideburns.

Bullying was no more. I began to resemble the institution that I had resented. I was being assimilated, absorbed into the fabric, as if the beatings and hypocrisy were simply a test, something every chap has to go through before he changes from a caterpillar to the right sort of social butterfly.

My status, I suppose, was best described as slightly eccentric but acceptable. All that was to change on a dark November evening in 1975.

The week leading up to my exit was unremarkable. I spent spare afternoons in the study of my guitar-playing friend Chris Bertram. An unlikely duo, we pillaged the B.B. King songbook, murdering the blues, and I discovered that I could scream like a banshee and rather overdid it, but then, that's what adolescence is for, isn't it?

By now I was in the sixth form, only months from taking English, history and economics at A level. There was no element of coursework; it was sudden death, three hours of essay writing, and if you kept your wits about you, you might do okay.

A couple of evenings before my demise there was a comical but depressingly despotic event that took place at a lecture on Machu Picchu and the archaeology of the Incas. It was delivered by an academic explorer who also happened to be a personal friend of the headmaster, the automotively initialled

B.M.W. Trapnell. Trapnell was a cosmologist by trade, and had an emollient effect on parents and also, one imagines, school governors. Five minutes into the lecture, the plug was pulled on the slide projector, and in the chaos the slides were cruelly rearranged in what was clearly a very cleverly executed hit.

The aftermath descended into a Nazi-style persecution. Names were taken and the order from the top was clear. Punishment beatings were in order; pride was at stake. A birch was used to personally beat those deemed to be the ringleaders, and it was administered by Mr Cosmology himself, a big man and, sadly for their bottoms, a very good fives player.

After the event there was tension in the air. The school was in an angry mood, but no one would storm the Bastille. Most inappropriately, therefore, two days later there was to be a celebration in Sidney House. The joyful construction of a new dwelling for our illustrious housemaster would be commemorated by the convocation of the entire authority structure of the school.

The flogging cosmologist, the deputy flogging cosmologist, plus the flogging rowing-kit fetishist and all the school prefects assembled at one dinner table. The food was to be cooked by the more minor prefects in the house.

There was an atmosphere of quiet anarchy. I sat in a study with Neil Ashford, who was 16 and pretty bright, to be honest. We had a one-ring electric hob and a bottle of cheap sherry under the desk. We were just chatting, minding our own business and slightly tiddly when there was a knock at the door. The sherry was hurriedly stowed, and a prefect stuck his nose round the door, holding a block of frozen runner beans.

'I say, I couldn't borrow your hob, could I? We've run out of cooking rings,' he said.

We nodded assent and consigned them to the saucepan. We watched the beans defrost, then start to bubble and boil. Around this time, we both felt the urge to urinate. Through careful coordination and impressive bladder control, we relieved ourselves into an empty bottle. I did have a flashback to being one of the three witches in *Macbeth*. As I poured our mixed consommé into the bubbling pan I found myself recalling 'Eye of newt and toe of frog, wool of bat and tongue of dog ... add thereto, a quarter bottle of piss'. A classical education is a wonderful thing.

The mixture bubbled away, and 15 minutes later the prefect appeared and pulled out a tasty morsel. 'Perfect,' he pronounced. We realised that the house was devoid of authority. All were busy fawning, bowing and scraping to the jailers and floggers, in search of self-promotion, I assumed.

So we tiptoed to other studies and, like a pair of Pied Pipers, managed to obtain the keys to the house bar in the attic, and then locked ourselves in with several barrels of beer. Down below, Neil and I could see the silhouettes and shadows of *The Last Supper*. Not for them, but for me, as it turned out.

We slowly sipped our pints of Marston's Pedigree and started to giggle. The rest of the bar, half-a-dozen errant souls, wanted to know what was so funny. Being daft, we told them. By break time, 11 a.m. the next day, the whole school knew. I realised that I was some kind of breathless hero, until lunchtime when one of our house prefects declared me depraved, disgusting and an abomination. After lunch, the abomination was summoned to the housemaster.

'There's nothing I can do to save you,' he told me. This was a surprise to me. I never thought of him as the messiah, and I certainly didn't now.

I was called to see the headmaster: the cosmologist, the wielder of the birch, the flogger of the minor transgressors – the king rat. I put on my overcoat and took a contemplative slow walk through the dark November fog. I would be out, but I would not be broken. After all the bullying, the fencing, the drama, the music, this was it – the showdown. Admitted to the warm head-magisterial study, I sat down in front of Mr B.M.W. His feet were crossed over – *very big feet*, I thought fleetingly. He spoke, almost absentmindedly: 'This is not the kind of behaviour we tolerate in a civilised establishment. Therefore I must ask you to leave the school.'

Therefore? You have to be kidding me. In what century, from what misanthropic ivory tower, did this creature originate? The hypocrisy, the twisted regime, the cover-ups, the maintenance of good order over all principles of humanity – therefore fuck you. But I didn't say any of that. I smiled and looked him in the eye and thought, *You have eaten my piss.*

'Any preference as to when you would like me to go? Next week? End of term?' I said.

'Tomorrow morning,' he shot back.

'Oh, that's clear. Is that it?'

'You may go.'

I closed the door gently, with a satisfying click. The cold, damp air felt good. I was out. I was on my own. I had taken a pot-shot at the system and, by God, I think I winged the blighter.

Lock Up Your Daughters

Winter, leading into spring and summer and culminating in my eighteenth birthday, was a period of cleansing and essentially re-entering the human race. I was allocated a place at King Edward VII School in Sheffield. It was an ex-grammar school, now a comprehensive, but with a good academic reputation. It was mixed, girls and boys, and – shock-horror – it was friendly. I waited for the hierarchy to become clear, for the punishment beatings, but nothing of that sort went on. I wondered about what might have been, had I not been packed off to boarding school.

There was little point in attending the school, except for the legal requirement to do so, because in a few months I would have to sit my exams, and unfortunately the exam board in Sheffield was radically different from the one in Oundle. I spent lots of time in the library, mugging up on my Norse mythology rather than studying.

I joined the Territorial Army as a private. My number was 2440525 and the sergeant said that I was too clever to be a private, and asked why I didn't wait to become an officer at university. I told him I just wanted to get on with it, so he issued me with kit and that was that.

Our unit – D Company, Yorkshire Volunteers – was, in theory, on 24-hour call in the event of a war. We would be sent direct to the front, with mortars and rocket-propelled anti-tank weapons, one of which was given the surprisingly cute name of the 'wombat.' Our life expectancy in combat, I was informed, was 1 minute and 45 seconds.

I got drunk with a lot of steelworkers, dug holes in inhospitable pieces of Northumbria and got to carry a big belt-fed general-purpose machine gun, which used a lot of bullets, all of them blanks.

Otherwise, I shovelled shit on the farm, of which there was a great deal, and drove tractors and dump trucks, laid concrete and constructed fences. I converted my anger into the physical, and I felt a relief from the rage that had burned continually at boarding school.

Then, one English class, one fateful lunchtime, I heard mutterings from the back: 'We don't have a singer for rehearsals tonight.'

I turned round, and suddenly recognised my drumming buddy Paul Bray. He had two very cool dudes who already looked like seasoned rock professionals flanking him.

'Er, hi ...' I began nervously. 'I sing a bit.'

They looked me up and down. I was a bit pudgy, with an awful short haircut and terrible trousers.

'Brilliant. See you at six o'clock.'

It would be nine months till I was due to start at university. Time to listen to Radio Caroline under the bed, draw fantasy stage sets and rehearse in my mate's garage on a Tuesday evening. Limbo ain't a bad place to be.

Our band had a real drum kit and two guitars, and the bass player had his own gear, a self-contained amp and speaker. The rest of us shared one Vox AC30. Two guitars plugged in plus the new vocalist: me.

My microphone had been snipped off the side of a portable cassette recorder and spliced via Sellotape onto a longer cable and thus into the Vox combo. It sounded truly awful, but the band were light years ahead of anything I had experienced up to then. They had learnt half of the album *Argus* by Wishbone

Ash, plus 'All Right Now' by Free and the inevitable 'Smoke on the Water'.

After one song and letting rip my Ian Gillan shriek a few times, they all nodded sagely: 'You are the new singer.'

I asked if they had a name. 'Paradox,' came the reply. I thought it was a rubbish name.

I regarded home in Sheffield as being a kind of holding pattern. I didn't feel as if I belonged, but then it wasn't an unpleasant existence. It just seemed as if I was walking on eggshells unless I was outside digging holes or shovelling horseshit.

The local pub was a 20-minute walk, which was arduous in deep snow, and on the way was the old German prisoner-of-war camp, complete with half-demolished prison huts. Beyond that, down a steep hill, was the bus stop and, above it, looming Bram Stokerish in the moonlight, the Fulwood isolation hospital.

On two occasions, walking back from the bus stop in the darkness and wind, I met people wandering in the road, confused. I had to wait until I could flag down a rare passing car to get them to safety. I suspect now that they might have had Alzheimer's. They would almost certainly have died of exposure, left to their own devices. In the seventies, people were simply 'loopy' and that was that.

Having done my good deed for the day, fate returned the favour. We actually had a gig. We debuted at the local youth club, with at least four people in front of the stage and the rest pinned against the wall in sheer terror as we hacked our way through 'Smoke on the Water'. I think they had the Four Tops more in mind.

I had spent 15 quid on a half-decent mic, a Shure Unidyne B, which had a ridiculous stand that could lose its legs and vertical integrity suddenly and for no obvious reason. I had a tambourine, and had saved up for a very old pair of Vox 4 ×

10-inch speaker columns. Signing on for the Summer, my dole cheque appeared in the post and I had enough to buy a 60-watt Carlsbro guitar amp from a secondhand store. Now we were all equipped, but with no gigs to go to.

I turned salesman. I went out and door-stepped publicans who had gigs. I scoured the ads in the local paper for bands and then went through the phone book to find the number of the pub where they were playing. I bullshitted for England, but there was no evading the awful truth that came with the question: 'Do you have a demo tape?'

Of course we didn't. I forget how we made one in the end, but anyway, it was awful. I think we just put a cassette recorder at one end of the garage and made a racket.

Somehow, we got a booking at a pub called the Broadfield, and we may even have done a second gig. We were paid three quid, as well as one dog-eared hamburger and a bottle of Newcastle Brown apiece, and had to sign a receipt.

Next was a council-sponsored Afternoon in the Park in Weston Park, by the university and just up the road from the Royal Hallamshire Hospital. A local DJ from Radio Sheffield turned up, but he'd been in the pub all afternoon and was quite possibly on acid.

The headline band was called Greensleeper, and they had that bored air of insouciance born of being the biggest thing in the postal district and doing gigs every weekend. They had a following, which turned up just before and left immediately after they played.

We were left to set up on the small stage in bright sunshine. There were some green fold-up chairs and some kids eating ice cream and squinting at us. We started to play. The drum kit was shifting around and the stage was not held together, so it started moving apart as well. At which point a ne'er-do-well gentleman jumped up on stage shouting, 'Shut up – I'm trying to sleep!' He pushed the guitar amp off the back of the stage, which was only two feet off the ground in any case.

I seized one of the fold-up chairs and hit him with it, and he just staggered backwards and then walked back down the hill, straight through the empty lines of chairs normally used for old ladies to sit by the bandstand.

Fuck, I thought. This is like the Who. But it wasn't really, and the DJ on acid said so on his radio programme that night.

Nevertheless, with our new-found notoriety I pressed hard for playing our own material and a name change. Paradox was too wishy-washy; we needed something legendary.

'How about Styx?' I suggested.

'Isn't somebody else called that?'

'Oh, they won't notice,' I stated confidently.

Our second appearance at the Broadfield was also our swansong, but our first as Styx. We even had badly photocopied handouts with wiggly letters, made by sticking individual letters to paper with glue, but not quite in a straight line. The tambourine was now polished aluminium, and it twirled around, but you had to be careful in case it severed the blood vessels around the base of your finger.

I was trying to be cool. Picture this: lumberjack shirt (because Rory Gallagher wore one), waistcoat with lots of badges on it, and Hush Puppies. Lock up your daughters, South Yorkshire.

We had one self-penned song, called 'Samurai'. The lyrics were not mine, but a fellow sixth-form poet who contrived to combine the Samurai with vultures and to rhyme flesh with crèche in the same line.

'Cool,' I said. 'Er, what's a crèche?'

We decided to split up on a high, citing commercial pressures plus the fact that the two guitarists had summer jobs wearing wooden clogs and cleaning out steel furnaces, which paid rather better than the three quid we got paid in our final appearance.

Among all this, it was easy to forget that I was meant to be taking my final exams. I had done little studying; actually, I had nothing to study. I had a box of history notes; economics I thought was a load of rubbish made up by academics to create jobs for themselves; and English was fun to create, but oh my God, just the cover of anything by Jane Austen made me want to eat my own leg rather than drag my way through it.

Anyway, I sat my A levels having not read a single book for the English exams or opened many textbooks for economics. History I reckoned I could probably blag because I was actually interested in it, which was probably a good thing because I would be spending three years of university ostensibly studying it. I can't remember what I wrote, but incredibly I passed all three with the lowest possible pass grade, an 'E'. Even more incredibly, I had an offer from a London university who wanted me so badly that they only required an 'E' grade in two out of the three subjects.

Thus, with no wasted effort, I entered the halls of academia: Queen Mary College, University of London.

Minibusted

I was in London, with an agenda, an aim but no plan, and a Government grant putting actual money in my pocket. My first problem was surviving the day I arrived. I was immediately summoned to the head of the history department, Professor Leslie. He held up the piece of paper with my A level grades.

'What is the meaning of this?' he demanded.

'Ah, well. I did have a little problem.'

'What ... problem?'

'Well, you see, I was chucked out of school and had to home study.'

'Why? Why were you thrown out?'

'Er ... drinking,' I offered.

He pointed at me, and his eyes looked like giant gobstoppers behind the twin television screens that were his glasses. He also had an alarming resemblance to Mr Toad.

'I have got my eye on you,' he declared. 'My spies will be watching you. A student needs only a bed, a chair, a desk and a suitably illuminated light.'

'Well, thank you very much,' I replied and, breathing a sigh of relief, I headed directly to the student union bar, where a fantastic pint of Bass lay in wait, priced at a quarter of the cost of beer in a pub. Happy days.

I had a plan cunningly concealed from my parents, and in truth even from myself. They were puzzled by my choice of a history degree.

'What use is that?' they asked.

'Useful in the army,' I replied. But the thought bubbles around my head told a different story.

I had a plot: anything to get out of here, and if I am going to be a rock singer, it must be London – but I can still join the army if it all falls apart. And here I was, almost out as soon as I'd arrived. I sipped my pint. *Priorities*, I thought. *Number one, virginity. Must lose it, and fast.*

I put an end to my military ambitions once and for all by joining the London University Officers' Training Corps. I won't dwell on the subject. I turned up to the drill nights and they were dreary affairs compared to running around the Northumbrian desolation of Otterburn with machine guns and steelworkers. It was more a gathering of chinless wonders intent on dressing up in ill-fitting uniforms and boots that had never seen mud.

I soon fell in with a lot of drunks, a very mixed crowd, and discovered they were called medical students. This, I thought, was the beginning of the end for virginity. So I began a career washing coffee cups late at night after the pubs shut, in the mistaken belief that doing useful things might make a 19-year-old dental student swoon. Eventually she did swoon, but not before I discovered that she was a virgin too, and worse, could recite chapter and verse the pharmacology of birth control. This removed the frisson of pure lust, but replaced it with a comforting reliability based on sound clinical practice. Practise we did, though.

That taken care of, I set off in search of rock 'n' roll and the secret of the universe. And it was only Friday afternoon.

You don't have to be Sherlock Holmes to spot musicians, especially rock musicians. Either wandering around in a daydream or driven by a burning ambition, they are often given away by guitar cases, drumsticks or a copy of *Melody Maker* turned to the classified adverts in the back. As quaint and faintly ridiculous as it sounds now, *Melody Maker* was the only serious magazine for adverts of musicians wanted, gear for sale, studios available, van for hire and all things rock and musical.

It was a broadsheet, and basically black and white. Interlopers like *Sounds* magazine had colour centrefolds of newspaper-grade quality – large sheets of toilet paper in order to try to make inroads into *Melody Maker*'s circulation.

So I just spotted a Gibson SG being carried, out of its case, by a slight, curly haired guy.

'Hiya. Nice guitar. What kind of stuff you into?' I asked.

'Priest, Sabbath, Purple.'

So in the space of 30 seconds we had a band. Martin Freshwater was his name and he knew a bass player called Adam. Then we unearthed Southend's very own Jon Lord, Noddy White.

Bits of Noddy looked like Noddy Holder of Slade, hence the name, and I never found out if he had been born with another one. Noddy taught guitar, had a double-neck bass and six-string combo, and an organ that didn't sound nearly as impressive as it looked. All we lacked was a drummer.

Steve was the only non-student, and I have utterly forgotten how we found him, but he lived in Catford and had more drums than I had ever seen in my life.

We found a large room in the disused kitchens of the halls of residence, set up some kit and made a noise. The walls were tiled and the stainless-steel sinks created a natural tinny reverb, so the whole experience was like playing inside a biscuit tin.

I asked Noddy to show me how to play guitar, and I slowly crabbed and clawed and contorted my stubby fingers into the requisite shapes. Immediately I started to write, and the first thrill of creation soon turned to frustration without the ability to create form and structure.

I never forgot the initial joy, the thrill of that moment of inception, of meaning. Even if it only meant something to myself, and even if it ultimately was deemed rubbish. There was a purity in the art of creation. By now, we had worked up a small repertoire, and all the material was our own. We were basically ready, or so we thought, to get some gigs.

But we needed a name.

Names are vexatious things. They can unwittingly define and doom a band to perdition, or, even worse, to be damned by faint praise.

A name creates the tightrope that every band walks. Rock music walks that tightrope for eternity: too pomp, too punk, too serious, too laughable, too out of tune, too technical – none of it matters as long as you stay on the tightrope. In fact, it's exciting to watch as you wobble.

But it's hell if you fall off.

In 1977 punk was in full flow, and Queen Mary College, Mile End, the East End, was smack-bang in the middle of it. The Pistols' secret gigs, the Jam, Bethnal – a punk band with a violinist. What's in a name?

We played way too fast, and the more excited we got, the faster we played.

'Speed?' Noddy suggested.

'Speed?' I queried.

'Yeah. Cos we play too fucking fast.'

None of us, and I mean NONE of us, had any idea that speed was a drug, and a rather popular one for a culture that hadn't discovered – and anyway couldn't yet afford – cocaine. Beer was the only drug in town. In the student union after 5 p.m. there was a gaggle of music fiends who stood by the jukebox and fiercely disagreed every day about the same things. They shouted at each other and remained friendly at the end of it. Future world leaders and football supporters, take note.

The union bar contained all shades of red, from light pink in high heels to communist scarlet, with blood-stained hatchets to bury in the heads of the filthy capitalist oppressors. As an avowed contrarian, I stood up and opposed a few of the more silly motions in public debates. It was worth it, just to wind up these po-faced and self-important arbiters of student political opinion.

The Socialist Workers Party rep was always polite but intense – a duffel-clad class warrior. We would have entertaining arguments before he decamped to plot the coming apocalypse, leaving me with the thought that I was *on the list*.

'The *Titanic*,' 'I reminded him, 'also had a list, and look what happened there.'

There were, however, departments in the student union that actually did things, as opposed to talking about doing things. Entertainment seemed absolutely the place to go. The entertainment officer was elected by students, along with his or her deputy, and essentially became a student-union-funded concert promoter.

Queen Mary had, and still does have, an extraordinary facility, the Great Hall. Built in the 1930s as the People's Palace, it had one of the largest proscenium stages in London. Now it has been modified as more of a multi-purpose space, but back in 1977 it was still a theatre with a seated balcony and a large floor, which, for gigs, was devoid of chairs.

I started out as a volunteer by pushing boxes around and loading in and out for various bands. I assembled the 'Atomhenge' for Hawkwind, and these days I drink in my local pub with the drummer, who is now one of the UK's leading authorities on waste recycling. At the same show were the reformed Pirates, minus Johnny Kidd himself, of course, who had been killed in a car crash some years before. The guitarist, sadly now deceased, was called Mick Green, and he is pretty essential listening for any guitar player.

Variously, Manfred Mann's Earth Band, Ian Dury and the Blockheads, Lone Star, Racing Cars and Supertramp all adorned the People's Palace stage. The BBC used it for a series of *Sight and Sound in Concert* broadcasts, and all the shows were open to the public. I did a bit of everything, from front of house to backstage and security – and a lot of truck loading.

From the sold-out psychedelia of Hawkwind to the smell of dirty old cookers and musty carpet was a reality check, but in our little rehearsal biscuit-tin Speed built up a repertoire that was an interesting but very odd mix. If we were a garden of sound, we would have been a mangled tornado of dead leaves and twigs, with the occasional daffodil visible through the browned gale-force fugue.

My two self-penned, very primitive guitar riffs were called 'FBI' and 'Snoopy'. I possessed a large stuffed version of the cartoon character created by Charles Schulz. Snoopy abuse was a prominent feature of the show. I wish I could tell you why.

Our first gig was at the Green Man in Plumstead, where we played to not a lot of people. Snoopy was disembowelled and we played extremely fast and largely out of tune.

It went down a storm and the promoter gave us a residency once a month.

To get to and from gigs, we stole – er, borrowed – the college minibus. It had seats and windows, so the seats had to be removed and the bus loaded up out of sight, then rapidly driven through the gates before somebody realised that the windows were full of Mr Fender, Mr Marshall and a big stuffed white dog with a black nose.

After all the gear was in, there was no room for people, so we had to travel by train. We would then sneak back after the gig and replace the seats before dawn.

My first year at university wasn't half bad. I saw a lot of bands and played in a band. I learnt to play bad guitar, wrote my first songs and did gigs. Time to move on, up and in – or maybe that should be down and out.

Going to the Dogs

If my account sounds strangely devoid of much in the way of historical studies, that's because as I progressed to my second year, I wasn't even turning up to most lectures. Very occasionally, I would drink two or three pints at lunchtime and wend my way into my medieval history tutorial. My tutor was a very nice old lady, and I think she might actually have experienced most of *The Cambridge Medieval History* she so adored. I can't remember anything about Charlemagne or Frederick II, but I do remember that the sunshine was very bright and interfered with my daydreams as it streamed through the hazy window that framed her silhouette.

I was now the full-on entertainment officer. I had an office, went to committee meetings and I had a budget. Most crucially, I had a telephone with an outside line and a hotline to every agent in town. Suddenly I had a freshers' week to organise: booking bands, discos and all that good stuff.

I think I ended up with Fairport Convention as the main event, and the whole week was extremely profitable. I made about 20 per cent on top of my expenditure. I was hauled before the committee and told I was a 'disgrace'.

'This is just exploitation of the student body,' I was informed.

'So you want me to lose money as a general moral principle?' I enquired.

After the inquisition, I gave the problem some thought. I had never seen Ian Gillan – one of my vocal heroes – so I phoned up his agent and booked him. Money no object, I said. In return, I suggested, might there be a few pub gigs he could point in my general direction? Speed was fun but constrained. To borrow a song title from my future, I had a 'Burning Ambition'.

The telephone, of course, gave me the ability to respond to adverts in *Melody Maker*. One in particular seemed promising: 'Vocalist required to complete recording project.' I phoned up. Just one problem: 'Do you have a tape?' Of course I didn't. The guy I spoke to was a recording engineer and also the bass player. It was free studio time, and I had never been in a studio in my life. The influences, though, sounded like a shoo-in for me: Purple, Sabbath and, delightfully, Arthur Brown. He, Ian Gillan and Ronnie James Dio are probably the three singers you could refer to and say, 'Aha! I see where Dickinson nicked that from.'

I should recount my history with Arthur Brown, one of England's wackiest performance artists, and one of rock music's most insanely talented voices. The first time I saw him was at Oundle when I was 16. Kingdom Come was the band, and the album was called *Journey*. The concert was, for me, a mind-blowing shamanic ritual. I have never tried acid or mushrooms or any hallucinogen, but with Arthur that night I didn't need to. Deep, *deep* analogue-synth sine waves scooped your eyeballs up and planted them in stereo where your ears should be. The single screen of blobs and lights and stars compressed time to a singularity.

Then Arthur hit the stage dressed in face paint and a gigantic headdress, standing like an Aztec king before a gigantic tripod, and raised his hands in sacrifice and intoned, in a dark, extended baritone, a command to strip the rust from your soul: 'Alpha waves compute before eternity began ...'

Who cares if it sounds like hippy bollocks? I can tell you I thought I had seen a glimpse of God that night.

In 1976 Arthur had a band with no drummer. On top of that tripod was not an altar, but a Bentley Rhythm Ace drum machine. Arthur wasn't sacrificing or blessing us; he was fiddling with the analogue tape loops of each individual drum, all of which ran at different speeds, and he was probably cursing frequently in frustration. No one but a madman would even have attempted it. There was a lead guitarist and a bass player, and two keyboard players, with every kind of analogue synth going, VCS3, Theremin and Mellotron.

Somewhere in the midst of this falling-into-a-musical-black-hole experience, two fellows came on stage dressed as brains to be beaten with a stick, and men danced around dressed as traffic lights. Inspired and deliciously potty.

'Fire' is the best known track of Arthur's, and this alone is enough to secure him a place in rock's pantheon, but all of his albums with Kingdom Come and as the Crazy World of Arthur Brown are worth exploring. Pete Townshend was the associate producer of *The Crazy World of Arthur Brown* – the whole idea of the Who's *Tommy* came from it – and it's a concept album, one of the first, about a man's descent into hell. When he opens that door, well, you guessed it: 'I am the god of hell fire, and I bring you, fire ...'

There was a black voice trapped in Arthur's body, because he could strip the paint off walls when he sang blues standards like 'I Put a Spell on You'. That night I saw him, Arthur planted the seed for what I describe as 'theatre of the mind', with music the proscenium arch and your brain as the stage.

Anyway, back to my immediate problem – I didn't have a demo tape. I would have to improvise. In my second year in London I had moved my lodgings away from South Woodford – a bland, characterless university halls-of-residence tower block that overlooked the motorway – to somewhere slightly more challenging, but so much more interesting.

The Isle of Dogs is the U-shaped bend in the Thames that features prominently in the credits of *EastEnders*. In the late seventies it was a desolate, windy and decaying place. Tower blocks sat alongside thirties council flats and houses, all built for the thousands of workers who once populated the London docks. In Tudor times it was a marsh and a refuge for criminals on the run from nearby jails. Because of the tidal flow a wall was built, which gradually formed the shape we all know and love. Water-operated mills were built on the wall, hence the Millwall, which ran down the west side of the Isle. Before basins were scooped out of the mud to form the docks, Henry VIII released wild dogs onto the marshes. He was fed up of spending money on chasing criminals, so he made sure the dogs were fed up in a rather more unpleasant sense.

Tate & Lyle still has a sugar refinery there, and tucked away, on Tiller Road, was the ground-floor flat that was my new abode and the location of my first demo recording. I had a flatmate, but I didn't see much of him, as he would disappear into his lair and only emerge at odd hours of the night. He had long hair, an Afghan coat, goatee beard and John Lennon glasses, and he giggled a lot to himself for no reason I could fathom.

There was an upright piano left stranded in one bedroom. Clearly not the object to sling in the back of the car when your days at university are over, it had a mostly operating keyboard but sounded like a load of dinner gongs being hammered with tortured dissonance. I had a cassette recorder, and only one cassette. On one side was a series of awful easy listening, and on the other I had recorded some Monty Python. Cassette fiends will recall the curious rituals involved in taping over pre-recorded commercial cassettes. I got busy with a piece of Sellotape and then fiddled with the innards of the recorder, and eventually had my cassette poised and paused, standing atop the piano.

I didn't bother playing the piano, because I couldn't. I stepped well away from the tiny built-in condenser microphone and just yelled a lot, wailing through scales and letting off a nasal shriek with a couple of different vibratos as it faded away.

I put it in the post, to the PO box listed in the advert. With it was a note in red biro: 'Here is the demo. If it's rubbish there is some Python on the other side for a laugh.'

With that, I resumed normal operations. Go to college. Open the post. Avoid going to lectures. Sort out a rehearsal. Daydream a lot. Drink three pints at lunchtime. Go to tutorial. Remember nothing. Make some phone calls to agents. Wait an hour for the 277 bus. Eat something. See the girlfriend. Pub. Bed.

'There is a message for you,' I was told a couple of days later, when I showed up to the entertainments office. 'This guy phoned back about a tape or something.'

I grabbed the message: 'Call Phil on this number ...'

I dialled 'this number', and a friendly, enthusiastic Brummie voice answered: 'Yeah, I really liked the tape. You were doing some mad melody ideas. A bit like Arthur Brown.'

It was 3 p.m. By 6.30 I had found my way to the studio. It was homemade in a garage. Lined with egg boxes and foam it was Abbey Road as far as I was concerned. For a small pro-am studio it was quite well equipped. It had a small drum kit in situ, and lots of cables, pedals and stands to weave past on the way to the vocal booth. I had no idea about recording. I understood what a tape recorder did, and I understood a bit of what a mixer did (mix, right?), but of multitrack recording, I had no clue.

The idea of headphones was totally new; a monitor mix was an undiscovered country.

Phil played me the backing track. *The guitar was pretty cool as well*, I thought: a little bit Peter Green, early Fleetwood

Mac, 'The Green Manalishi' feel. The song was called 'Dracula', and it had some corny *Carry On*/'Fangs for the Memories'-style lyrics, but played absolutely deadpan serious. Try 'My only sense of humour is in a jugular vein' and 'Your neck is on the menu tonight' as a taster and you get the idea. I started to sing, having learnt the song in the control room. Phil leaned forward and pushed the talkback button: 'Erm ... how long have you got?'

'All night if you want,' I replied.

I could see him leaning back to dial a phone number.

Phil played bass and had called his big brother, Doug, who played drums. Together, we all listened back at four in the morning. I had never double-tracked, or harmonised with myself, but I did that night: three-part ascending choir vocals, big doubled choral pieces. If only the owner of the three-bedroomed semi whose garage it was knew what he started that night.

'We'd better start the band, then, I suppose,' said Doug.

I was most impressed by the fact that they had a battered blue transit van. It performed parcel deliveries by day, and at night it would turn into the most exotic four-wheeled magic carpet, transporting our merry souls to la-la land until dawn, when we all went back to the pumpkin patch with the rest of humanity. But before we could sprinkle fairy dust into that petrol tank, we had to find a guitarist.

So an ad was put in *Melody Maker*: 'Guitarist wanted for pro recording band. Good prospects.'

My God, I came over all a twitter. Pinch yourself, Dickinson, here comes the Big Time.

Dope Opera

Speed was not so speedy anymore. We had all moved and were spread across East London. Varying degrees of work plus geography put paid to us, and in any case our drummer couldn't get off from his job in Catford. Plumstead became Glumstead as we played our last gig, but not before a puzzled audience saw me disembowel Snoopy on the stage at the People's Palace. I knew they were puzzled because I could clearly see the bemusement on the six faces in the cavernous venue. Perhaps they thought they had encountered a strange art installation, or they were simply so appalled that they stayed to see the car crash.

Actually, we weren't that bad – just not that good.

Doug and Phil lived in a rather swish rented mansion block in Battersea in south-west London. In the seventies – and the eighties, for that matter – rents in London were affordable, and houses were cheap. One enterprising lad on a social-sciences course actually bought a flat during his time at university, using his grant as a deposit. Smart cookie.

I did something quite different with my grant money. I spent most of it on a PA system for the new band. It consisted of two large pieces of furniture with 2 × 15-inch speakers buried in the cabinetry. Sat atop were a pair of integrated double 12 inches with a tweeter on top, powered by four 200-watt valve amplifiers, designated as slaves, powerslaves, in fact. I had upped the ante in the microphone stakes and now gripped a gold AKG-something-or-other, with a cannon plug at one end and a jack plug at the other. I was halfway to paradise at least.

All of which depleted my bank account to almost zero. The nice people at Barclays had given me a chequebook, a bank card and what seemed to be a free overdraft, which was how I fed myself. I was also responsible for not paying my rent. I managed this by not being present between the hours of nine and five, Monday to Friday, or if I was present, I hid behind the cooker.

After a couple of terms of this, letters started to arrive. Quite a lot of letters, really. *Never mind*, I thought. *One day all of this will be in a book.*

In the meantime I manned the telephone in the rather swish mansion block in Battersea and waited for prospective guitarists to phone. By day three I was losing the will to live. If auditioning disciples was like auditioning guitarists then no wonder Jesus ascended to heaven. At first I listened and they talked, and talked ...

I had maybe a hundred names, and we booked them in over three days at a rehearsal studio above the Rose and Crown in Wandsworth. I made notes on their stories and their influences and styles.

'Well, I think I'm as good as Jimmy Page, but maybe not as clever.'

'I like to think of myself as a cross between Ritchie Blackmore and Mozart.'

'I think the guitar is, for me, an extension of my entire personality.'

Phil and Doug just jammed on a couple of chords and we watched as the helpless, the hopeless, the hapless, the naive and the outright lunatic failed to negotiate any musical material or collaborate with any rhythm at all, not even their own pulse.

At the end of three days, and after nearly throwing myself off Albert Bridge into the Thames in frustration, two shiny nuggets appeared. Both were over 30, which seemed an impossibly distant age. There was a fantastic Irish guy who had played in showbands, a total pro. Music was like flicking on a light switch for him. But then in walked Tony Lee. Tony was a chilled-out Australian with presence, and when he played, which he did effortlessly, he gurned in a most-agreeable manner. He was 30 years ahead of his time as far as facial hair was concerned. In short, he looked great and, boy, could he play guitar.

We called ourselves Shots, but we could have called ourselves Anal Catastrophe and only had to change one letter. It was the era of punk, after all. I thought it was a rubbish name as well, but I couldn't think of a better one.

We set about rehearsing material and creating an image. Not being experienced at either past-time, I went with the received wisdom. After rehearsals, or lengthy discussions over vats of tea in Battersea, I would bounce around trains, tubes and the 277 bus before arriving back at the Isle of Dogs.

One random night, I unsuspectingly fell under the evil spell not of bell, book and candle, but of glass, resin and matches. Marijuana had arrived, and in the finest tradition of toilet archaeology, shit was about to happen. I had been hammering on the keys of the dilapidated piano when there was a knock at the door.

Peering around the door handle was my grinning, pixie-faced flatmate, he of the Afghan coat and John Lennon specs.

'Fancy a glass?' he said.

I had no idea what he was talking about but, in the spirit of 'What Does this Button Do?', I feigned nonchalance.

'Why not?'

I tentatively followed him into his lair. It was full-on hippy-headband, joss-stick heaven: carpets on the walls and ceiling – even on the floor. It was a male boudoir, and a temple to a fragrance I couldn't quite identify. He giggled a lot. He was still giggling when he took a badge from his lapel (students always wore at least 10 or 15 badges) and laid it down, bending the sharp end of the pin to vertical. This was intriguing behaviour.

He then crumbled a piece of a brown mud-like substance away from its bigger brother, and rolled it into a greasy lump. He impaled it with great care on the badge like a surgeon would treat a fragile liver before transplant.

Suddenly he lit the lump, swooped a glass over the top of the whole issue and, lifting the edge of the inverted glass, inhaled the resulting smoke before going very red in the face. I was nonplussed. Finally, he exhaled. The glass was still full of the joys of combustion.

He nodded at the glass.

I inhaled to maximum effect. My lungs felt singed, my epiglottis ravaged by a Brillo Pad, but for some reason I rolled on my back, put my hands and feet in the air, and I was suddenly on the ceiling looking down at myself. I had a few more puffs, and by now had figured out that this was a resinous form of marijuana. Things became funny that were not so before, and I spent several hours perforating the fabric of the universe looking for the joke. Though I am loath to admit it, that little puff of dope opened what They Might Be Giants would have called the little 'Birdhouse in Your Soul'. That and a desire to eat doughnuts.

I never got the chance to thank my flatmate because the police arrived and took him away a few days later. He was a generous soul, and had sent a large lump of hash in the corner of an envelope via Her Majesty's postal system. Whether impaired by his own fumes, or simply impaired in his judgement, he addressed the envelope to the wrong house. The recipient opened it, called the police and kindly gave them the name and address of the sender, helpfully provided within.

I think he was fined £400 and I never saw him again, but whatever was in that piece of dope had not gone away. My yearning was to transfer the theatre spinning through the cosmos of my brain into the very soul of an audience. But there was the problem of image. It was clear to me that I didn't look the part. I also couldn't bring myself to fall into the mire of the fake American rock 'n' roller. Image in entertainment can be everything and nothing at the same time.

I had to be substantial. I had no choice, because judged on image I was a walk-on disaster. In case you think this judgement too harsh, there is a wealth of photographic evidence. Because the recording of 'Dracula' seemed to be in the right vein, we concocted a sort of pastiche Screaming Lord Sutch bargain-basement shock-horror band personality. Our lanky Australian wore a cape and a lot of eye shadow. Our bass player wore a rubber 80-year-old man mask and I wore green army long johns, boxing boots and a grandad shirt. The *pièce de résistance* was a gold lamé jockstrap. In case you think this may just have been a terrible accident during a game of blind man's bluff in a charity shop, I had the gold jockstrap handmade.

Up in Hackney, East London, was a legal squat, basically a commune of three streets in a triangle. In the middle of it were all manner of vegan cafés and rainbow coalitions. There dwelt a lesbian seamstress who measured me up, somewhat unimpressed, and produced my sparkly willy-cover.

I had in mind Ian Anderson, he of the tramp overcoat and codpiece on Jethro Tull's *Aqualung*. Although I didn't sound like Ian Anderson vocally, I was a massive Jethro Tull fan, and of course Glenn Cornick, the founder of Wild Turkey, had been an original member.

I started to use my limited dramatic skills. A great deal of prancing went on in confined spaces during rehearsals, and twirling inanimate objects while standing on one leg.

Fast approaching was our first gig. The owner of the Rose and Crown took pity on us, I suspect because we spent a lot of money in his rehearsal room. There was one person in the audience and there is nothing quite so lonely as one man in a disco. He sat at a table in the middle of the dance floor, the blue flashing lights reflecting off the mirrored walls. No matter how many mirrors, it still didn't look like a crowd.

More gigs followed, and our fame spread as far as Croydon. There, we suddenly came to the attention of an agent, who wanted to sign us. He made all the right noises but said all the wrong things.

He had red hair and a comb-over, and was an agent for rockabilly bands, fifties revival acts, Teddy-boy cover groups and any form of novelty to entertain awful people.

'Brilliant, lads,' he said. 'Love it. Comedy heavy metal. Hilarious. Love the banter. Come up to the office and sign the contract.'

And then he was gone.

The office was on a damp-smelling first floor above a curry house in Finsbury Park, just around the corner from the tube and not too far from the Rainbow Theatre, a legendary rock venue (now sadly an evangelist church). That, of course, was where we really wanted to be, but this seemed better than nothing. We signed the contract. It said that we promised to do everything, and he promised to try to do something but with no guarantees.

'Brilliant, lads. Fantastic, great, comedy heavy metal ... bring the house down.'

We went away feeling strangely glum and unfulfilled.

After a few weeks of nothing in particular from this gentleman, we were offered a gig at an army base in Arbroath, Scotland. Research, plus a map, revealed the truth about economics espoused by Dickens: 'When the petrol bill to drive from one end of the country exceeds the total fee available, result misery.'

Arbroath being notable for its smoked fish, I went down to the fishmongers and bought some boil-in-a-bag kippers to give us a taste of what might have been. Our agent protested: 'Well, frankly lads, you're blowing a great chance. Extremely disappointing.'

We consigned our agent with the Donald Trump comb-over to the bargain basement of history, and headed south-east, beyond even the mighty metropolis of Plumstead.

Gravesend is one of those town names, like Leatherhead or Maidenhead, which make Americans scratch their heads and wonder, *Why?* The why in this case was probably nautical and may have alluded to the end of the line for ships of the line. The Prince of Wales didn't live there, but he certainly gave rise to a few pubs in his time, and Shots appeared one dull evening, setting up in front of the bar, with the gents' toilet entrance just to one side of the non-existent stage.

Masks on, jockstrap firmly strapped and silver tambourine twirling away, we were enough to stop conversation at the bar, which is always a good start.

The big challenge came when patrons attempted to use the toilet facilities, and I decided to conduct a few improvised interviews with them as they stepped onto our territory. The more humiliating the better, and the landlord rebooked us.

Word got around about the prancing singer, the old geezer on the bass and the increasingly uncomfortable Tony Lee on black Gibson, black mascara, black lipstick and no work permit. As we returned to the scene of the crime weeks later the place was packed and then, after that, more packed. The landlord was delighted.

'Love the banter,' he'd say, 'love it.' And he would buy me lots of beer.

Summer of 1978 was, for me, stunning. I was free to roam the London streets with only dreams as my guide, and even then, the liberty to forget at will. I had resigned as entertainment officer, so I just pottered about the East End, getting a builder's suntan.

Because of punk and its DIY attitude to records and record companies, everyone was in on the act now. Self-produced singles on vinyl were standard for rock bands too, but as Shots we were at a disadvantage. We didn't have the cash to have one pressed. Tony, our Antipodean vampire, was showing signs of ultimatum fever. He was older, had actually earned money out of music and was in a reasonably tearing hurry to do so again.

Throughout my third and final year at university, we resumed our gigs in small pubs and clubs around London. We could have papered the walls of a small hamster cage with rejection slips for 'Dracula'. The Prince of Wales was starting to get bored of us, and I think the feeling was mutual. There are only so many times you can try the same gags and the same songs before people begin to drift. One evening, however, we were out loading the van and I was standing, temporarily unused, when I was approached by three odd-looking individuals.

Paul Samson had a bowler hat, leather jacket and a moustache, plus shoulder-length hair in curls. He was not unlike a King Charles spaniel. Chris Aylmer was tall, had a mullet and seemed really quite mature. Barry Purkis had dyed red hair in ringlets, a Nazi-stormtrooper dress jacket, fluorescent earrings and bright-red trousers.

''Allo,' started Paul. 'We're Samson. We've got a deal, an album and management, and we want a singer. Interested?'

'Gary Holton, Heavy Metal Kids – that's the sort of thing we're after,' chimed in Barry.

'I can see the Ian Gillan influence,' Chris intoned reflectively.

'And Kiss, and the Residents. Mad shit,' Barry added.

'Mad,' Chris muttered.

'Yeah, mad,' Paul chuckled.

'Well, I am very flattered,' I replied. 'But I've got to finish my final exams in three weeks so I can't do anything until I've got that over with. Is that okay?'

'Yeah, alright. We'll be in touch,' Paul said, and he wrote down his phone number. I had become more and more preoccupied with exams, and for the six months before my finals had decided to catch up on the previous two-and-half-years of academic insufficiency.

With no wasted effort, I got a Desmond, a Tutu, or, more correctly, a second-class honours, lower division.

By the end of the exams I was starting to imagine that I was almost getting the hang of this academic business. My brain was creacking in all the right places, and I began to wonder if all this activity might have created some permanent impact.

I finished my last exam before lunch. I took a deep breath as I turned my back on the great white-fronted main building on the Mile End Road. I took the 277 bus down to the Greenwich foot tunnel and walked under the River Thames to the old wharves that lay on the south of the river. Wood Wharf Studios was a rehearsal room with a panoramic view of the water, but for today my destination was the small portable shed around the back.

Head still buzzing from cabinet papers about Munich, appeasement and the fall of France to the Nazis, I opened the studio door. It was 1979. I was 20 years old and I was about to start singing full-time with Samson.

A Heavy Metal Crusade

It was not quite what I expected. There was more gear than I had ever seen in a rehearsal room: Marshall amps, weave-fronted Marshall speaker 4 × 12-inch cabinets, Paul's Gibson SG, Chris's Fender Precision bass and, of course, the greatest number of drums I had ever been in close proximity to.

While the equipment was certainly not lacking, the will to do anything was curiously absent. I was raring to go, but we immediately decamped to the pub. Thus fortified, we made a start. Sort of.

'Shall we start?' I asked.

'Nah. Let's get wrecked first.'

And so it began. It was to be two years of madness, and yet we still managed to pull off some decent music, plus some variable gigs, although secretly we quite liked it that way.

The immediate task at hand was to get wrecked, so I went back to the pub and had a third pint. When I returned, the wreckage had already started. Although I'd been in a band called Speed, I had no idea that there was a drug called speed until a couple of years later. There was a light white crusting on the tip of Chris's nose. He was unusually active, being as he was fairly languid under control conditions.

Paul, on the other hand, was carefully rolling one of several joints using resin crushed atop tobacco removed from a Marlboro cigarette. This, plus a new echo machine, made for pleasant interludes of overlapping feedback that went on for several minutes.

Barry, or Thunderstick, as he had named himself, was wearing a blue boiler suit. As the engine room of the band on the drums, he didn't seem to be his usual bouncy self. This, I discovered, was because he had washed down a handful of downers with his pint. After half an hour or so, we launched into a number: stoned guitar, speeding bass and a drummer on downers periodically losing consciousness and threatening to fall off his drum stool backwards. Fortunately there was a wall behind that prevented this, and which meant he would suddenly wake up and thrash his kit much faster, as if to make up for lost time.

I did a bit of singing. *Three pints*, I thought, *is not enough*.

In the midst of this quick, quick, slow and stoned routine, the door opened and in walked what I thought might either be a travelling salesman or a minicab driver. He stood and watched. I have never liked being watched in rehearsals. I don't even like being watched by people I know, truth be told. Rehearsals are where you can screw up and feel safe to experiment.

Now he started tapping his foot and nodding his head, pursing his lips in the way that people who know absolutely zero about music do. He thought he was important, but he was just irritating.

We stopped, but not all at the same time. It took a while for Thunderstick to realise and slowly collapse onto his tom-toms, fast asleep.

'Hello, can I help?' I offered.

'Ah, yes. I'm Glyn. Alistair sent me down to have a listen. You know, see how it's going.'

He had quite a strong South African accent, and I was right: he was a minicab driver. The Alistair he referred to was Alistair Primrose of Ramkup Management, Samson's manager.

'We're just knocking it on the head,' Paul announced.

Short but sweet, the first rehearsal ended up back in the pub. Glyn had a cash float and we figured we may as well convert cash into food and beer. After an hour or so we went back to retrieve Thunderstick, and found him on the roof staring at the sun with his eyes closed. He was in no state to walk so we all sat on the roof while Chris and Paul smoked a lot more joints. We waited for our respective chemical states to stabilise so we could go home.

I found communication as I would normally understand it quite arduous with people who were out of their gourds. It's difficult enough when you are straight. I resolved to adapt. That's what evolution is for, I reasoned. If the mountain wouldn't move in my general direction, then I would jolly well find out what all the fun was about and clamber aboard.

Day two of rehearsals was looming large, and I was sure that eventually we would play something in tune that started or finished in time. And, dear reader, that's exactly what happened. So there. Samson did have a record deal and they had produced an album as a three-piece with Paul on lead vocals. The album was ready to be released, but the slight technical hitch was the addition of a fourth member, for whom no useful purpose could be assigned on the record.

The record label was an independent one, Laser Records, and the album was called *Survivors*, featuring a kindergarten bad-taste painted sleeve with the band standing atop a mound of dead rock stars. On the credits were instructions to 'play loud when wrecked', and it was certainly advice that we heeded for the next couple of years.

It's safe to say that almost every mishap, catastrophe and legal disaster that could befall a band happened to us over the next two years. We were sued, injuncted, arrested, on the run for various offences and utterly misunderstood by everyone except our own mothers.

The management were all accountants or company secretaries, and their skill set was recruiting accountants and financial personnel. They had offices on the top floor of a building in Blackfriars, wore suits and were drunk for 50 per cent of the day as part of their job description. There was some money they had obtained from a mystery backer, and that funded their foray into music. The other group they managed were the UK Subs, a hardcore punk band led by the evergreen Charlie Harper.

I received a pay cheque, £30 a week – in fact it was an advance, so just a loan really. It was thought great sport to fill in my first cheque payable to 'Bruce Bruce', as they had tied themselves in knots one drunken evening trying to remember the 'Bruces' Monty Python sketch.

I wasn't very amused because I couldn't cash the cheque and I had to eat.

'Bruce Bruce' then went down the slippery slope of acceptance as my stage name, something I was not entirely happy with. I thought it pretty stupid, really. Although not nearly as daft as the name of the movement that I had suddenly been co-opted into, unaware as I was of its existence.

The New Wave of British Heavy Metal was cooked up as a musical movement during a boozy lunchtime session involving journalists from *Sounds* magazine. Fed up with being seen as the idiot brother of the *New Musical Express*, they decided to fight back with a new wave of their own. It was a preposterous title, shortened to the equally incomprehensible NWOBHM, pronounced 'Newobbum'. The bands involved suddenly found themselves in a national music paper, to their great surprise in some cases.

The NWOBHM was nothing of the sort. It was an 'old wave' that had been ignored by the mainstream media in favour of punk, which, with its Vivienne Westwood fashion links and faux-class-war rhetoric, was more palatable to journalists who had aspirations beyond mere music.

The bands that inspired this NWOBHM were solidly traditional and, in the main, still going strong. To read contemporary music criticism you could be forgiven for thinking that rock music had ceased to exist in 1979. Far from it. Judas Priest, Motörhead, the Scorpions and various offshoots of Deep Purple were all selling out theatres and arenas, in spite of the media attention lavished elsewhere.

In Samson I was suddenly a member of the NWOBHM. Alistair Primrose claimed to have invented the roadshow that feted the movement. 'Dear boy,' he would say in his high-pitched country-reverend voice, 'we're going on a Heavy Metal Crusade.'

Two of my earliest shows with Samson were Heavy Metal Crusades, and they were eye openers. At a half-empty Surrey University I sat and watched Saxon do their stuff. I hadn't seen them or heard much of them before. They came from Barnsley, not a million inches from Worksop, and had a biker-boogie sort of sound, with epic overtones of Vikings, crusades and subsequently plummeting Boeing 747s.

Biff Byford, the singer, produced a large knife on stage, which he brandished triumphantly during one song. I watched with great interest as he tried to hurl it into the wooden stage, where it would embed itself menacingly. Except it didn't. It bounced off and clattered all about the floor. Bending over and picking it up to try again did not improve the situation, and even though it did end up stuck in the wood eventually, the drama had rather vanished.

Note to self: when things go wrong on stage either ignore and move on, or make a meal out of it and create its own narrative within the performance. Oh, well.

Samson nearly always headlined at Heavy Metal Crusades, mainly because our management paid for the shows. And thus the world discovered Barry's alter ego, Thunderstick. The key to the persona of Thunderstick was not just Barry's adoration of Kiss, but also of bands like the Residents and Devo, strange bedfellows as far as image went. Going round to Barry's house was like being in a surreal suburban Kiss encounter group. The first realisation was that the plywood units you were sitting on all contained old 12-inch guitar speakers, and were all connected to industrial-size amplifiers, which in turn were connected to the turntable, and on it, of course, was Kiss. As the cushions hoisted your bottom upward, his Alsatian dog would run into the room, bite its tail and run around in manic circles. As the walls of the terraced house began to crumble under the onslaught, Barry's wife would bring tea and biscuits, seemingly oblivious to the trench warfare going on beneath the furniture. Going round to Barry's was a seismic event.

Samson's intent was similar, and to achieve it we intended to blow things up and set fire to everything. Thunderstick took his Kiss-inspired concussive living room and tried to achieve the same effect in clubs. The character of Thunderstick was entirely separate from the band, and that's where the problem arose. Fee Waybill of the Tubes was part of a theatrical performance-art group that happened to play rock music. Barry would have loved that to be the case with Samson, but it was only the case for himself.

Paul in particular never engaged with it in any meaningful sense, and I think audiences saw it as a gimmick rather than an artistic endeavour. The Yorkshire Ripper didn't help much either. Gimp masks were not the flavour of the month.

Another Heavy Metal Crusade was at the Music Machine in Camden. Samson stood a bit of a chance in our south-east London stomping ground but, this far from home, in spite of a masked Thunderstick adorning various magazine covers, the audience was, to say the least, a bit sparse.

Still, we set about setting the place on fire – something we were about to do more literally. At the Music Machine I was introduced to our pyromaniac-in-chief Scotty. He was, as his name suggests, not English, and he was roadie, driver and blower-up of things. He laid mortar charges, set off confetti cannons and taped incendiaries to pieces of masonry, which were hopefully incombustible.

At first our gigs were few and far between. In 1979, after a few Heavy Metal Crusade road shows, we had only one gig between us and world domination. The album *Survivors* had a release date in the autumn, but there was no tour. We had an agent. I phoned him and decided he was useless. I was back to being entertainment officer again, with a telephone and a list of promoters, but at least I had a single, 'Mr Rock 'n' Roll', and a supply of cheap shirts to send out as promo items. I cold-called and bullshitted for England once more.

'Oh yeah, and a HUGE light show – and pyro. Front cover of ...'

Blah, blah, blah.

It took three weeks of hard work but I booked us a 20-date UK headline tour. I phoned our agent and told him he was a lazy shit. He sacked himself.

Life goes in circles. The next domino to fall was a pitifully short 20-minute opening slot for Ian Gillan, featuring Jimi Hendrix's psychedelic clone Randy California as special guest. Gillan had returned to his metal roots after a few years of jazz rock, and the effect was transformational. Ian's bass player, the sumo-sized John McCoy, had also played on and produced the *Survivors* album.

This was the first time I had ever set foot on a big stage, with a real crowd who actually wanted us to be there. Plus I was able to watch my childhood hero doing his stuff every night.

It was not quite what I expected. Which is to say, I had no idea what to expect. Ian was having vocal problems. That was obvious to me and quite a few others. Something had happened to his upper register, and the scream with a vibrato the depth of the Grand Canyon had been laid low. The purity had been replaced by a gruff rasp, and some nights I could hardly bear to watch. What I found incredible, though, was his undimmed self-belief, best summed up by 'look 'em in the eyes and mean it'.

At the end of the show he walked on with his guitar for a cover of 'Lucille'. He was strumming away, looking very uncomfortable, it must be said. Lead vocalists seldom look comfortable wearing a plank, especially so when it's hoisted up to nipple level. 'Lucille' would suddenly stop, and Ian would punch out some strange a cappella bluesy incantation, beautifully in time and in tune, but incomprehensible.

I stood on the sound desk every night trying to make out what he sang.

'I can't hear the guitar,' I'd say.

'It's not switched on.'

'Oh.' I thought for a moment. 'What's he saying at the end?'

'No fucking idea. He's pissed and just says random shit.'

Not only was he standing there with virtually no voice while randomly strumming a nipple-high electric guitar, but he faced off 3,000 people with every syllable hung on by a variety of drunken Glaswegians: 'Who far gits on the soul. Phara wooorgh ... gits inda backa macar ... yeah!'

Ian impressed me not just because he had one of the greatest rock voices of all time, but because he had courage. Here was a showman and a trouper. He didn't leap around; he spoke between songs with a quiet humour, or menace, if required, which is best summed up in one of his lyrics: 'He's got style. Got a reputation, no one dares to question.'

Except for me. I door-stepped him after a show, during the load out. He had a bottle of Bell's whisky in one hand and a Rothmans cigarette in the other.

'Er, hi,' I started. 'How is it with your voice on these long shows. Are you okay?'

He looked at me, then at the bottle and his cigarette, then back at me.

'Ulcers. Got some ulcers,' he said. He glanced back at the Bell's whisky. 'Sorts 'em right out.'

And with that, he turned away. I felt touched he'd even bothered to reply, but I was genuinely worried for him. The voice is a precious instrument, an emotional instrument. There is nothing between you and your audience. There is no guitar plank to hide behind, no giant stack of keyboards, no battery of tom-toms. There is nothing and no one to blame except yourself, and an audience will murder you and dance on your grave in a heartbeat if you let them.

Survivors came out and did okay, not brilliantly, but the tour and the press were fantastic. We got front covers of national music magazines, but, of course, it was all about Thunderstick. I was credited with backing vocals and guitar on the album. All absolute rubbish. I was nothing to do with it and all the songs were in the wrong key for me. My voice was barely getting warmed up singing them.

We set about a new album with the prospect of a new record label, Gem Records, distributed by RCA and with some real funding. Incredibly, I had not been in a recording studio since 'Dracula'.

We parked ourselves back in the Greenwich studios to write, but this time we could stare out at the river through the panoramic window without a minicab driver to disturb our endeavours. The time spent in the library at King Edward VII School ripping pages of Norse legends out of books came in handy after all, and 'Hammerhead' came into being. 'If I Had a Hammer' was already taken as a title, and Afro-Caribbean it certainly wasn't. There was such a profusion of different influences on the album that it's amazing we wrote anything coherent, but actually it works as a sort of period piece.

In no particular order we were throwing Rainbow, Journey, Devo, Kiss, Deep Purple and Peter Green-era Fleetwood Mac plus ZZ Top into a blender. 'Add thereto a tiger's chaudron, for the ingredients of our cauldron.' Whatever Shakespeare was smoking, we smoked an awful lot more of it during that album.

I screamed and shrieked, harmonised and crooned. Thunderstick broke milk bottles and we recorded it. Paul tracked, double-tracked and echoed his way around the songs. John McCoy, our producer, would watch, sporting a top-knot and smoking a firework-sized joint. 'Yeah, man,' he'd say. 'It's fucking mad.'

Indeed it was. The walls of Ian Gillan's Kingsway Studios in Holborn, where we recorded the album, were covered with gold, silver and platinum records. I had never laid eyes on such artefacts and would peer wide-eyed into the grooves, waiting for each indentation to reveal its secrets and stories. Deep Purple were there, of course, but there was also the disc for the original soundtrack of *Jesus Christ Superstar*. All a bit jaw-dropping for a 21-year-old. I quickly moved my gaze, lest I should be decreed uncool by my bandmates for showing too much interest and enthusiasm.

We finished the album and played it back several times, easily convinced of our own genius. It was called *Head On*, a name dreamt up by the label. The cover featured a gimpish executioner clutching an axe, which formed a rather tenuous visual pun with the title.

We'd all been imbibing in the Newman Arms, the pub above the studio, before returning several pints later for one last self-congratulatory moment. We lounged on the well-worn sofas that lined the back of the control room. The recording engineer was celebrating the mix by sprinkling some rather aromatic concoction onto our standard Marlboro Man tobacco-hybrid joints. At that moment in walked Ian Gillan, hair down to his waist, vintage Rolls-Royce in the underground car park and rock god in every sense of the word.

The engineer offered a joint. Ian waved it away as he sat down and rested his chin on top of the mixing desk: 'Nah, mate. I'll just stick to an oily.' (Oily rag equals fag equals cigarette, for our American brethren.) He looked around the room. 'Well, let's have a listen,' he said.

I heard my 21-year-old self ripping off most of Ian's phraseology in the vain hope of licking his vocal boots. I was passed a joint and took a few puffs. I was nervous, watching my hero listen to my version of himself. He waved his hand and McCoy paused the playback. 'Who's the singer?' Gillan asked.

Obviously he had no recollection of the upstart who had the temerity to question his vocal prowess at the Carlisle Market Hall a few months earlier. I elevated my hand feebly. 'Err, me,' I said.

'Cool vocals. Great screams,' he said casually.

I realised at that moment that I suddenly and very urgently wanted to vomit. It wasn't something he said; it was the something I'd smoked on top of four pints in the Newman Arms. I'm still not sure what temple balls are, but I can tell you they disagreed with me. I opened my mouth to reply and just managed to get out 'Thank you – I have to go' as I almost ran out of the control room and into the toilets. My head fell into the porcelain bowl and, with the soundtrack of the new Samson album playing down the hallway, I threw up for the foreseeable future.

I was sick, dizzy and weak, on my knees on the cold lino floor, groaning and gasping into the bowl. I heard voices progressing towards me from the studio: 'He's in here, is he?' The door was kicked in and a strong pair of hands dragged me backwards. Ian Gillan wiped the vomit from my mouth, sat me upright and put me in a cab home. This was not my finest hour, as he would remind me every time we met for the next

20 years: 'Hiya, mate. You're not going to throw up all over me again today, are you?' How not to meet your maker.

Home in this case had moved to the other side of the Isle of Dogs, where I paid the princely sum of 10 pounds a week to stay in what was essentially a post-student flophouse. I had nowhere formal to sleep, like a bed, but after the last of the bongs had been smoked I wrapped myself up in sheets and slept on the floor beside the unguarded gas fire. The windows were sealed with sheets of polythene and the single bath had spectacular growths of mould suspended from the ceiling, which at least gave you something to look at while having a soak. The address was Roffey House and it was the only property on the floor that was not boarded up, but its fourth-floor balcony still stank of piss and dog shit.

It was a relief to go out on the road on tour somewhere – anywhere, in fact. We were moving on up, and our self-booked tour plus Ian Gillan had finally attracted a half-decent agent.

Ham of the Gods

The future was looking almost rosy. Our album had charted at number 34 and we were on the radar of a new and very progressive publishing company, Zomba Music, run by Clive Calder and Ralph Simon. They represented songwriters and also record producers, having realised that it was often the producers who controlled the recording output and through them they could effectively control the output of the music industry. They were shrewd, but in a business full of charlatans and dreamers they were as close as you could get to being straight.

They managed Mutt Lange, who had just produced AC/DC's *Back in Black*. The engineer on the album was Tony Platt, and they were anxious to develop his career. He was the man who knew what most buttons did in a recording studio, and he was to have a profound effect on me in particular. He reshaped my voice, and it became the voice that people recognise today.

Samson went in to Battery Studios in Willesden, north-west London, to record a third album, *Shock Tactics*. By chance, there was another Zomba-managed producer working right next door. His name was Martin Birch. He had produced some of the greatest, if not *the* greatest rock albums of all time, with bands like Deep Purple and Rainbow. He was a legend.

He was making an album for a band called Iron Maiden, called *Killers*. I had first seen Maiden at the Music Machine in Camden. Samson were headlining, but the Maiden tribe turned up and packed the place out. Uncompromising, intense and with a savage execution, they were the cutting edge of the new metal movement. When I'd listened to *Deep Purple in Rock* and *Speed King* from behind a closed door at 15, I'd felt an upsurge of adrenalin, of chills running up my spine and out to my fingers. When Maiden launched into 'Prowler' I got the same goosebumps. This was a modern-day Purple, but with a theatrical side. I regret to say that, from the moment they took the stage in Camden, I knew I would be their singer. This was going to be a theatre of the mind, and I could do it with them. Darth Vader didn't stand there hissing and clanking saying, 'It is your destiny.' He did not have to. They had Eddie.

Iron Maiden's first album had gone straight to number 4, and they were now a worldwide band. Unusually, their uncompromising leader was a bassist, Steve Harris, and their no-nonsense manager was called Rod Smallwood. They had earned a reputation for firing a lot of musicians. I didn't have a problem with that; nobody rides for free. Dave Murray, the guitarist, was Steve's right-hand man; left-hand man was Dave's childhood friend, Adrian Smith, who had joined the band just before *Killers*. The pairing made for one of the UK's most formidable guitar attacks. Clive Burr was the drummer.

Clive had also played a year before in Samson and found our juxtaposition highly amusing. He was a very open, warm and friendly individual who was chatty about drums, women and designer sunglasses. Maiden all wore a boy-band-style uniform, based on a hybrid 'typical metal' fan. In the case of Steve Harris it didn't matter, because he always wore tight jeans, white trainers and a leather jacket. I think Mr. Smallwood wanted to make sure there were no backsliders who might head down the slippery slope to Hawaiian shirts or, in my case, red floppy hats.

Samson termed it their 'cunt kit'. As in: 'Morning, Clive. I see you have your cunt kit on.'

The truth was that behind the slightly bitter terminology was a streak of jealousy. Maiden were better players, manifestly better managed and properly funded by a record company, EMI, which actually gave a toss. There was a seriousness about them. In sharp contrast, Samson lolled around making smart-arse comments until the dope ran out. The cracks were already starting to appear, and I could see the end of days for us as a unit. Still, for now, we had written what I thought was our best material.

Tony Platt came from the Mutt Lange school of production, and he had some strong views on how things should get done. The major problem was that Thunderstick couldn't really play the drums very well. Barry envisioned his style as being somewhere between Kiss and the Police, which entailed hitting everything in sight and kicking various clanging and tingling items of percussion while constantly ignoring the simple requirement to keep time. Twenty-four track, two-inch tape recording meant that the drums had to be put down with some semblance of accuracy. Our backing tape looked like Frankenstein's facelift, full of splices, cuts and edits – hundreds of them – all designed to keep Barry in time.

Paul's guitar sound got less echo and more presence, which he hated. In general we examined what we did in quite some detail, which required a degree of sobriety. I found that quite a relief. I was bored with pissing about. It was time we made a proper-sounding record.

So finally it was my turn. Tony had dug up a Russ Ballard song, 'Riding with the Angels', and decreed it should be the first single. It seemed fairly straightforward. I did two or three takes.

'No. Pitch the whole thing up a couple of intervals,' Tony said.

So it began. My voice was stretched and my head hurt. The falsetto screech became almost an irrelevance as my natural voice extended into the back of my eyes. There was so much power from my engine room going into those top notes that the falsetto simply had nowhere to go. It sounded weak, and I was shell-shocked. For me, listening back to *Shock Tactics* was a shock. More shocking still was that everyone else loved the new voice, over a copy of someone else. This was actually me. I hated it.

We started to rehearse for some shows; I was hoarse after half an hour. We played the Marquee Club; I couldn't speak for two days afterwards. I was in despair. I had sung on an album that was getting great reactions, but I felt like a fraud. My voice couldn't do it. I moped around for a couple of days, crying into my beer, before my subconscious drew my attention to some sage guidance I'd received from my dentist ex-girlfriend. As an ex-pupil of the very prestigious Cheltenham Ladies' College, she'd had quite extensive singing lessons, and she kept a notebook.

'I think you've got a jolly nice voice, but it needs a bit more control,' she said, lecturing me in her plummy tones.

This made me grumpy – but interested. 'For example?'

'Well, can you do this with your tongue?'

I peered down her throat. Anybody watching might have thought I was trying to retrieve a goldfish, but I was in fact examining her ability to flatten her tongue like a squashed toad.

'Hmm.' I borrowed her exercise book, and took to the library in search of the voice and how it works.

Remember the little singing notebook, and the hours researching breathing and resonance in the library? my subconscious said. *Remember stupid exercises with candles, holding chairs in front of you, squashing your lower back against walls and a multitude of other bizarre things to do to strengthen your diaphragm and develop resonance in your chest voice and head voice?* it said. I started to pay attention to it.

Technique is just empty unless you apply it. You have technique to apply to your new voice. Stop feeling sorry for yourself and be smart. Learn how to be you. Teach yourself.

I started to enjoy my new-found pipes. I began to see that a whole new landscape had been opened up. If I was a painter, it would have been like being given a massive canvas and a whole palette of new colours.

Theatre of the mind was becoming very exciting, but I wasn't sure if it would be with Samson. A&M Records were now interested in us. Rather more specifically, they were interested in me, which was made abundantly clear at a photo session in which I was certainly in the foreground, the band consigned to the middle distance.

Reading Festival that year was much more straightforward, but with a different drummer. Barry had left; Paul wanted him gone. I liked Barry but had to concede that in the actual business of drumming, there were certain shortcomings. Mel Gaynor stepped in. He was in about four bands at the same time and had a very active social life. He was an unbelievable drummer. Our swansong at Reading was rather good. I rolled out my new voice, everybody cheered and no one seemed to miss the gimp mask.

The festival was awash with gossip and rumour that night. There was no mud – it was fine and dry – and alcohol and chemicals were doing a fine job of creating mental instability and inability. In the middle of a clearing, surrounded by hospitality chalets and beer tents, was a single large pole, with bright-white lights on top. I was in a corner of a beer tent when Rod Smallwood approached me, saying, 'Let's go somewhere quiet where we can talk.' We walked out and stood, illuminated for all the world to see, under the pole in the middle of the backstage area. I felt sure he was working up to something.

'Do you want to come back to my room for a chat?' he said. I felt sure he didn't have any etchings for me to see. Reading Holiday Inn became a low-ceilinged rabbit warren of debauchery for a week around the festival if, of course, you could get a burrow.

Back in the room, away from prying eyes, Rod laid out his cards. 'I'm offering you the chance to audition for Iron Maiden,' he said. 'Are you interested?'

There had been enough beating around bushes and tap-dancing around issues, I decided, so I told him what I thought: 'First of all, you know I'll get the job or you wouldn't ask. Second, what's gonna happen to Paul, the current singer, and does he know he's going? Third, when I do get the job, and I will, are you prepared for a totally different style and opinions and someone who is not going to roll over? I may be a pain in the arse, but it's for all the right reasons. If you don't want that tell me now and I'll walk away.'

The speech was a combination of pissing in beans, injustice, sleeping on floors, bravado and genuine invention. If Iron Maiden wanted to play with the hammer of the gods then bring it on. If not, take a hike and get someone more boring instead. As the saying goes, we should all be careful of what we wish for because we just might get it.

Neighbour of the Beast

I was asked to learn four songs for the Maiden audition. The band had two albums by now, so I learnt all the songs. I didn't exactly have a great deal else to do. The existing singer was going to be fired after some Scandinavian shows the band was already contracted to play, which was made clear to me. The niceties of filling a dead man's shoes did not sit comfortably with me, but it wasn't my soap opera. At least not yet.

I turned up to the rehearsal studios in Hackney, and if I had been looking at the group as a military unit, I would have assessed their morale as being rock bottom. The atmosphere was weary. They needed cheering up. I had no idea what had been going on or the disagreements that were ongoing and, frankly, I didn't care. My job was to sing and, above and beyond mere singing, to create my cinematic, musical mind-vision.

All the songs were in very comfortable keys. My voice was barely ticking over, so I let fly with a few improvised embellishments. We started to play for fun, odd riffs, verses from our favourite influences, bands of our adolescence; of course, we all had the same influences. We all shared Purple and Sabbath, and even Jethro Tull got a look in; Steve was a huge fan. We bonded musically, and I was left to ponder the sad state of affairs that had led to such profound apathy in the face of such amazing potential.

Steve wanted to book a recording studio the same day. I remember him shovelling coins into the payphone while talking to Smallwood. Like when a football player is transferred to a new club, there were still checks to be done. One of them was to be forensically tested in a recording studio, just to make sure that the musicians had not been swept up in the emotion of it all.

I had to wait a few weeks until Paul Di'Anno had been fired, and then I found myself back in Battery Studios. I overdubbed vocals on four live tracks. It was, frankly, not hard. I was coasting, but salivating at the chance to show what I could really do – to open the taps on my voice and blow the doors off. Management and band huddled together in the control room as I stood in the vocal booth. There was a discussion. I got the job.

We celebrated by gatecrashing the UFO gig at the Hammersmith Odeon that night, and getting quite drunk. The hard work began the next day.

'Ever done any shooting? Right-handed?' The audiologist grinned cheerfully as he reviewed my results. I nodded.

'Absolutely typical,' he said, in a very lilting Welsh accent. 'Down at four kHz – you see?'

'Is that anything to worry about?' I asked.

'Nooo, not really. Probably when you get to sixty-five, but you won't be bothered by then, will you?'

Second World War rifles plus GPMGs, grenades and 7.62 mm SLRs with no hearing protection had excised a chunk of my hearing at 4,000 Hz. In the meantime I had eye tests, blood tests, drug tests and insurance companies crawling all over me. I was delighted to hear that I was a venereal-disease-free zone, and there was no reason why I shouldn't go on the rampage for the next few years with a rock band.

As a musician with no fixed abode, I was living with yet another girlfriend, above a hairdresser's in Evesham, Worcestershire. The commute to London was cheap as I still had a student railcard, and the trains were interesting and the

Cotswold Line quite beautiful. It was still possible to find Class 50 locomotives, the odd class 47, and, on special occasions, a High Speed Train would sometimes whistle its way through the otherwise quiet Evesham station.

I was a minor local celebrity in the pubs where the metal fans hung out. There were quite a few bands, and a lot more pubs. The area was steeped in Black Sabbath, AC/DC and the occult. The last recorded human sacrifice was on nearby Breedon Hill. People still believed in witchcraft, and the whole area seemed to run on a tape loop constantly repeating from around 1973. Aleister Crowley, the self-styled Beast 666, was born up the road.

Mostly weekends were spent at Elmley Castle consuming mind-altering amounts of Scrumpy, a hallucinogenic cider. The pub sat at the bottom of the hill that led up to the castle ruins. The landlady had posed nude for *Mayfair*, and the pictures were available on request. Cider was dispensed in plastic containers, often with lemonade to give the cloudy liquid a bit of fizz.

Regular drinkers sat catatonic in the saloon bar. All the furniture faced outward, and there was a pentagram on the floor. In the corner was a TV, suspended from the ceiling. Watching it meant using the mirrors that lined the tops of the windows. The whole scene resembled shell-shocked corpses slumped in their chairs facing the wrong way, mouths awash with cider. At the end of the evening they would all drive home, some of them in little blue invalid carriages.

I left this paradise for lunatics in favour of the mighty metropolis. Joining Iron Maiden meant being paid the enormous sum of a hundred pounds a week, so I rented a room in a house in Stamford Brook, West London.

I made my way across town to the Maiden offices, an upstairs flat in Danbury Street, Islington. If I was to pick a character for myself from *Winnie the Pooh*, I'm sure it would be Tigger, full of boundless enthusiasm. And boundlessly I leapt up the rickety staircase to the first-floor office and presented myself: 'New singer, reporting for duty, sir.'

Smallwood was unimpressed: 'Go and get some fucking clothes – you look like a roadie.'

I asked Clive how I could possibly contrive to look like a cunt. He told me. Motorcycle bomber jacket, stripy T-shirt, white hi-top trainers ... the only issue was the stretch jeans. Fine in principle, but designed for people with legs six inches longer than mine. Sheer laziness dictated turning them up at the bottom. I paid in cash, and gave Rod his change with the receipt.

Music was so much easier. Off the Caledonian Road was a rehearsal studio called Ezee Hire, and we parked ourselves there every day to write. It was a fruitful time. The choruses that formed our first album together were honed there, although some were written in the Hackney studio where I had my initial audition.

Before going in to record the album, some shows were booked, culminating in a headline slot at the Rainbow Theatre. The irony was not lost on me. I passed it in Shots wistfully, I filmed a ludicrous video in it with Samson, and now I was headlining it with Iron Maiden.

We did some warm-up shows in Italy beforehand. I had never performed outside of the UK up till then, and apart from a school trip, had hardly been abroad. We drove there on a tour bus. I had never been on one of those, either. There was a toilet that was almost useful, although it was forbidden to shit, which made it just a figment of a fevered imagination in the event of intestinal catastrophe.

The first shows were nervous affairs for me as the new boy. We were trying out some new material and gauging opinion. I had bought a pair of black spandex pants, de rigueur if you didn't wear jeans or straight tights like Steve, and we did photo sessions with Ross Halfin, the band photographer at the time. We were encouraged to gob at the camera and look suitably feral. Later, we discovered the shower-room shot, the long concrete-corridor shot and various other setups at which Ross was extremely adept.

The Rainbow Theatre show was a success of sorts. The press wrote nice things as I recall and, in general, their reviews were positive for the new vocal interloper. Of course, having been in Samson helped one's notoriety, but fans of the previous singer, Paul Di'Anno, remained unimpressed. One wrote a letter of complaint, detailing his horror at hearing his favourite songs being played through an 'air-raid siren', and there may well have been an uncomplimentary remark about a cement mixer as well.

Rod immediately seized on the 'air-raid siren' remark and repurposed it as testament to my not-yet legendary tenor howl, as showcased on songs like 'Run to the Hills'. I became the 'human air-raid siren'. There was always an element of feeling like the Elephant Man in all of this. Rod was not so much the ringmaster of the circus as he was the impresario, the organiser and manipulator of the artists and acts, all controlled from the anonymous caravan behind the big top, where the money was counted as well.

Having a management-appointed nickname was standard practice. Even the road-crew names were interspersed with unwanted epithets. Our producer, Martin Birch, would turn up to rehearsals in his Range Rover, with straw attached to his boots. Thus his credit on *The Number of the Beast* reads: Martin 'Farmer' Birch. It was all harmless really, and it took a few years before it became tiresome.

After the Rainbow show we really set about the new album. As well as being the first album with a new singer and a totally different vocal approach, it was also the vexatious and critical third album for the band. Traditionally, it is the third album that determines whether it is the end of the beginning, or the beginning of the end for a band or artist.

Album culture, the cult of the 40-minute LP with two sides, still persists to this day, even in the days of digital. I think there are several reasons why this is, and the recording format itself has shaped the artistic vision in positive ways.

To write tight, concise material that takes a listener on a musical journey is quite a demanding task. Doing 40–45 minutes of new music every 14 months is complex and hard work. Commerce demands that albums follow in quick succession, that tours can be enabled and follow-ups can happen, based on the sales of the previous record. All this puts a strain on the creative elements in the group. Write album, rehearse, record, perform for eight months, then do it all again ... and then do it all again.

After two cycles of that kind of behaviour, many bands would simply be emptied of ideas and exhausted by touring, or dispirited by lack of success. The third album, then, becomes the watershed. Even successful bands, and Maiden were very successful when I first joined, were fragile. With our third album, we had the whole world to play for. If we dealt the right hand of cards, we would be the leader of the pack.

Any sense of pressure was swiftly negated by sheer enthusiasm. The act of creating and rehearsing have always been sacrosanct for Maiden: no managers, strangers, outsiders, fan clubs or minicab drivers.

The cocoon of the rehearsal space was our musical playpen, and we were discovering new toys and new playmates. Everything was duly recorded, and still is, on a cheap boombox cassette recorder. This becomes a reference as we try to remember what on earth we did in rehearsal when we come to put it back in order in the recording studio.

Martin Birch turned up right at the end, for one day. He had a listen to the songs. He made no comment; he just looked thoughtful and paid attention to them. Much later down the track, Martin and I had a few beers, and he opened up on his philosophy of production.

'There are two types of producer,' he said. 'One type thinks that it's his record, and he's going to make a hit record that will sell shitloads and everyone will say he is a great producer.'

He sipped his beer and looked around the bar with disdain. 'And then there are producers who are just a mirror. We reflect the artist in the best way to let their message, their sound, come through.'

'And what if the band is shit?' I asked.

'I don't do shit bands.'

I thought back through his catalogue. Deep Purple's *In Rock* and *Made in Japan*, Black Sabbath's *Heaven and Hell*, Blue Öyster Cult and quite a few little surprises: Leo Sayer, Jimi Hendrix, and Wayne County and the Electric Chairs. *You could learn a lot from Mr Birch.*

We moved from the Caledonian Road straight back to Battery Studios in Willesden. We had only five weeks to record and mix the album, including a single and B-side, which had to be finished first, as it had to be released almost immediately.

Even today, with digital desks, this would be quite a tall order, but with two-inch tape and an analogue desk, no memory or mixes or automatic fades, this was old-school craftsmanship.

A mixing desk is just like a telephone exchange. Instruments come in at one end and are routed to magnetic tape, where they are recorded. In between entering and ending up on tape, the signal is modified for tone, level and amplitude to make sure the molecules of iron oxide on the magnetic tape are kept in a faithful, happy state, and not splattered all over the place. To mix, however, the entire process is not simply reversed; it is completely rebuilt. The taped instruments now re-enter the desk, but this time they are combined to produce the nice stereo vinyl record we so desire. The only way of recording the settings of the hundreds of knobs on the desk was with small chinagraph pencils and sheets of A4 paper with pictures of the controls, and biro marks so that the desk could be reset. To flip-flop the whole process twice in five weeks was huge, but that's what we had to do.

We were using an old mixing desk made by a company called Cadac. It was on its last legs, and this was its last job. The rest of the studio looked like a building site as well. The vocals were done in a demolished kitchen with wet plaster still drying on the walls. There was plenty of beer on hand, and a fair amount of cocaine for those of that disposition.

Steve and I were non-participants, while others varied from occasional to 'quite' often. Despite small amounts of coke, the main consumption was of Party Fours, a half-gallon-oil-can-sized beer container. We built a wall of empties to rival the Great Pyramid by the end of the album.

Outside, the winter weather was slush, cold and foul. Someone was murdered at the bus stop and the chalk outline remained for several days. Martin's Range Rover was hit by a minibus full of nuns, and the repair bill was £666.66. We laughed, but Mr Smallwood seized the day, and all manner of stories about curses, hauntings and evil spirits were dreamed up. One of the more creative ones had to do with Steve's bass gear being possessed by the evil one during the tracking of 'The Number of the Beast'.

It is true that there was an evil moaning and groaning sound on the tape that we could not account for. It was only when we checked the talkback mic that we discovered the culprit. It was Steve 'Evil One' Harris himself. Steve insisted on standing by his bass gear when recording. He wore headphones and was unaware of his vigorous, rhythmic chanting. Still, it made for a good story.

We had two spoken-word pieces on the album, one from the Bible, and the other from the Kafkaesque TV series *The Prisoner*. The latter was my idea, so Rod had to call Los Angeles to speak with Patrick McGoohan, *The Prisoner*'s creator and star, and owner of the rights. I was there when he made the phone call, and I have never seen him so nervous. The short conversation was priceless.

'Hello, this is Rod Smallwood from Iron Maiden.'

'What? Who are you?'

'Er ... we're a band.'

'A band! WHAT sort of a band?'

'Well, we're a heavy metal.'

'Metal, you say?'

'Yes, we er ...'

'What do you want?'

'Well, you have a bit about "I'm not a number, I'm a free man", and we wanted to use it – on a track.'

'What did you say you were called?'

'Iron Maiden.'

'Do it.'

The phone went dead.

'Fucking hell!' said Mr Smallwood.

Much the same response sprang from his lips when he spoke to the agent for Vincent Price. Although it is a cliché, 'I'm afraid Mr Price doesn't get out of bed for less than 10,000 dollars' certainly put a marker down in the sand.

Fortunately, I used to listen to the ghost story at midnight on London's Capital Radio, being quite a fan of radio that displayed any semblance of imagination. When Vincent priced himself out of the market I suggested using the guy who read that, and to this day many people believe it *is* Vincent Price reading the classic biblical lines at the beginning of 'The Number of the Beast'.

The Capital Radio voiceover performer came into the studio, and in half an hour had given us five absolutely corking performances. He was a lovely man, an actor in his sixties and a total professional, with a subtle delivery. He was utterly unfazed at being in the midst of one of the world's more disruptive rock bands.

The first song we recorded was intended to be a B-side. It was called 'Gangland' and featured a writing credit for Clive Burr, on the basis that the drums were as integral to the track as the guitar riffs. We were all like little puppy dogs recording it. We stayed till four or five in the morning, listening back.

'Too good to be a B-side' was the general feeling. I wasn't so sure; I thought it a bit presumptuous seeing as we had nothing else to compare it to. I was the new boy, however, and at least everyone had their tails up before the main event, which was a track called 'Run to the Hills'.

The layered harmony vocal was such a colossal change for the Maiden sound. Our jaws dropped as we heard the rough mixes. There are some songs that you can feel in your bones will be huge. In our case, the third album, the expectation and the curiosity all colluded to make 'Run to the Hills' the perfect storm as a showcase to the world of the delights to expect from the forthcoming album.

The only slight disappointment, in hindsight, was the choice of B-side. With 'Gangland' destined for the album, we had no spare tracks save 'Total Eclipse', an excellent presage of global catastrophe, climate change and the end times. It was an extra track on the Japanese version of the album, and I suppose it was an unexpectedly good B-side.

The title track of the album, 'The Number of the Beast', needs little in the way of description, as it's one of the greatest metal tracks of all time. Steve had a habit of whistling softly into a portable cassette machine, and then transposing this into a vocal line or guitar riff. I only discovered this when he played me his original songwriting tape for 'The Trooper', which sounded like a cheerful postman walking up the garden path to deliver the mail. I suddenly understood why a lot of Maiden vocal lines were virtually unsingable, or at least required careful attention to phrasing to ensure you didn't bite off the end of your tongue while wrapping your gills around the unnecessary consonants.

For Steve, the words exist in rhythmic space first and foremost, then perhaps lyrical or poetic space, and lastly in a format designed to make the most of the human voice. It took me years to figure this out, and when the penny finally dropped it was a relief. I didn't get nearly so cross and frustrated at the melodies and lyrics produced by Steve once I understood his motivation. In return, over the years, Steve has learnt to live with the voice as an instrument, which bends and shapes to create moods, and is not simply an assembly of Lego bricks.

Clive found 'The Number of the Beast' very tough, in part because the drum timing is very much an extension of the melody, and thus it is almost spoken, as in the song's intro. The problems lay in interpreting the lyrical riffs in Steve's head and placing them into a definitive format that musicians could write down and reproduce. In sharp contrast, a track like 'Hallowed Be Thy Name' is utterly straightforward.

When the time came to sing before Mr Birch, it was a mixture of curiosity and frustration. The frustration was born out of Martin's tactic of making me wait; the curiosity was finding out what he could teach me. This was a guy who'd had some of the greatest voices, and some of the greatest vocal performances, on his watch.

I wanted to get stuck in to bashing out the vocals, to bask in the glory. Martin was not interested in such frippery, and in the nicest and most polite way he taught me not to take things for granted.

Consider the opening sequence to 'The Number of the Beast'. Before the blood-curdling scream à la 'Won't Get Fooled Again' is an almost whispered intro building into the climactic shriek. It's not very high and it's physically undemanding. I thought I could polish it off in a few takes and move on to being loud and bombastic.

Martin, Steve and I spent all day and all night on the first two lines. Again and again, until I was so sick of it I threw furniture against the walls in frustration, taking big lumps out of the damp plaster in the half-completed kitchen.

We took a two-hour break. I sat glumly with a mug of coffee. Martin was positively chirpy. Bastard, I thought.

'Not so easy, eh?' he grinned. 'Ronnie Dio had the same problem on "Heaven and Hell".'

My head, which ached, and my eyes, which ached, started to pay close attention. 'Like, how?'

'Well, he came with the same attitude as you. Let's bash this one out. And I said to him, "No. You have to sum up your entire life in the first line. I don't hear it yet."'

Of course, I know the song. The opening line.

'Your whole life is in that line,' said Martin. 'Your identity as a singer.'

Dimly, I started to see the difference between singing a line and living it.

I went for a walk around the rest of the studio. It was deathly quiet, no musicians around. The silent drum kit, the guitars lying around and the faint odour of dust roasting on the valves that were still switched on in the amplifiers.

'*I left alone, my mind was blank. I needed time to think to get the memories from my mind ...*'

And that's who I was when I went back to the microphone. '*Just what I saw, in my old dreams ...*' and so it went on. It was like Martin was a can-opener, and I was the can of beans.

Once the crack had appeared in my self-constructed dam, the flood happened. The wall I built was my ego. Everyone needs one, especially if you want to own 100,000 rock fans, but you don't bring it into the studio. What possesses you in the studio should be the song, like a film that unfolds before you. All I do is sing the words that paint the picture. I thought I'd invented theatre of the mind, but Martin Birch had been doing it for years.

The level of intensity involved in all of this was considerable, and the stress and strain on Martin even more so. We had an engineer to assist him, the very amiable Nigel Green, who was on his last mission as engineer before being a producer in his own right. For reasons lost in the mist of time, Nigel was nicknamed 'Hewitt'.

From somewhere at 2 a.m., 'Hewitt' would be commanded to produce cases of beer. He was a combination of highly accomplished technical engineer and concierge of dubious legality.

As musicians, we got to relax with a pint after our performance was done. Not so for Martin. He worked every day, no breaks, until he would unexpectedly call us in and declare, 'I'm having a day off tomorrow.'

This, I subsequently realised, was possibly what Dr Jekyll said to himself in the mirror shortly before meeting his alter ego, Mr Hyde.

Martin had an alter ego. We called it Marvin. Over the years Marvin has provided us with hours of entertainment and near-death experiences. The first time I met Marvin I was confused. In fact, I was in Samson, and during the recording of *Shock Tactics* we were invited over to listen to some finished mixes of *Killers*, which had recently been completed.

Marvin was out, loud and proud. And foolishly I introduced myself, and was sober at the time. Marvin was not.

'Sit down, boy,' he said.

He flamboyantly hurled the producer's chair on its rollers so it bounced off the rear wall. He put his hands on my shoulders and shoved me into it. I started to feel just a tinge of apprehension.

'Now, boy. Listen to this ...'

He slammed the chair up against the mixing desk, wedging me in place, and played *Killers* till my ears bled.

'Whaddidyathink of that?' he challenged, just audible over the cochlear cataclysm that was my inner ear in shock.

'It's, er, very good,' I said.

'Heh, heh. Yeah, yeah – very good.' And he just walked out muttering to himself, and left me alone in the studio with the tapes for the new Iron Maiden album.

At the end of recording *The Number of the Beast*, Martin played back the album, mixed and super loud. 'I'm having a day off tomorrow,' he announced, as the madman peered out from behind his eyes and Marvin took charge.

'Hewitt,' he demanded, 'how old is this desk?'

'Don't know, Martin,' Hewitt replied, looking slightly nervous.

Marvin seized the flexible metal cord built into the desk, which held the studio talkback microphone. With one wrench he uprooted it and tore it from the desk. It looked like a forlorn tulip with its roots dangling down as the electrical connections were left hanging.

'It's broken, Hewitt.' He tossed it over the back of the desk.

Hewitt visibly winced.

'And which channel doesn't work, Hewitt?'

'Er, channel 22,' Hewitt replied.

Marvin stood up and unscrewed the channel, a piece of circuit board about three feet long and, up till that moment, potentially quite valuable.

'Piece of shit,' Marvin muttered, and snapped it in half.

Hewitt could see his job prospects going down the pan fast, but kept his sangfroid and smiled nervously. I think he was beginning to enter into the spirit of things.

'Now, what else is broken, Hewitt?'

Thus ended that particular desk, consigned to the scrapheap by Martin Birch, ably assisted by a man called Hewitt.

The next day Martin was gone. Zomba had him straight on a flight to LA to start another album with Sabbath, or Whitesnake, or whoever. I saw how much he put into making records, how much of his psyche was chucked into a mincing machine every time. I wondered how long he would be able to keep up the pace.

For us, though, the pace had started to quicken – and there was no going back now.

The Big Dipper

Being in a band in global demand with a number 1 album was like being on a rollercoaster. The difference in our case was that the rollercoaster didn't stop, or even slow down, for the next five years. We had cranked our way up the clunky railway and now stood at the threshold of the drop. As we toppled over the edge and tumbled into free fall, we went straight down, screaming, hair standing on end, adrenalin pumping. Five straight years of this sort of thing can seriously wobble whatever internal gyroscopes you might rely on. For now, however, we just enjoyed the rush.

Almost as soon as the album was mixed, the single, 'Run to the Hills', was released, and sold nearly 250,000 copies in the UK. Before the album was officially released we were in the midst of a UK tour, and we had the first of several spats that would crop up over the years.

We were on a totally ridiculous schedule: eight shows, day off, seven shows, day off, and so on. These were two-hour shows, and the vocals were not the world's easiest. The on-stage set-up caused friction immediately. I was quite traditional about basic stagecraft, like, hey, if I'm singing, I stand at the front. If you're playing the solo, you stand at the front. That sort of thing.

Steve Harris had other ideas. He wanted to stand in front of everybody and run all over the stage. I wasn't having it. I wasn't going to sing to the back of the bass player's head.

The wedge monitors we used were equally spaced out across the front of the stage, which meant there was no focal point when I sang.

We did the soundcheck, then we did the show. The first thing I did was move my wedge monitors to the front and centre of the stage. Steve grumbled, and the roadies moved them back. So I moved them back again to the centre.

When I was singing, half a bass guitar was being stuck up my nose, because clearly there was some demarcation zone I had infringed. I countered by putting ludicrously long legs on my mic stand. The base of it now resembled a TV aerial, and in my peripheral vision I could see Steve careering towards me, so I positioned it as a sort of anti-bass-player tank trap. I have quite a few chips in my teeth as he would still run into it full tilt.

It all came to a head when we played Newcastle City Hall.

We had driven down from Edinburgh at ridiculous o'clock in the morning, because Rod thought it a good idea to shoot 'The Number of the Beast' video there all day, immediately before the show. We brought in ballroom dancers to use as extras, with 666 pinned to their backs. I think that might have been my idea.

Anyway, we had to hold the doors because we were still filming half an hour or so before the audience were due to come in. Of course, we were all exhausted. We went on stage, quite a small stage, and Steve and I spent a bad-tempered show like two rutting stags locking antlers.

Rod needed to separate us backstage. We were both busy rolling up our sleeves to go outside and sort each other out. Steve was yelling at Rod as he separated us, 'He's got to fucking go!'

Well, I didn't fucking go. Can't say I didn't warn you, guys – this will be a little different. Get used to it.

We came to a compromise on the location of microphones and monitors, and established that, in the case of who stands in front of whom, good manners trumps boundless enthusiasm. It was a small breakthrough, but it set us on a path to a new level of theatricality and presentation.

We got the news that the album was number 1 when we were checking out of a cheap hotel in Winterthur, Switzerland. The celebration was somewhat tempered by the necessity to push a full-size tour bus down the hill in order to jump-start it. The driver explained in quite unnecessary detail that the emergency brakes depleted the battery and that this gizmo drained that gizmo ...

He could have just owned up and said that he'd left the lights on.

We played all the countries I had heard of and never been to. I got a chance to practise my dodgy French, which was much more successful than my non-existent Spanish. At the show in Madrid I attempted to concoct a phrase that translated as 'you are the best singers in the world'.

Well, I thought, *El Mundo* was a newspaper, and it was pretty obvious what that meant. Cantante was something to do with singing. Hey, how hard could this possibly be?

Whatever I said, I said it boldly, and they cheered.

So I said it again, and they cheered a bit less.

Thinking they hadn't heard me right the first time, I said it slowly and, I thought, very boldly and clearly.

There was near silence.

After the show I asked the record company what had happened.

'Aha. You say that you are the best singer in the world.'

Hmm. Loud, confident and wrong.

Now we were out of Europe, having triumphantly bashed our way around anywhere with a government worth speaking of. We were off to the United States, a place so impossibly exotic I couldn't bring myself to go to sleep for a week thinking about it.

We landed in Detroit, Michigan, in the summer. Next stop, Flint and various other places I had never heard of. We were in the heartland of motor-city USA, before water scandals and property crashes ripped the heart out of it. To start our US onslaught, we were third on the bill to a most peculiar pairing: Rainbow and 38 Special.

The last time I'd toured with Rainbow was when Graham Bonnet was in the band. He was notable for having a monstrously loud gravel-voiced tenor, and a very florid taste in stage-wear allied to a haircut better suited to James Dean than the sidekick to the 'Man in Black', Ritchie Blackmore.

I was, and still am, a big fan of Blackmore. I understand his penchant for wearing pointy witchy hats and dressing up a band as strolling minstrels. This tour, however, was not that. The singer was now Joe Lynn Turner, an American with what Ritchie hoped would be a radio-star voice to give Rainbow the leg up they required in the USA. It's ironic that had Rainbow stayed with Ronnie Dio, the world might just have turned in their direction after all, but that's all 20/20 hindsight and speculation.

Anyway, this was Ritchie, with the now legendary hair weave and abundant locks, plus Joe, with equally abundant locks and a less-sophisticated trichological procedure – as in a big wig.

On the other hand, 38 Special were equipped with five singers, one of whom was basically a mascot. The guitarist was the principal songwriter and the principal male voice, but there was a Van Zant, Southern rock royalty, in the band, complete with Southern rock trilby hat. There were two, perhaps three backing singers, all wearing prodigious crinolines better suited to a Mississippi river boat of the 1900s.

Then there was us. Five English terriers snapping at everyone's heel and pulling faces at frightened Americans who thought they had come to see some adult-orientated rock, and instead got 20 minutes of West Ham laid across their stoned brains like an iron bar.

We actually got on quite well with everyone, but all was not peace and love between the Southern rock fraternity and the darkened offspring of Paganini's ghost. There were constant arguments about who should headline, which revolved around who each band manager thought had sold the most tickets, and the system of alternating headlining status started to break down. In the end, Iron Maiden headlined one show, because no one could agree who should go on last.

Rod Smallwood had determined that a tour bus was a waste of money, so we drove around in two large Ford LTD estate cars, one driven by Rod, the other by our tour manager, Tony Wiggens. There was always plenty of space in Rod's car.

It's silly things that start a corrosive process in a band. In our case, it was Clive Burr's luggage, which exceeded the allotted space and meant we were often delayed leaving hotels. Dark mutterings were heard. Of course, if we'd had a tour bus no one would have cared.

America was an undiscovered country, with strange procedures and unusual devices to which a lad from Worksop had not been exposed. We stayed in the road crew hotels, and on the first night at the Ramada in Flint, Rainbow's sound engineer introduced himself, saying, 'The lads are going to a hot tub party if you fancy it.'

Well, this left a curious image in my mind. What was a 'hot tub', and in what way would it involve a party? I thought of apple bobbing, but I couldn't understand why the water had to be hot. Perhaps they were toffee apples, I mused. Otherwise, why would people have a party around a warm bath?

My curiosity piqued, the cab pulled up outside a sprawling single-storey suburban house, and I had my first glimpse of American teen spirit.

The kitchen was full of girls drinking wine. The lounge was full of boyfriends, who weren't speaking to the girls, because they had lost the ability to speak. Elmley Castle had come to Michigan, but instead of hallucinogenic cider, great mushroom clouds of dope billowed up towards the ceiling as they concentrated on playing *Pong*, a primitive video game.

My Falstaff days were long gone. I drank beer, but that was it. I moved through to the back, which is where I discovered the bubbling Jacuzzi full of roadies, and females who were not roadies. Apple bobbing was not the game in town, and the other American invention, the waterbed, was available for relaxation in the bedrooms.

I went back into the kitchen and struck up a conversation about the motor-car industry and the local economy with a girl who seemed to have a bit more about her than the others. After only a few moments she tired of the subject, asking, 'Shall we go to the hot tub?'

I couldn't help but notice her broken arm, firmly set at right angles in a very robust cast. 'Aren't you worried your cast will get wet?' I said.

'Oh no, I'll rest it on the side.'

My first hot tub was an interesting experience. Rainbow's sound engineer served us drinks as we bubbled our flesh, but conversation was somewhat stilted with the other occupants of the tub. It's difficult to have a chat about backdrops with your stage manager when he is about to ejaculate.

The bubbles temporarily ceased, and I leaned over to the silver button. *I know exactly what this does*, I thought.

We drove around the USA in our LTD Fords. We stayed in strange motels and ate hamburgers in Louisiana served by men with faces full of warts. We were pulled over several times for speeding, à la *Smokey and the Bandit*, and we finally finished the tour in Norman, Oklahoma.

We were due to fly to Canada for a short headline tour before returning to America to start a special guest slot with Scorpions. I have always loved Canada, and Canada returned the favour by faithfully following Maiden for years. Canada espoused the band well before the USA, and eschewed the vagaries of fashion and radio popularity to support us, which it continues to do undimmed to this very day.

Canadians share a very similar sense of humour and a refreshing lack of hysteria. Perhaps because of their closer Commonwealth ties and French culture, their sense of history is embedded, giving places like Toronto a comforting sense of permanence.

Despite this starting to sound like a Sunday-school outing, I was due a rather nasty injury, and one of our road crew almost got his head blown off at Massey Hall in Toronto, where we were being recorded for a live broadcast. An M-80 firework (equivalent, it is said, to a quarter of a stick of dynamite) was thrown on stage during the band changeover, when our guitar technician was peering at a pedal board as he squatted on the floor. The device landed on top of the board and exploded. Bill was concussed and blinded by the detonation. I grabbed the mic and had a rant about the stupidity of the individual involved, and we came close to cancelling the show. Thankfully, he lived to tell the tale and his sight returned.

I am not 100 per cent sure what possesses someone to throw something at a person on stage. Is it an act of homage or attempted murder? The same goes for racist football hooligans who chuck projectiles at players on the pitch.

Sometimes the objects are genuinely intriguing. On stage at Donington one year, I discovered a fully formed, inverted sherry trifle, *sans* bowl, on the front of the stage. Was there a sherry trifle trebuchet cunningly concealed in the beer tent, and if so, why was there only a slight crack in the custard, like a miniature rift valley?

By contrast, in Portugal one year I spied blood-filled syringes sticking out of the lino stage flooring by their hypodermic needles – quite disgusting, and really quite hazardous. Live ammunition, ball bearings, coins, wallets, sunglasses, brassieres, panties, T-shirts, flags, hamburgers, beer cans, bottles of piss and hundreds and hundreds of shoes have all rained down on our parade.

In Argentina so many shoes ended up on stage that I proposed constructing a shoe cannon to fire back their cheesy odour-eaters in what a Napoleonic artillery man might have termed 'a whiff of grapeshot'.

The mystery of the shoes perplexed me for years, until the mechanism was finally revealed. Why would anyone take off a shoe (for only ever a left or right arrived, never a pair) when they would need footwear in order to get home? Alternatively, perhaps all their rucksacks were full of shoes that they brought specially for the purpose of lobbing. The question still remained. Why? The truth is that the shoes are stolen mainly from people who practise crowd-surfing. Opportunistic rascals steal the sneaker and toss it on stage. That's all there is to it. Case closed.

Well, I'm glad we got that out the way, because it preoccupied me for a long time whenever a shoe landed on stage. In Canada, though, I had other things to worry about. I had virtually lost the use of my left arm.

My problem had begun on the European leg of the tour, a couple of months before. Every night on stage I would thrash my head up and down. By now I had grown a heavy mane of hair, which had quite a momentum to it, twisting my neck this way and that. Headbanging was a pretty effective way of losing all track of time and space and wobbling your brain to the music.

My neck seized up, and I could not move it without a great deal of pain. I was sent to a German doctor, who gave me a

Me, aged 15, with awful anorak.

Uncle John, not on holiday in Malta.

Back to School

First day back at school, ~~felling feeling~~ feeling very worried indeed, because I did not know what the boys would be like.

I had a very great surprise when I discovered that my lessons were not the same.

When I got back to school everybody thought I was going into 3A. I ended up in 4A. There was also another surprising feature about going back to school, Everybody who had previously hated me were now friends with me.

I hope you can set your work out better than this.

English Prep: Write your own account of what you felt like when you came back to school.

Early efforts at sarcasm.

TUTOR'S REPORT Name: DICKINSON P.B.

As so often, Paul's performance in academic work has failed to match his potential. I only hope that he will do himself justice in the 'A' levels and that he realizes how important these will be for him. Several colleagues have kindly offered help with revision notes etc. and perhaps Paul will write to let me know of any areas where such help would be most appreciated. I was pleased to learn that a school has been arranged for next term. As he considers his plans I hope he will not dismiss too lightly the exciting stimulus of university life, nor the future advantage of a degree. He is lucky to have the offers he does.

After defending and driving Paul so closely for 4½ years I was very sorry indeed that he should leave us after such an unspeakable and inexcusable yet transient and contingent aberration. Looking back in time over the bullying and clashes one realises what a great success he has achieved, when the cards have often seemed stacked against him, to establish himself as a positive personality capable of winning and deserving respect for his achievements, as in fencing and corps, and at the same time to retain without bitterness or chagrin so much of his unsquashable eagerness and unfailing resilience. His tongue has always been his undoing; perhaps the shock of his expulsion will teach him humility and self-control.

He has my sincerest best wishes.

Early predictions of rock rebellion.

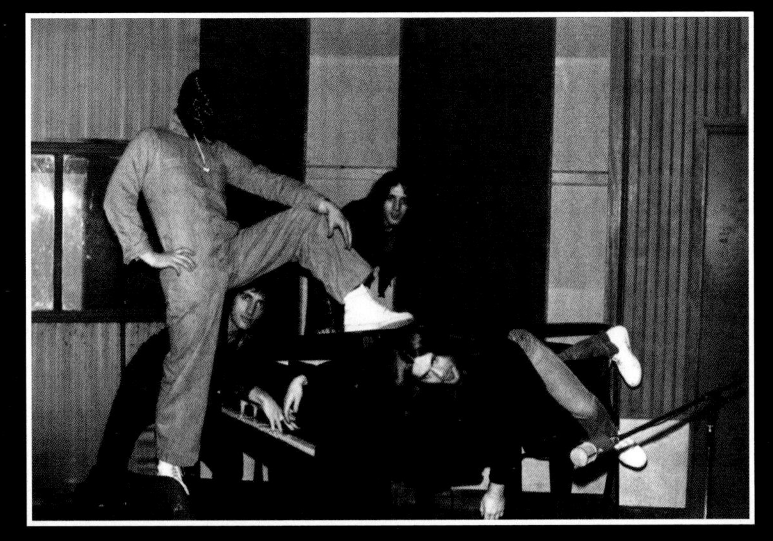

Samson playing loud when wrecked. Thunderstick, Chris Aylmer, Paul Samson and yours truly.

Samson's last gig at Reading. No Thunderstick. Hours before the Maiden meeting.

I explain the aerodynamics of this plastic goose to Clive Burr. I'm in Samson, he's in Maiden.

'How many fingers am I holding up?' Doing my best Ian Gillan impression onstage at the Marquee in Soho.

Above: Early fruit and vegetable shot. From left to right: Adrian Smith, me, Steve Harris, Clive Burr and Dave Murray.

Below: Rod Smallwood in his element.

Matching hair and trousers.

First ant into space.

Singlehandedly holding up the Russian airforce.

He's not the Messiah, he's a very naughty boy!

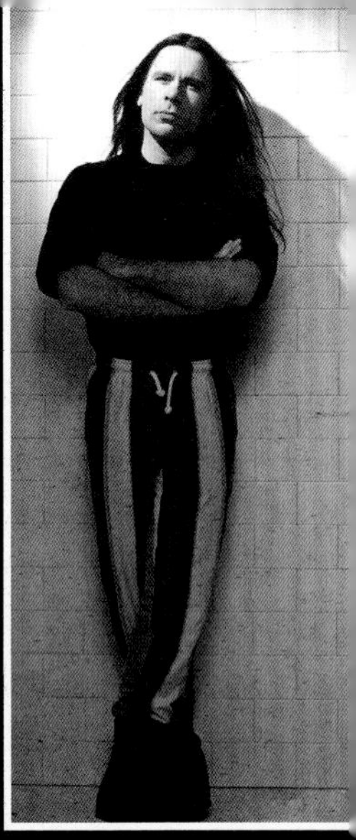

All in the best possible taste.

couple of injections and laid me down under two huge heat pads for half an hour. He then sent me away, a bit stiff but all seemed well.

However, the damage my headbanging had caused to the discs between the vertebrae in my neck had not gone away; only the symptoms had been temporarily alleviated. By the time they returned, things were much worse. In Canada I could barely move my left arm, which cramped and spasmed, continuing into the left side of my neck. The pain was intense and unrelenting, and I lost all fine motor control in my left thumb and first two fingers.

I tried ice packs. They didn't work. Massage made it worse. Heat made it worse. I could not sleep. I was sent to a local doctor in Ottawa.

'You have muscle spasms,' he said.

Tell me something I don't know, I thought. 'Why do I have muscle spasms?'

He was busy writing the prescription. 'Take these.'

Librium, Flexeril and Butazolidin were the end result. I lasted one day, after which I realised that I had lost the ability to speak and I could not actually feel my gums when I brushed my teeth.

The shows carried on and we got to Montreal. I went to the hospital. They took X-rays and stuck pins into my thumb.

'Can you feel that?'

I said I could.

'Hmm. Neurologically normal,' he wrote on his pad. He swivelled his chair to pin up the X-rays.

'Aha!' he said.

'What is it?'

'See those?' He pointed with his pen to cloudy areas around my scapula. 'They are muscle spasms,' he proudly pronounced.

'No shit, Sherlock,' I said.

He told me nothing I didn't already know, except about the pills I had been given.

'Good lord, who gave you these?' he said.

'A Canadian doctor.'

'And he gave you a liver-function test?'

I didn't shake my head; it hurt. My eyes did it instead.

I threw all the pills in the bin. Next stop was New York. There had to be somebody there who knew what they were talking about. I paid 100 dollars for five minutes with a sports doctor. He had treated Muhammad Ali, ballet dancers and American football players. He pressed with his fingers.

'Here?'

'Ouch.'

Then he cradled my head and gently lifted upwards, taking pressure off the spine.

'How's that?'

He took an X-ray. It wasn't pretty.

'You have a herniated disc at the top of your neck, C4 and C5. I can fit you in for an operation on Monday.'

'Whoa there, Doc. What operation?'

'Well, I take out the cartilage and put a plastic piece in instead.'

'I have a gig in Chicago before Monday.'

'Oh, well. In that case it's traction.'

'How long does that take?'

'Eight weeks.'

'Well, that won't work either. What else?'

He sighed. There was a golf course in his future, I sensed, and I was delaying him.

'Okay, home traction unit and a neck collar. Best I can do.'

A home traction unit was a badly designed gallows that fitted over the top of a wardrobe door. A water bottle was hung from one side and my head was lifted up from the other. It looked pretty stupid.

Finally, Tony Wiggens, our tour manager, came to the rescue. His American girlfriend recommended a chiropractor.

'A chiropractor? That's like a fortune teller who uses dead bodies.'

'No, that is a necromancer.'

The chiropractor was actually very good at telling this dead body exactly what was going on. He gave me good advice, the best of which was to stop hurling my head around as if it's trying to achieve escape velocity from my torso. Wear the neck collar and throw the rest of the apparatus in the bin, he told me. I was advised on ways to modify the way I moved, ate and drank to give my neck the best chance of healing given the punishing schedule.

A silver American Eagle tour bus was in our future, and a long series of overnight trips criss-crossing the USA in pursuit of the Scorpions. We were the special guests in a three-act show, with a good chunk of time to develop a connection with an audience who were ripe for conversion.

It's taken a while for European tour buses to catch up to their American cousins, and back in 1982 there was simply no comparison. The American Eagle was like a whorehouse on wheels.

Bus life soon established its routine. The front lounge was misery, where Rod plotted, played cards and was grumpy, and where Steve watched hours of videos. The back lounge was naughty, where Clive, Davey and Adrian disposed of a lot of vodka. I flipped from one to the other and found the whole process a tiny bit frustrating.

The Number of the Beast tour was when we did most things on the road for the first time. As time went on it became clear to me that the novelty would soon wear off. The joy of getting brainlessly mashed every night just to get through the next pointless 18 hours soon paled into a hopeless numbness until the next show brought light and life to our world.

The biggest factor that changes 'Saturday night out with the lads in a band' to 'every Saturday spent in rehab or therapy' is money and drugs. Access to either can seriously damage your mental health. We didn't have much money, actually – I don't think any of us had a credit card between us – but everyone wanted to give us drugs, lots of them, and all for free.

I'm loath to attribute drugs as the root cause of Clive's growing estrangement from Steve, but slowly yet surely niggles and arguments crept in backstage.

Clive's luggage was an issue – Clive got more luggage. Steve jumped on the drum riser, telling him to play faster – Clive slowed down. The front of the bus became the front line, and the back of the bus turned into a bunker for the bad boys.

They had such a terrific on-stage row in Kiel Auditorium, St Louis, that Clive went into slow motion in protest. I didn't help matters by bringing out a pillow and two blankets and pretending to go to sleep in the middle of the stage in protest.

'I thought that was a bit out of order,' Steve said.

'Fair enough,' I replied.

Once the rot starts in a band, it's like a dog with a bone: always there, waiting to be gnawed on. We were too busy to talk about it, too close to escape from it and too tired one minute and full of adrenalin the next to be rational about it.

The juggernaut rolled on, but one wheel was wobbling.

On the Bandwagon

Oh boy, did we move on. The word was out in the USA, and halfway through our Scorpions tour we returned briefly to the UK to headline the Reading Festival.

Might I be permitted to pinch myself? I must be dreaming. One year before I was in debt, in a failing band, and standing under a lamppost being offered an audition at the very same festival we were just about to headline. We looked a very different band to the fresh-faced boyishness on the back cover of 'Run to the Hills'. There was an air of confident lunacy about us. The Faustian pact we had made was still a one-way street all in our favour, oh yes, and my neck was feeling a lot better, thank you very much, just in time for us to scramble on a jumbo jet and resume operations in the USA. By now we were genuinely snapping at the heels of the Scorpions.

The bus rolled on, and we went from the West Coast to St Louis. It was time to begin with Rob Halford and Judas Priest, and the combination was one of the hottest tours in the country. Priest were incredibly reliable, and their sound engineer was phenomenal. The last time I had seen him was in a hot tub in Michigan. Life really did seem to be going in ever-increasing circles.

We had the aura of otherworldly beings, at least in our universe. Without realising it, circumstances led the rest of humanity to assume that we were rock stars. Deep down, when I was aged 16, I thought it would be an amazing experience to be a rock star, and do all those things that are read about in the newsprint broadsheet weeklies. Rock stardom was lived vicariously by journalists as envious as they were pretentious in many cases. It was a seductive and easy pit to fall into, and made easier if your will was addled by industrial quantities of coke and hash.

What saved Maiden from this depressing fate was our gradual organisation into an unplanned triumvirate of me, Steve Harris and Rod Smallwood. We each offered different ingredients to the overall pie, and as we gained knowledge of each other's contributions, we started to fiddle about with each other's domains. Not exactly a democracy, but at least a sort of guided autocracy.

There is a reluctance on the part of bands to admit that they are not democracies. The only member of a band who is quite happy to say 'of course we are a democracy' is the local dictator, because he knows he will never be contradicted.

The lesser beings, talented as they may be, have to put up with the largesse of the main man, and that's just the way it is. It doesn't have to be unpleasant. The reason so-called 'supergroups' so often fall short of expectations is because the monumental egos, when taken out of context and placed in close proximity, do not act as a force multiplier. Imagine putting Napoleon, Hitler and Stalin in a room together, setting aside any political differences, and just observe whether any sensible decision could be made to advance a common cause.

The interpersonal chemistry required to sustain a global rock group over many decades is nothing short of a miracle. Too many chiefs and not enough Indians; all Indians and no chiefs; one chief and rebellious Indians; stupid chief and clever Indians: all are doomed to fail. The temperature of the porridge has got to be just right.

The American tour concluded. All was well in the world. Rod was in his element, brimful of statistics, headcounts, merchandise dollars per head and countless other measures of our success in prising open the vault of the biggest music market in the world.

As the weather turned autumnal, we bent nature to our will and flew south for the winter to the land of Oz, which, after the gratuitous insanity that was touring the USA, was very much more Anglo-Saxon, but equally painful.

The flight, of course, was lengthy. Like 99 per cent of the rest of the world, we flew with our knees up into our chest in economy class, and stood in bleary-eyed line to be searched for peanut butter and any other food products that might silently take over the Australian ecosystem overnight. Apart from a cartoon strip dedicated to their existence, I could not for the life of me see what possible point there was in the continuing existence of funnel-web spiders. There are perfectly inoffensive English spiders that could do the job, but not kill you as you take a crap in the loo ... sorry, dunny.

The Kings Cross district of Sydney had a club called the Manzil Room, a good rock 'n' roll dive. I had my drink spiked with speed and stayed up for 48 hours, wired out of my skull. I called a doctor because I had a show that night and couldn't actually speak after staying up and rabbiting ten to the dozen uncontrollably. I drank lots of water, slept all day, got up half an hour before the show and reset the gyros that kept my voice upright.

Thank God it worked. Twenty-three is an amazing age for the immune system.

The girl on reception in the hotel was very friendly, and so we found ourselves on a boat in Sydney Harbour with all the crew: cold beers, darkness, the Harbour Bridge lit up and twinkling on the dappled black water. We took a small yellow inflatable dinghy out into the harbour and a lot of beer. A shark's fin appeared a few yards away, then another. My rowing experience came in handy.

Nothing in childhood is ever wasted.

Things had moved on from the days of the gold lamé jockstrap; in fact, they had become more transparent. Steve was now wearing a pair of black plastic trousers, tights basically, that looked like they had been sprayed on. Trouser envy took over, and I found the same type in Paris, but in red. The singer of UFO, Phil Mogg, was once asked about his trousers, and volunteered the comment: 'Yeah, underpants are naff.'

I think we all subscribed to the same tailor. Not to be outdone, Clive wore a silver spandex skin-tight onesie. Line-up photographs, viewed at crotch level, resembled a vegetable shop well stocked with red peppers, aubergines and silverskin onions.

Our on-stage trousers eventually wore out. Mine in particular had the PVC coating worn away by friction with the microphone stand, leaving a rather horror-movie special-effect blistered finish. While strolling around Sydney I spotted the very thing in a shop window: two pairs of Harlequin ballet tights for blokes.

To date I had been using a pair of white boxing boots from Lonsdale. Steve's personal helper, Vic Vella, had left them in front of an electric fire to dry out after they were soaked in one of our sweat-stained theatre shows. One boot survived, but the other parted company with its slightly shrivelled sole. Moments before going on stage I made the fateful discovery. The only solution was the universal panacea of gaffer tape. I taped around the top and bottom of the front of the foot, and it worked just fine. When the tape on the bottom wore out, I just added more. I got fan mail about my boots. One girl wanted to know where she could find the boot with the black stripe on it. Well, the answer now was in the dustbin.

Newly suited and basketball-booted, my next appointment was the check-in desk for the flight to Tokyo. I was on my way to the land of samurai and sumo, bullet trains, temples and Mount Fuji, and electronic gadgets and video-game nirvana.

Maiden were already big in Japan. The band had a live EP, *Maiden Japan*, which obviously was a pun on one of the greatest live albums of all time, Deep Purple's *Made in Japan*. When I stepped off the plane and went to immigration at Tokyo Narita airport, a couple of things struck me immediately. First, it was unbelievably clean. There are hospitals in the UK that could only aspire to the antibacterial regime clearly prevalent in Japanese transport hubs. Second, this was the first country I had ever visited where not just the language but the alphabet itself was alien.

The latter problem was solved by a combination of bilingual forms and traffic lights. While awaiting your bags arriving in the operating-theatre sterility of the luggage carousel, you simply pressed a button and a green or red light directed you to a stern customs guard.

Very politely, your luggage was searched with white gloves, and very politely you were sent on your way.

The words 'Live at Budokan' marked a band as a worldwide phenomenon, and being big in Japan was so sought after that an American band called Riot named their album *Narita* after the international airport. 'Gatwick' or 'Heathrow Terminal 5' doesn't have quite the same ring.

The concert organisation ran like a precision chronometer. We travelled on bullet trains to the shows, and these ran with a reliability and timekeeping that must have commenced with the ticking of the first atomic clock.

For all their legendary status, the actual concert halls were very modest theatres. We were not at Budokan level yet, but even Budokan is not quite so exotic when you realise it is just a medium-sized gymnasium that gets used as a martial-arts centre.

The phase 'big in Japan' is also very misleading. The Japanese have two entirely separate chart systems, the international and the domestic. Selling 50,000 records would catapult you handsomely towards the top of the international chart; 50,000 records on the domestic chart would barely register. It was rare for an international artist to make a domestic-chart breakthrough, as, for example, Sheena Easton did.

Maiden were young and growing. It was 5 p.m. Tokyo time and we had finished the soundcheck. The show would be over by 8. They started very early to ensure minimum disruption of the school or working day that followed, or so I assumed.

There was an eerie silence before we went on; just the occasional cough or shuffling of feet. There was no support band. Such things were not the norm.

The theatres were 1,200 to 2,500 seats in the main, and the wood and carpets muffled the sound, although I remember the Osaka Festival Hall as being just the right construction for a mix of ambient sound and non-reflectivity.

Blue-uniformed ushers would patrol the aisles lest a foot should stray or emotion get the better of obedience. At the front of the audience there was no barrier. There was, instead, an invisible Japanese force field. It was a piece of string between us and the crowd.

We, of course, were down the front edge of the stage, Steve machine-gunning with his bass and staring them out with crazy eyes. Every so often one of the crowd would crack, shaking in a frenzy on the spot. Emotion would take over, and they'd step out of line, then back, as if struggling against a moral tractor beam that pulled them towards the obedient masses.

Like a shot, a little blue-suited man delivered a swift blow with a rolled-up newspaper to the poor chap, who snapped back to his seat, head bowed, arms by his side, looking like a robot that had just been switched off.

In later years I discovered the Japanese expression often used in schools to describe an individual who was overly individualistic: 'The nail that stands up is always hammered down.'

We were coming to the end of 187 shows, plus writing and recording an album, all in under a year. We were to spend a very brief spell in the UK at Christmas then straight into writing and recording another album and starting another enormous tour. I had traversed the globe, east to west and north to south. All my wildest fantasies had been fulfilled: number 1 album, big in Japan, US tours, headlining the Reading Festival.

My hotel room was covered in the spare junk of the intercontinental rock star. Suitcases never big enough for the T-shirts acquired. Fake samurai swords to take home, along with gadgets, posters, books and a stereo system, which I played super-loud in my room to the annoyance of anyone sleeping next door – usually Rod Smallwood.

After the last show we got very drunk. I was mixing hot sake with cold-beer chasers. Back at the hotel I was hungry. Room service had stopped for the night. I crawled on my hands and knees down a hotel corridor till I found a used room-service tray with two old bread rolls and a slab of butter. I caught sight of my reflection in the mirror by the lift.

There is a William Blake painting, *Nebuchadnezzar*, which is on the cover of Atomic Rooster's album *Death Walks Behind You*. The king's face looks out in horror as he realises what he is becoming: he is transforming slowly into a beast.

That painting was my reflection.

What has happened to you for the last year? I asked myself. *And what can you do to stem the insanity?*

I checked if my foot was morphing into a beast's. It wasn't – not yet, anyway. There was still time, and I did have two bread rolls in hand.

New Battery

Christmas was a strange affair: life not on the road. I owned a house now. A small new-build terrace in West London – the spoils of war and having a number 1 album. Rod Smallwood came round for dinner. His Christmas present was an ornate box to hold playing cards, because he was quite fond of gambling, but only in the right circumstances.

The cards came out. After he won hands down, he pocketed the cash from everyone at dinner then left. It was, I suppose, his managerial instinct. If you invite a sabre-toothed tiger round for a cup of tea, don't be surprised if it eats you. It's not to be taken personally; it's just what sabre-toothed tigers do.

The next three albums and tours equated to the next five years of my life. All of it, though, would be done without Clive Burr, let go at the end of *The Number of the Beast* tour.

It wasn't about luggage, and it wasn't about partying, or girls, because anybody and everybody was guilty of that at some time or another. 'Artistic differences' would be to overstate his creative input. The closest phrase I could get would be 'self-fulfilling irretrievable disagreements'. The breakdown of the relationship between a drummer and bass player is pretty fundamental, especially if the bass player also happens to be the principal songwriter and band leader.

Clive always regarded the Maiden set-up with a jaundiced eye, even as he was held in high regard by fans. I loved his drumming feel, essentially because his sweet spot was of the big-band swing-time variety that guys like Ian Paice of Deep Purple had going for them.

Where we didn't see eye to eye was in the intricate and often eccentric fills and time signatures dreamt up by Steve. Their personalities were increasingly on a collision course. Steve was shy off stage, but aggressive and precise on stage. Clive was Mr Outgoing off stage, but often Mr Approximate when it came to precision on stage. Throw the whole melange into a pot and it got messier and messier throughout America. By the end, Steve took me to one side and said, 'He's got to go. I can't fucking take it any longer.'

On the one hand, Steve and I had come a long way since near fisticuffs in Newcastle City Hall. On the other, I would be sad to see Clive go, but things had clearly been bubbling under for a long time.

We entered a whole new world with a leap of faith and a new drummer. Nicko McBrain was a professional musician and had known almost nothing else for his working life. Technically he was totally overqualified for us. The drum parts to date were busy, but not a problem for Nick in the slightest.

He had toured with the French band Trust already, and when they supported Maiden I'd watched him play from the side of the stage. Steve and the rest of the band were Trust fans, having toured with them previously.

Being a frustrated skinsman myself, I love watching drummers. They evolve a personal movement style over the years, which I find fascinating. Some sit, body upright, with their arms flailing like a syncopated spider as the wooden sticks whirl around their head. Some drum as if in a trance, while others act more like madmen trying to batter their way out of a prison cell, and others still look like accountants until you close your eyes and listen rather than look. Nicko was a dead ringer for Animal from the Muppets. His face would light up as he started to play, and the drums would each receive their individual encouragement vocally, very similar, in fact, to Steve's nocturnal mumblings on *The Number of the Beast.*

When cymbals were struck, and Nick has always liked to spank a nice piece of metal, they were always treated to special intimacies: 'Fuck off ... Fuck OFF ... Feeer ... Feeer ... Fuck off ... Fuck off!'

Over the years we have considered gagging him in the studio, but live there is simply no concealing the musical Tourette's that comprises the McBrain damage. His volatility extended to his long-suffering drum roadies. A few months after he joined, I was woken up by a commotion outside my hotel window in San Sebastián, Spain, where Maiden were doing pre-production rehearsals. There was Nicko's drum roadie sitting in a fountain, clutching a brick and shouting: 'Kill me. Kill me now.'

Nicko's advice had sound therapeutic value: 'Fuck off and don't be a twat.'

Otherwise, it was a very pleasant Sunday evening in the town square.

We enlisted the services of Steve Gadd to look after Nicko. Steve was also a drummer, and had quite a distinguished career with the band Charlie. He understood the mania that inhabits the drummer's brain, but for him it manifested in a gently ironic and very relaxed view of the universe. It was as if he had some invisible duck on his head, and all the water thrown on it just rolled off its back. Eventually, Steve got time off for good behaviour and became our most-trusted assistant tour manager.

In the New Year of 1983, the band decamped to the island of Jersey, together with Martin Birch. We took over Le Chalet Hotel in its entirety. Sadly, it no longer exists. It has been erased from the hillside on which it perched; either that or it fell off.

For the next two albums it was our writing home. It had a bar that was open 24 hours a day, so help yourself, and a small ballroom, which we turned into a rehearsal room to write, eat, sleep and breathe music. The internet did not exist and neither did the laptop or mobile phone; there was one television and a pool table.

The Atlantic gales blew against the windows that faced the storm-lashed, five-mile beach below. At night the Corbière lighthouse shone eerily, and by day (if the tide was out) you could scramble up the causeway strewn with driftwood and seaweed. I couldn't help but think of Van der Graaf Generator's masterpiece 'A Plague of Lighthouse Keepers'.

With the image of Blake's *Nebuchadnezzar* and my two bread rolls firmly in mind, I decided to take my fencing kit with me. My mental salvation from rock 'n' roll torpor would be to dust off my foils and get stuck in to some training. Incredibly there were two fencing clubs on Jersey. I put a training plan together and showed up.

Fencing interested Martin. One evening he recounted his struggle with the music business. An engineering prodigy marked for greatness, and with early greatness achieved, he was dragged off on tour with Deep Purple as a live sound engineer.

He was a black belt in Shotokan karate, and he would take his kit everywhere on tour with Purple and train as an antidote to the madness. He would talk of the power of 'one blow'. At one stage he came very close to quitting music altogether to study karate full-time in Japan.

I was busy writing. My little four-track cassette recorder held a few ideas, and I had started a writing partnership with Adrian that would provide Maiden with a seam of material to line up as potential singles or radio tracks.

Japan had nibbled away at me. I had bought a copy of Miyamoto Musashi's philosophical *The Book of Five Rings*. Touted as the go-to text for business warriors, it was written as a treatise on combat, life and art by one of Japan's most legendary rōnin.

Musashi's life has been serialised and put into an epic novel, and as a character he impinges on much of Western movie culture, from *The Magnificent Seven* to Clint Eastwood and *The Outlaw Josey Wales*.

The Japanese ultra-nationalist Yukio Mishima became obsessed by him and caused mayhem when, as one of Japan's most-revered poets, he disembowelled himself and was decapitated by a faithful assistant during a failed *coup d'etat*.

The inspiration for our song 'Sun and Steel' came from one of Mishima's best-known novels. But the lyrics are not about Mishima; they are about Musashi. The song is short and quite simple. I kept the guitar riff straightforward because I am not very good at guitar. Adrian plays it far better than I could have imagined.

Ross Halfin turned up and we stood on rocks by the lighthouse, windswept and trying not to look freezing cold. 'Flash bang wallop, what a picture. What a photograph.'

Steve rolled out 'The Trooper' after whistling a happy tune into a Sony Walkman, and I pinched a verse from *The English Hymnal* for the first lines of 'Revelations'.

The opening drum sequence to 'Where Eagles Dare' I can take partial responsibility for. It was based on Cozy Powell's intro to 'Stargazer', by Rainbow, although it's the effect, rather than the notes played, that I was after. We toyed with different things, and I mentioned that there was a terrific tom-tom fill I remembered on an obscure hit from a guitarist called Gordon Giltrap.

'Oh yeah, "Heartsong". That was me.'

Of course it was – classic McBrain drumming. We took that fill and infilled it with triplets before it goes into the main riff. The bass-drum part was extreme. It was like Woody Woodpecker having an epileptic beak attack.

'You can't play that on a single bass drum. It needs a double pedal,' Nicko declared. I was inclined to agree with him, but that wasn't the point.

'I bet you Ian Paice could do it.'

The work rate required to get his single foot to play the pattern was extraordinary. To his eternal credit, he worked at it for days and he succeeded.

'Fuck me, I'm glad that's done. We aren't ever gonna do that live – fucking hell.'

We ended up opening the show with it every night. Oops.

Rod Smallwood showed up and we all drank heavily. Apart from writing and rehearsing, there was not a great deal to do. Steve organised a pool tournament and arranged for an enormous trophy. There was one rock night per week in a desolate pub down by the beach. When we turned up we instantly doubled the attendance figures.

In the bar, arguments ensued and questions of philosophy were answered. The meaning of life, according to Rod, was simple: 'Pride and ego. Pride to do your very best and ego to take it that bit further.'

I thought there might be more to it than that.

Martin had also pitched in and Marvin made an appearance, as he started standing on the furniture muttering, 'Death, one blow,' and striking one-legged karate poses.

We thought it might be a good contest to see who would win between karate and fencing. I fetched my foil and we moved the furniture away from the bar. Rod had moved on from philosophy to physics: 'I was so immensely strong, I could lift five navvies on the end of a shovel.'

Combat preparations momentarily ceased as Martin and I both looked askance.

'How does that work? That's bollocks,' we said.

'No, it's not. It's bloody physics, that's what it is,' said Rod.

I failed physics O level, and Rod studied architecture at Cambridge, but clearly not bricklaying.

Anyway, Martin and I squared off. He bowed, and I gave a fencing salute. After a bit of unsteady toing and froing he unleashed a roundhouse kick that sent bar stools flying; I stopped toing and knocked over a plant pot, and somewhere in the midst of all this two-bulls-in-a-china-shop chaos, the point of my foil had nestled comfortably in the middle of his chest.

'Ahhh ... ippon,' Martin said, bowing deeply. The only injuries were caused by collisions with furniture. I think we decided, on balance, that the furniture won in the end.

More Atlantic gales; the bedrooms were damp and draughty. 'Still Life', 'Quest for Fire' and, of course, 'Dune' came from Steve's muse.

Actually, 'Dune' wasn't 'Dune' at all. The author Frank Herbert didn't like heavy metal and caused us no end of problems, so the name was changed to 'To Tame a Land'.

'Flight of Icarus' began life in a toilet. Adrian was fond of playing guitar in bathrooms – he liked the ambience from the tiles – and, while he was noodling away, I heard a sequence of chords and started singing along to them. The chorus of 'Flight of Icarus' just started flying like an eagle as a result.

I quickly realised that we potentially had a song under four minutes that could do the unthinkable for Maiden: airplay on US radio. For the lyric, I flipped the story of Icarus on its head and made the father the villain of the piece. Driven by ambition and ego he forces his son to fly, with terrible consequences as his son, in youthful exuberance, flies too high and his wings melt. Basically the pushy parent revisited.

One of my favourite songs on the album is 'Still Life'. Atmospheric and dark, it deals with themes familiar to many of Steve's songs: fear, powerlessness, betrayal and inescapable prophecies. Unless I am very much mistaken, Iron Maiden don't do love songs. The closest any of us gets is melancholy or anger at lost love or love betrayed. Closet psychologists, eat your heart out ...

Anyway, we now had some great songs, but what were we going to call the album? Basically, we have Eddie to thank for the name.

Eddie is Iron Maiden's mascot, monster, alter ego – call it what you will. Part supernatural, part primal, part aggressive adolescent, Eddie is a super anti-hero with no backstory. Eddie doesn't give a fuck. He just is.

Eddie also gets us off the hook as individuals. Eddie is far bigger and more outrageous than any badly behaved superstar. Eddie makes rock stars obsolete.

This comes in handy when you get to your late fifties and rather fancy a quiet night in after playing to 25,000 screaming metal fans. Eddie can take care of the after-party, probably by disembowelling them and eating their brains, which is often more than they deserve. He had become an on-stage superstar during *The Number of the Beast*, all down to a bit of lateral thinking from Dave Lights, our, er, lighting engineer.

He had seen some giants – on stilts – at an opera, and asked if he could commission the building of a giant walk-on Eddie.

I remember the unveiling at the Rainbow Theatre. The roller shutter went up and there was a gasp as we beheld the giant. We realised right then that this one piece of theatre was going to be transformative. We could upstage just about anyone on the planet by having our gory ghoul amble on stage for 30 seconds and bob his head around.

Until then, Eddie had been a rubber mask on a human wearing leather jacket and jeans. Mr Smallwood was quite effective in costume and denied all knowledge, although, actually, he was very good at frightening small children.

The giant walk-on Eddie opened up massive stage possibilities, and one of them was to remove Eddie's brain on stage. The heart didn't feel like the right thing to do, and by removing his brain we could consign him to a straitjacket. The Beast on the Road had been shackled, lobotomised and put in a padded cell. This all seemed to be a promising album cover.

The top of his skull was Velcroed in place, and the skull casing filled with women's tights stuffed with chunks of foam, stained bloody brown. Ripping out his brain actually looked more like pulling out several feet of pork sausages, but the thought was there at least. The photo for the gatefold sleeve features the band seated around a banqueting table, regarding a large brain, which we are clearly about to consume.

The working title for the album was 'Food for Thought'. It was a pun, but not a very good one and, as is often the case, the answer came one Sunday afternoon in a pub called the Mermaid, just by Jersey airport.

'Why don't we call it *Peace of Mind*?'

'Oh, no. That's *Piece of Mind*, not *Peace*.'

The artwork was sensational – and who cared if it was nothing to do with any of the songs on the album. Although we did slip in a reference to 'Piece of Mind' during 'Still Life', and the final twist came one evening while watching *Omen II* in the TV room, full of band and crew. As the credits rolled there was a scrolling verse from the Book of Revelation with the line 'neither shall there be any more pain, for the former things have passed away'.

I was rather hoping that a bit of tampering with the Bible might provoke yet more controversy. *The Number of the Beast* had generated plenty of hot air from the waffling middle classes and religious bigots, so we hoped for a bit more.

I'm sorry to say it didn't work. No one seemed to care that 'there shall be no more brain, for the former things have passed away'. Our adulteration of the Book of Revelation went unpunished, but it made us chuckle a little.

The great rollercoaster hurtled on and deposited us in the very much sunnier climate of the Bahamas to record the album. Making records in a tax haven was beginning to sound a bit Rolling Stones – but we soon put a stop to that.

In the early eighties drug-trafficking was ravaging the island, and while out by Compass Point Studios life seemed suitably laidback and beach-hut friendly there were places in the capital, Nassau, that were potentially unfriendly.

Cruise ships docked and boatloads of either elderly or drunk-and-crazed college kids descended into town at regular intervals. There was still an air of faded colonial splendour, and the British ex-colony just about vied equally with the new American economic colony in a contest for the hearts and minds of whatever remained of island culture.

It still resembled the island where Sean Connery filmed *Dr. No*, even if the bauxite mine which doubled for so many other locations in that, and subsequent Bond movies, had been dwarfed in economic significance by the arrival of bags of cocaine and hash.

Up the road from Compass Point Studios, along the beach, was the Traveller's Rest. It could have been pulled straight out of a Hemingway novel. Concrete tables, black-eyed peas and rice, conch fritters and smudder grouper were all on the menu. The cool, damp evening breeze flowed through the open windows, and the only entrance was a pair of Western saloon-style swinging doors. The deadliest concoction on offer was a banana daiquiri of such quality that it rendered you both potent and impotent at one and the same time.

The band all lived and slept in small, neat townhouses by the beach. Only a few yards over the road was the studio. Each townhouse had three bedrooms and the road crew occupied the spare rooms. In the evening the waves broke gently on the beach with a peaceful whoosh.

My small house had a downstairs balcony with the sea below it. The reef was several hundred yards out and the water was clear. Being close to the equator, the sun rose and set at very similar times throughout the year. If in any doubt as to what time it was, I just had to wait till the stingray flapped lazily past my balcony every day at 4 p.m.

At night, small ticks nibbled away at us. The locals called them 'no see 'ums', for obvious reasons. Sea snakes cavorted around in the shallows and dogs were potentially rabid so best avoided, unless you knew the owner. The one exception was a delightful little mutt called Biscuit, who belonged to our neighbour, Robert Palmer. More of him as the story unfolds.

Now it was time to do some work. The studio was spacious and comfortable, but with a few eccentricities. Island power was sometimes unpredictable, so there was a backup generator. All well and good, but the power spike when the generator kicked in would send a surge through the magnetic tape heads of the 24-track recorder, erasing or damaging whatever content happened to be in contact with the head at that moment.

A power cut was therefore a critical moment. The room would suddenly plunge into darkness, and tape operators would lunge for the recorder to pull the tape away from the heads. You had about 10 seconds to do it before an entire swathe was wiped from the tape.

Except when it came to the power supply, we took our time. Rod had decided to go for broke in the USA, and had gambled on us being able to do the business as an arena headliner. Social media did not exist. It was radio that ruled the roost, and if we could get a radio track away, we were home and dry – hard work and touring would do the rest. I told him that 'Flight of Icarus' was the one.

When we recorded the track I had a stand-up row with Steve over the tempo. He wanted to play the whole thing much faster, almost like a slow shuffle. I stood nose to nose with him and he reluctantly caved in and let me dictate the timing.

'This is nothing to do with getting it on the radio, is it?' he demanded.

'Oh, no. God forbid. Of course not,' I lied.

Well, we did it, and it was a top 10 radio hit, out of the box. As it happens, I think it is the right tempo regardless, but I'm sure Steve would disagree because we haven't played the song live for 30 years.

'The Trooper' was a monster, and the galloping bass line and iconic sleeve was like red meat to hungry wolves in Europe. 'Revelations' occupied the space normally taken up by a song like 'Children of the Damned', and for reasons of musical insecurity I sported a guitar to play the opening lighter passages.

I was not exactly overconfident playing in front of several thousand people, and I'm pretty sure that whatever I played was never actually broadcast to the audience on the grounds that it might have been crap.

The laid-back rhythm of island life soon ceased. The hard grind of another world tour lay ahead. The UK was carpet-bombed from Hull to Southampton with shows, Europe similarly, but the big event was the headline tour of America and Canada.

Organ Pipes

Singing is hard at the best of times, and doing it with a band like Maiden posed some unique challenges. The vocal strain was intense. We had never given very much thought to vocal monitors, and the longevity of my voice was never considered as a limiting factor when booking the gruelling tours. With the kind of singing I was doing, it was inevitable that my voice would fail.

The closest analogy to a singer losing his voice is a football player breaking his leg. He may never play again, and the voice is such a precarious instrument that similar emotions prevail. Simple vocal strain can be dealt with by rest and silence. Living like a monk goes with the territory. More critical is disease, and singing while carrying a vocal infection like laryngitis can be career-ending stuff.

The pressure on singers in these situations is unrelenting and often self-inflicted. Of course you want to do the show, and the guilt involved in cancelling is enormous. Managers, agents and the like are often unsympathetic at worst, and neutral at best. Thankfully, it hasn't happened too often over the years, but the work rate and lifestyle for the first five years meant that some degree of incapacitation was bound to happen.

The best way to preserve a voice is to get loads of sleep in a quiet room with no air-conditioning, just an even temperature and good humidity. Preferably take regular rest days, and avoid unnecessary speaking and especially shaking hands with lots of strangers – absolutely the best chance of catching colds and flu. Have an even and unremarkable diet with plenty of fresh vegetables, avoiding too many dairy products and other foods that produce excess mucus.

Excess or sticky mucus is the death of the singing voice. The pathetically fragile vocal chords need only the tiniest blob to adhere to them, and the uneven vibration that results sounds like a piece of paper being played through a comb.

Vocal polyps, essentially callouses caused by harshly rubbing the vocal chords together repetitively (as in shouting for days on end), are permanent manifestations of the same phenomenon.

A German opera singer wrote a treatise on the subject of phlegm in which she identified more than 50 different types – almost as many words as the Eskimos have for snow.

It goes without saying that drugs of most description are eventually fatal to the voice, especially ones like cocaine and speed, which are snorted into the delicate mucosa in the sinus cavities.

Cigarettes and hash appear to work for some people, but certainly not for me. Lucky if you can survive the onslaught, but how lucky not to do it at all and sing even better.

The vocal chords are only the start of the process. My style of singing is very physical, and I am drained at the end of a rehearsal; my belly aches, my head hurts and my eyes feel like they want to pop out of my head.

The diaphragm is the engine room of the voice, and singers breathe in a way more familiar to people who meditate or do yoga. Very seldom will you observe the shoulders of a good singer rise up when he takes a breath; indeed, taking breath may be almost imperceptible.

This is because the singer has trained his lungs and belly to relax and be inspired by simple air pressure from the atmosphere. If the body is relaxed the lungs simply fill up. The interesting bit is that most of the lung capacity is located well below the nipples, in the lower back.

I am the king of the elastic waistband as a result. Restrictions around the belly are extremely uncomfortable and lead to inefficient production of wind from the diaphragm, the bellows of the body.

Singers train their diaphragm to become stronger and train themselves to stand with their lower back slightly flattened to permit maximum expansion of the lung cavity. Eating before a show can thus be a very uncomfortable, even hazardous activity.

Once the diaphragm has metered the amount and velocity of air going through the pipes, the vocal chords add the note to be sung by stretching or relaxing, much like a reed in a clarinet mouthpiece.

That's not the end of the story. This raw-data note now arrives at the base of the tongue, which shapes and echoes the sound, moving and directing it around the resonant cavities of our soft palate and the hard, bony spaces of the sinus cavities.

With practice, singers find their own sound from within the shape and space of their own bodies. The ground rules remain the same, however, and if you choose to make your idiosyncratic vocal style by vocal abuse, just make sure you know the rules before you try to bend them. That way you stand a chance of having a voice that will survive more than five years.

A voice is, after all, just that. It's a voice for a story, a way of making people feel something and, to that extent, the end justifies the means.

After this brief description of what goes on, you're probably wondering how we get beyond our first vowel sound without a college degree. Fortunately there are babies to teach us. We have forgotten how to be babies, to our eternal shame, but they make the most extraordinary noises, as anyone trapped on an aeroplane with one for several hours will testify. The vocal power that comes out of that tiny package is remarkable.

Rock stars, of course, have long had the capacity to act like babies but have not had the sense to sing like them.

Powerslave

The *Piece of Mind* tour was shorter than our previous one only because the album took longer to write and record. We gambled in the USA and went for the jugular, headlining Madison Square Garden in New York. It paid off.

Piece of Mind was us laying down the gauntlet to America. Even though we had a radio track with 'Flight of Icarus', it was clear that we would not last long as American media darlings because we were simply un-American. We disliked limousines and were more likely to be found playing darts than smoking crack.

We despised fashion, hated the cult of celebrity and thought the concept of 'all you can eat' as disgusting as its obese participants. In contrast, Canada seemed much more sane, and ice hockey seemed to make much more sense than American football, at least at the time.

We bashed our way round the States and the UK and Europe, and then Europe some more, and finally finished at a German TV festival at Westfalenhallen in Dortmund. It was the end of two years on the road. I had had herniated discs, paralysis of my limbs, laryngitis, bacterial bronchitis and a crash course in cultural assimilation.

The bill at Westfalenhallen read like a who's who of eighties metal: Ozzy, Scorpions, Whitesnake ... everyone was there. There were two stages at each end of a huge arena and a scaffold mixing tower in the centre.

I remember being very tired, but the adrenalin kicked in and the show was good, in that unsatisfying way that TV shows are 'good'. Seldom are they actually really wonderful. TV kills live music. Cameras are the enemy, but people are your true friends.

After the show I got very drunk and abusive. I behaved appallingly. I was swigging from a bottle of champagne as I climbed the scaffold tower to the mixing desk.

A very earnest journalist asked me what I thought of the sound. I responded by pissing on the mixing desk. I was asked to leave.

Unchaperoned and with my willy hanging out, I interrupted a photo session of Quiet Riot and inserted my dick in the singer's ear, thus becoming a new member.

I was escorted from the building and placed in a car, with the driver given instructions to put me to bed. Unfortunately I was in the front seat, which was bad for him, as I insisted on selecting reverse gear when he was at traffic lights. After I attempted to open the door at high speed I was escorted from the front of the vehicle and put in the back, where there were child-proof locks.

Who said we had forgotten how to behave like babies?

Piece of Mind had given us a new confidence, and a desire to break out of the 'angry East End punk metal' identity that we had been saddled with by the media, and which we never were. Fierce, yes. Punk, never. And East End? Well, that was almost true.

I had been busy fencing away, and was taking lessons from the British national coach, Brian Pitman. His son, Justin, happened to be a friend of mine, and he also placed fourth in the world under-20 championships, alongside future world champions. We became sparring partners, and a certain amount of drinking was involved.

Fencing is a paradoxical sport. It has the appearance of some aristocratic past-time, partaken of by a rich elite. This is a very convenient and lazy way of thinking, but since when has rigour ever got in the way of a good cliché for an idle journalist?

The paradox in fencing comes in the conflict between availability and opportunity. It should be taught and trained in the toughest inner-city schools, and not wasted on those who can merely afford it. That is not to say that it should not be inclusive. Merely that the net should be spread far wider than it is at the moment. In many respects, it is similar to tennis in its requirement for dedication and individual coaching.

It is, of course, a combat sport. The aim in times past was to kill your opponent, and sport had very little to do with it. I have a collection of old fencing books, and books on duelling. There is no more lethal way to dispense with a human being, other than a firearm, than by running them through with a sword.

I took my fencing kit with me on tour, and in every town we played I tried to train and fight at the local club. It made a change from the rock 'n' roll ghetto of the tour bus. I just turned up and fought, and then we went off and drank beer and talked about fencing, and very little about music, because nobody was bothered one way or another.

I entered competitions if I could prise my way out of tours. I still have some of the bizarre medals I won around the USA. On one occasion I ended up fencing outdoors at the Renaissance Faire in California, amidst a crowd of pointy-hatted wenches and stout gentlemen wearing Elizabethan dress shouting 'prithee' in a Californian twang in 100-degree heat. After I cleaned the cow dung off my kit I was presented with a rosette that read 'For valour'.

Errol Flynn, eat your heart out. Actually I took lessons from the fencing master who taught Errol Flynn, and who doubled for him in several movies. Ralph Faulkner also taught Basil Rathbone and Stewart Granger, I think and, well, pretty much anyone in Hollywood. He had his own studio, Faulkner Studios, out in East Hollywood, in what is now a low-rent district. He must have been well into his eighties and still teaching.

Drumming and fencing have much in common. Both require tempo, but the combat element requires timing, which is quite different, but reliant on tempo. Timing is the ability to deliver the punchline, as the secret of a good joke is ... wait for it ... TIMING.

In the space between people's intentions, or the space between successive actions, there is time to strike. It's like watching a great boxer effortlessly jab his way to victory, seemingly reading his opponent's every intention and being two moves ahead.

Ralph wasn't very mobile, but his hand speed and precision were extraordinary; his hand moved as if guided by a preordained groove in the air, and I struggled to achieve the required accuracy to manipulate the point of my foil around the worn aluminium guard and onto the target, his weather-beaten brown leather plastron.

From beneath his mask he barked commands. His voice was gruff, and it was quite difficult to understand. He would raise his mask and stare through the thick lenses of his wire-rimmed glasses: 'Parry four, I said.'

'Oh, yes,' I'd reply.

There was another club in LA run by former Japanese Olympic fencer Heizaburo Okawa, who was also a Kendo champion and a bit good at golf. Not too much eye-hand coordination at work there, then.

I felt at home with fencers because they were nearly always eccentric, smart and liked a beer. My biggest problem in trying to improve was a lack of consistency in training and coaching.

You simply can't get anywhere without a solid input from a proper coach. We would all be back in Jersey shortly to write the next album, but coaching was limited on the island, so I made plans to import my buddy Justin to spar with.

The Doomsday Clock kept by nuclear scientists was ticking at two minutes to midnight. That sounded like a song title. Ronald Reagan was expounding about the 'evil empire' of the Soviet Union and, just for shits and giggles, Steve threw in an epic song recounting *The Rime of the Ancient Mariner*.

In an ironic touch, I wrote the song 'Powerslave' as a partial allegory of life as a rock-star pharaoh, taking all the acolytes with him as he goes. In the end it's all just an empty tomb, so what was the point of it all? Bleak magnificence was the sentiment in my heart, and it was starting to become what I would feel at the end of the tour: 'A slave to the power of death ...'

The song started life as a little Egyptian-sounding riff on a guitar, and I always loved the image conjured up by the phrase 'slave amplifier'. A bit of daydreaming and staring out the window on a rainy day did the rest. The song gave us our album title, too.

What *Powerslave* really did, though, was give us the gift of Pharaoh Eddie, and the magnificence of the *Powerslave* stage set. Suddenly we had a walk-on Eddie mummy, plus a giant mummy that rose from the back of the set in a stunning finale. The theatricality was sensational. For 'Rime of the Ancient Mariner' we turned the same stage set into on old galleon. This was old-school painted backdrops, *trompe-l'œil* effects and props. It was proper theatre rather than insubstantial gimmicks. It was theatre of the mind.

When we came to make a video for '2 Minutes to Midnight', the director was keen to show how cinematic his storyboard was, so he met us to show polaroids of locations.

The Greenwich foot tunnel was one of them. It brought back memories of college and walking under the river to catch the bus to the Green Man in Plumstead. He then produced a series of drawings describing the mercenaries' hangout.

'We found this fantastic location. It's disgusting, full of rats and piss – horrible,' he said.

He flipped over the polaroid.

'I used to live there,' I muttered. It was 22 Roffey House. How the world turns.

Iron Curtains

Returning to the Bahamas to record *Powerslave* seemed almost like coming home. Although we all had homes, none of us had actually spent any significant time in any of them for over two years. None of us could really comprehend that it would be another two years before any semblance of a normal existence began to impinge on us, and even then, only briefly.

We mixed the album in the city that never sleeps, so good they named it twice: New York, New York.

I love New York, and over the years the city has returned the favour. It is a daydream of cinematic proportions, and it is in the smallest details that it reveals itself. The patter of the cops, the hustle and bustle, and the brash vulgarity that in any other city would be gross, but in New York it verges on inspirational. Early morning, winter's day, cup of coffee steaming out of a paper cup as the dustcarts hammer their axles round the potholes, you are in *The French Connection* and Popeye Doyle is going to step out of that office building right ... now. Or maybe not.

I had found a fencing *salle* (that's club in English) run by a world-class Ukrainian defector. Stan was a hero of the Soviet Union in terms of sport, and the national coach of Ukraine. He had smuggled himself out and managed to make his way to New York. He was an eccentric and industrious individual and, as well as running a fencing school, he had a business manufacturing and importing fencing clothing from around the world.

I spent hours training every week. I would hop on the subway down to 23rd Street with my kit bag around 11 a.m., warm up, then have a one-on-one lesson for 45 minutes. Reduced to a small ball of sweat and goo, I would go to the local deli and bring my lunch back to watch as he gave lessons to the next batch of modern-day musketeers. A couple of hours of sparring, and that was me done for the day.

Electric Ladyland Studios, where the record was being mixed, is tucked away in a basement in Greenwich Village, which was only a couple of stops down the street, or a pleasant walk. Take a listen back, have an opinion and let them get on with it. Steve loved the process of mixing, but I preferred to leave them to it and come in as a second opinion. It's very easy to get too close to a mix, so that it becomes very hard to make an objective judgement.

Later on, when I was in the middle of my solo career, I had to get more involved in the mixing process. Nevertheless, I would give guidelines and would always deliberately leave the crew alone to determine their own mix as they saw fit. You can't paint a picture if all you can see is what's at the end of the paintbrush. It's also very easy to get bogged down in technical minutiae, the creative equivalent of quicksand.

With the mix done, we rehearsed for the upcoming tour in a wonderfully tacky nightclub in Fort Lauderdale, and stayed in a cockroach-infested sea-front motel.

Soon enough, the holiday was over. It was time to emigrate to the Evil Empire, behind the Iron Curtain, as it was in 1984, to Poland to open the *Powerslave* tour.

The Tupolev Tu-134 is a small, twin-engine jet airliner, and it was the vehicle of choice to transport us to Poland. LOT Airlines was using all-Russian machinery, and this was the variant that had a bomb aimer's cupola in the nose, which was all rather thrilling.

We were tucked into the cramped fuselage, festooned with netting instead of overhead bins, while unidentifiable meat products and boiled sweets were delivered by the cabin crew, whose morale could best be described as homicidal.

Warsaw was forbidden fruit. We were received in scenes reminiscent of the Beatles when they landed back in the UK after playing Shea Stadium. We stepped off the plane, initially oblivious to the hundreds of Poles besieging the airport with banners, placards and albums.

The welcome committee was cordial, relaxed and the complete opposite of any preconceived notion we might have had of some Stalinist apparatchik or Stasi-style stooge organising our trip.

We walked down the aircraft steps and shook hands with the promoter's rep. There were grins all round. We smiled, he smiled, the sun shone, and the heat wrinkled the air around the concrete apron.

'Where is Rod?' the rep asked. Rod Smallwood had chosen this moment to make a bold statement. He had purchased a white suit (although, to this day, Rod insists it was beige) and dark sunglasses. As the aircraft door opened, he surveyed the reception committee, who ignored him. We ambled down to the ground and chatted to everyone, but Rod stood on his own, suited and sunglassed.

We had queried his choice of clothing when we boarded the plane.

'I've got to show them who's boss,' was his reply. I seem to recall none of us were too sure that a white suit would be the sort of thing to go down a storm in Warsaw.

By the time we had gone through customs and immigration, it was quite clear that the whole apparatus of the state had been infiltrated by Iron Maiden fans. Anyone with a gun wanted an autograph, and when we tried to get on the coach outside the terminal, it took all of my minimal rugby skills to batter my way through.

On the bus, the subject of the white suit was broached. Rod was a little uncomfortable at not being the centre of attention for all the wrong reasons. I did, I confess, try to take the mickey.

Rod had the unpleasant habit of striking people across the top of their head with his knuckles if he disapproved of the conversation. Record company execs lived in fear, but back in the Macho Man culture of the time it was tolerated, the same way females were ogled and touched up and accepted it by gritting their teeth and mentally kicking the offender in the nuts.

'Oh, shut up,' Rod said, and reached out his fist to rap me across the top of the head.

I grabbed his wrist; we locked arms. This was getting interesting. Finally we wrestled ourselves onto the floor of the coach with Rod muttering, 'Bloody hell, you're quite strong for a little bloke.'

After our undignified rutting, the white suit was white no more. Covered in dirt and dishevelled, it was never seen again.

The Poles were sensational. For me, it also represented the first country that had never seen the band with the old singer, so everything was new to all of us.

The shows went off, predictably, with barely a hitch. Such was the enthusiasm of the fans, and such was the palpable feeling of liberation in the air, that we could have stood on stage in our underwear waving white flags and the reaction would have been the same.

As we travelled through Poland it was like reliving the past 40 years of history, from the horrors of Auschwitz to the grim and obvious failure of communism, and the slow but growing sense of a new future, somewhere groping in the distance.

We had been given the services of a very bouncy young chap, Josef, who was to be our security guard for the duration of the tour. Josef spoke very little English and had been trained to kill people in imaginative and unexpected ways by the

Soviet military. He was a member of Spetsnaz, or special forces, as we would call them. Luckily for us, Josef was not inclined to execute or assassinate us, which might of course have changed if we suddenly went to war.

Josef was on permanent furlough after his parachute failed to open properly when he jumped out of an aircraft at 300 feet. The injury to his back meant he was now put out to pasture, guarding decadent Western rock stars.

After a couple of days we turned him, and he defected to our way of looking at the world. Initially, Josef's reaction to the glorious disorder whenever we arrived at a hotel was to kill them all. He carried a gun, not that he needed it, because, as he demonstrated one evening when turning out the light, his feet never ran out of bullets. Instead of using his hands, he kicked forward and backwards at head height, and finally, with astonishing deftness, he flicked off the light switch with his foot.

We explained to Josef that the audience were actually our friends, and that we really shouldn't try to kill them, because they were only trying to be nice. He seemed to take this on board, and over the next few days his English improved noticeably, even if his topic of conversation was more illuminating than we had bargained for.

Some of the crew had found some dope, and we persuaded Josef to try some. The results were immediate and, I fear, long lasting. Josef stood on the bed, in very good spirits, and signalled for silence.

'This is good woman,' he said, squatted down on a virtual penis with two virtual willies in either hand, and with his remaining orifice stuck his tongue into the side of his mouth and sang 'The Blue Danube' while moving up and down and side to side in admirably persistent rhythm.

'Very good, Josef.' Clearly there was a bit of work to do, but we were making progress.

As we drove through the Polish countryside to the venues, he would point out landmarks: 'There is secret military base.'

'MiG?' I enquired.

'YES! MiG 21.'

I liked Josef. Actually, I liked all the Poles we met.

The towns were, in general, quite depressing. We stayed in the upmarket hotel in Warsaw, but one drunken evening I woke up in a Warsaw apartment, I know not where, with people I didn't know who spoke no English. It was my fault for drinking with Howard Johnson, a journo who was out to cover the show. We had ended up in a car, been stopped by the police, and our chaperones had told the police we were Polish and thus we ended up sleeping off our hangover and listening to their cassette tapes compiled from the radio.

The bright sunshine was painful. We had a few zlotys, the country's currency, and we stepped outside to find ourselves in the middle of a high-rise housing estate. The buildings were drab and in poor condition, the queues for the tram or bus were building, and there were a few vendors with a horse and cart, which had vegetables for sale.

We waited for an hour or so before we found a taxi, and although we had no money it was obvious we were foreign, and despite our long hair we wanted to go to Hotel el Posh. Just as well because the band was missing a lead singer for the show that night.

The rest of the cities we visited were similar. We were taken shopping in a department store. There was precious little to buy. The building was little-changed from its former occupation as the headquarters of the Gestapo. Some of the venues were sports halls and, in a fabulous folly, the Spodek was built to resemble a gigantic flying saucer.

In Wroclaw we played the Centennial Hall, which was a chilling experience.

In the vast hall, a red velvet curtain hung to cover the centre of the dome. The reason became evident. A gigantic stone Iron Cross formed a central plug, which effectively kept the roof from collapsing.

Backstage, there were spyholes built in the walls so that the Gestapo could observe the audience, and presumably measure their individual enthusiasm for the Nazi floorshow. It was rumoured that the tunnels beneath the building extended down almost 17 storeys.

The relics of Nazi Europe seemed to follow us around. We had been in Jersey, itself occupied and fortified. Much of the concrete was still there, and the workers who died, some of them Poles, were reputed to have been buried in the walls where they fell.

By far the most sobering and depressing manifestation of the ghosts of Europe's past was our visit to Auschwitz, where death was planned, orderly and brutally, clinically inevitable.

Genocide has lost its power to shock in our visually overloaded world. The Khmer Rouge, Stalin's purges – they all seem to blur into one. Genocide is going on right now somewhere in the world, but it is the innocent plight of a child about to die that cuts to the very soul, unless, of course, you have given up on that idea, exchanged it for 'just obeying orders'.

No birds fly over Auschwitz. It is as if the very soil contaminates the air with the stench of death and the evil of those who walked upon it and planned the horror. It is the banality of industrial-execution planning contrasted with the screams of the gas chambers that is the true measure of the terror. That terror, I believe, is the secret fear that we may all be such monsters deep down. It makes me shudder even to think it.

I cried a lot after the visit. I was angry and silent. Not until I drove into Sarajevo 10 years later, during the siege, would I feel that same intensity.

Snow, Leather and Bondage

We left Poland with a documentary made, a Polish wedding attended and a drunken version of 'Smoke on the Water', along with a new-found respect for vodka.

Onwards, then, as the trucks rolled into the rest of Europe. Of course, we were all busted for drugs in Germany. Actually, we weren't. It was the great Iron Maiden drugs bust that wasn't.

Asleep in my bed, there was a knock at my hotel door.

'No maid service,' I groaned.

'This is the police.'

I opened the door. A very polite young chap in plain clothes showed me his ID.

'We are looking for drugs. Do you have any?'

'Er, no.'

'Do you mind if I take a look?'

'No, no. Go ahead.'

He very politely poked around my bags and said, 'Thank you.'

'Excuse me, but what's going on?'

'One of your truck drivers has been smuggling them in,' he said. 'We have two kilos of heroin, plus weed. When we found him, he was so out of his brain he could not even stand up.'

Well, that was a big 'wow' moment. I phoned the tour manager's room and looked down the corridor to see a bleary-eyed assistant tour manager being led away. I believe there was a half-smoked joint by his bedside. Never mind the drugs – that's a serious fire risk.

I got dressed and went to the restaurant. Sitting in one corner, on the naughty step, were half the road crew, all paying small fines for possession of minimal amounts of dope. On the roof were police with binoculars. It was all serious stuff, until it wasn't.

Whoever had alerted the police to the contents of the truck driver's cab had jumped to a few conclusions, and the police in turn jumped to a few of their own, all involving following the crew buses to their destination, which also happened to be our hotel.

The truck driver had been driving all night and had the next day off, so to relax he drank a fair amount of his minibar as a homemade sedative before going to sleep.

Blind drunk, he was dragged from his deep sleep and was thus unable to explain that he was diabetic and he liked to bake his own bread. Two kilos of self-raising is not to be sniffed at.

Autumn turned into winter, and Europe turned into North America.

We made landfall on the east coast of Canada, in Halifax. Interesting place, Halifax. We stayed for several days, preparing the show, and I ended up advising a budding dominatrix on the building of her dungeon. By day she was all crimplene slacks and a very professional radio-promotions girl, and by night it was ball gags, rubber and whips.

Not that I indulged. I was merely shown the catalogue after our vanilla amorous encounter.

'What do you think about the stocks?' she asked.

'Very nice. Is there any other choice of colours?'

I asked her how she had become so enamoured of S&M to want to build her own dungeon.

'Travelling salesmen,' she replied. It turned out that Canada was awash with S&M travelling salesmen, all carrying their kit in a little briefcase like freemasons.

I suppose all those dark winter nights have an effect on the soul. As the Icelanders say, 'What do you do in summer?'

'We like to fish and we like to fuck.'

'What do you do in winter?'

'In winter, fishing's not so good.'

I took the train to Quebec City, which took a bloody long time. I discovered that there are only two types of tree in Canada: those standing up, and logs. That's all there is to see apart from snow.

We were heading west in winter, and the further we went, the colder and colder it got. Toronto was almost tropical by comparison, and this, my friends, was where I met the mighty Johnny Cash. We were doing our soundcheck at Maple Leaf Gardens, and I noticed five guys sitting among the empty chairs at the back of the hall.

'Who are those guys?' I asked.

'That's Johnny Cash's band.'

I wandered backstage after we finished. The area was strewn with ice hockey detritus and rubber floor tiles. Standing above it all was a leather-greatcoat clad giant, with thigh-high leather riding boots. He extended his hand and shook mine.

'Hi, my name's Johnny Cash,' he said. 'I wondered if you could sign something for my daughter. She's a fan.'

His voice rumbled and resonated, but not in a loud and brash way. He was a terribly humble soul, and the sheer size of the man made him more impressive because of it. All I could think was: I shot a man in Reno, just to watch him die.

'Yes of course,' I said instead. 'Very fine boots.'

'Yes, had 'em made in Texas.'

I signed a photo and he passed me a promo photo of himself, playing pool, entitled 'The Baron'.

'Thank you very much,' he said, and then he was gone.

I too was gone, and nearly out for the count in Winnipeg. Outside the hotel it was minus 25 Celsius. I decided to go for a walk to see what would happen. Halfway around the small square in front of the hotel my eyes and nostrils had frozen – I could barely breathe, let alone see – and I just made it back to the lobby. Do not fuck with Canada.

We were fully in the grip of a continental winter. It took 36 hours to get over the Rockies to Vancouver, with snow chains and escorts, crawling at four or five miles an hour. I had never seen weather on such a big scale so close up. When people say 'bad weather' in Britain it usually means it's wet. In North America 'bad weather' means you might die.

Christmas was brief and shell-shocked. We finished at the Rosemont Horizon near Chicago, and stir-crazy did not begin to describe the atmosphere. We were so desperate to return home we paid to go on Concorde.

There was a super-early flight on a 747 from Chicago to New York that meant we could catch the 9 a.m. Concorde, to arrive that evening in London. Before leaving we partied like it was 1999, and I dressed up as Sherlock Holmes and wandered the hotel with a walking stick, beating up light bulbs.

After a brief period of unconsciousness (as opposed to sleep), I somehow ended up in first class at 7 a.m. in the pitch dark of a Chicago winter morning. The cabin crew came round and asked for drinks orders. I wanted a glass of water. The businessman behind me grunted loudly.

'I think I'll have a Bloody Mary,' he said. 'Guess it's gonna be one of those days ...'

Drunk as I still was, it already was one of those days.

Concorde was small, the seats were cramped and the menu was amazing. There was lobster and champagne, and ...

I woke up in London. I had passed out and slept through the entire experience. Not a single morsel of food had passed my lips. Seeing as it was Concorde, though, they gave me a bottle of champagne to take home as a consolation. So out of my brain I don't remember Concorde. That's almost rock 'n' roll.

The Boys from Brazil

Rumours were afoot of a dramatic and exotic development – an undiscovered continent. Iron Maiden world was about to go Brazil nuts. We were headed south, to Rio de Janeiro. I had never heard of Varig Airlines or held a Brazilian banknote. I had no idea where Copacabana Beach was or the Corcovado or Sugarloaf Mountain. I had never met the Girl from Ipanema and never tasted a caipirinha. Brahma was an Indian monk, not a beer, and I had no idea that wiggling your bottom could be a national sport. I also had no idea who Frank Sinatra's lawyer was.

Rock in Rio, the first one ever, was a 10 – on any scale of 1 to 10. I suppose I could get picky about the band, or my performance, but actually that isn't the point. It was a show that broke Iron Maiden in an entire continent overnight.

Initially, we turned it down. In the throes of selling out American shows back to back, a two-week break in Brazil seemed like madness. Yet the Rock in Rio offer seemed too good to be true. At every turn their lawyer just said yes.

'We want you for two shows in two weeks.'

'We only do one.'

'Yes.'

And so it went on. First-class travel, a massive fee, merchandising equivalent to a week of sold-out US shows, personal spending money, luxury hotels, guaranteed air freight for 30 tons of equipment – the answer was always, 'Yes. Anything else?'

On arrival in Rio, our clothes were almost torn from us by screaming fans, many of them extraordinarily good-looking females. We were pursued to our hotel on Copacabana Beach, which itself was surrounded 24 hours a day by hundreds of fans.

For the next week we would be prisoners in the hotel, along with several other artists, until the moment we were released to go to the festival, and what an incredible enterprise the whole thing was.

Three full stages had been created with a railway track laid down to rotate them before a specially designed and constructed festival set-up with a capacity of 300,000 people.

The biggest stars from the international music world, plus all the biggest local talent, were playing in a non-stop orgy of entertainment for two weeks. The TV rights alone were worth a fortune. Cynics might say the whole operation was a huge money-laundering operation. One thing was for sure: there was certainly a lot of it washing around.

We just enjoyed the ride, quite literally. The last time I had been in a helicopter was when I was chucked out of the side of a Westland Wessex in a tick-infested forest in Thetford. Today was somewhat more luxurious as we climbed aboard for the 10-minute ride to the festival site.

We were not yet headliners; that honour belonged to Queen, who were on stage after us. Even so, it was clear that there was massive expectation for Maiden.

The festival site itself was a chaotic blur. Tempers and tension were running high backstage. There was a barely visible sense of order, and a sense that disorder might break out at any time.

Two rival security firms were at each other's throats. Both had dogs and both had guns. They were involved in a standoff outside our dressing room. Leashed, fanged beasts with spiked collars were being held at bay at opposite ends of the corridor.

We waited in our dressing room for the signal that the stage was ready, oblivious to the commotion. In the hallway outside, guns were brandished and there was much trading of insults, and presumably aspersions cast about family members in Brazilian Portuguese. Once it all cooled off and the guns were holstered, we got the green light.

Rio was the biggest crowd I have ever played, and probably ever will. It seemed to disappear beyond the horizon, past the hazy floodlit pools of colour and into the blackness.

The surge of adrenalin as we ran out was immense, like a dozen Olympic 100-metre starts rolled into one. All these people, all that emotion, and … the sound was awful. We had brought our own monitors, but some of the gear was local, and the monitor engineer was a stranger. I waved my arms, trapped between a rock and a hard place. You can't stop in front of 300,000 people and do a soundcheck.

By the time we got to 'Revelations' I had put on my rather natty electric-blue Ibanez guitar. It matched the rather stylish electric-blue acoustic Ovation that I still have. The anger built as I tried to communicate with the engineer at the side of the stage. Hot and bothered, I wrenched the guitar off, over my head, and split my forehead open on its wooden edge.

My head was bleeding profusely as I approached the monitor board.

The engineer saw the blood and looked horrified. 'Fucking fix the sound – don't fucking stand there like a goldfish,' I ranted.

I expect I looked like a raving lunatic, which at that moment I was. To prove a point, I smashed my guitar across the mixing desk, and broke it halfway down the neck.

'FIX IT!' I screamed.

The sound did not improve, so I threw all the wedge monitors off the front of the stage. Crowds love this sort of thing;

they think it's show time. Sometimes it may be, but sometimes it's not. This whole spectacle was being shown live on TV across millions of Latin American households.

I did a bit more singing and then went behind the amps to calm down a bit. A roadie gave me a towel to wipe the blood away from my eyes, and then another member of the crew showed up, very excited. He looked carefully at the wound.

'Rod says can you squeeze it and make it bleed some more,' he said. 'It looks great on the telly.'

Next day, the picture was front-page news: sweaty, blood-stained me, and 300,000 new Iron Maiden fans.

We relished it all, and the comedown from the show lasted all night. It was a late show in any case, so it was four or five in the morning when we got to the hotel. Our ears were still ringing and alcohol seemed to have no soporific effect; the adrenalin rush was still overpowering the body's efforts to sleep.

I walked into the hotel lobby at about 6 a.m. There were no fans. The road was deserted out to the beach, and the sun was deliciously eyeball-roastingly warm, just before it would become scorchingly unbearable.

It was a strange feeling to be free after six days under siege. I indulged in the forbidden fruit of escaping without a minder and slowly crossed the road, took off my shoes and sat down on the beach, wiggling my toes in the hot sand.

Not long now, and then back on a plane to the middle of winter. *What a fucking weird life this is*, I thought to myself. I looked to my left. There was Brian May, eyes closed, face towards the sun, probably thinking something similar. I left him to it. Funny old world, really.

Much Ado About Cutting

Arriving back in England, I promptly took myself off for two weeks to a fencing camp in Sussex and arrived back with a coaching qualification. I was rapidly coming to the conclusion that being a rock star was not all it was cracked up to be.

The rest of the summer I spent training with Great Britain Olympic coach Ziemek Wojciechowski. The fencing competition season kicked off in early September, so it was good for me to try prodding and poking someone other than Americans.

I was, I think, ridiculously fit. I was training up to five days a week, sometimes twice a day, and if I had a competition, one of those days would be the competition itself.

Fencing competitions tend to be one-day affairs. As many as 200-plus fencers are whittled down to a final of two by early evening. To get to a final eight would normally involve starting at around 9 a.m. with a pool of five others – so five fights up to three minutes each. The next part involved sitting around and getting cold and bored. Then the same again. Sometimes there would be a third round, until the remaining fencers were placed in a knockout tournament, either from 128, 64 or 32.

When it came to the knockout encounters, the fights became three rounds of three minutes each to score up to 15 hits on the opponent. Over the years this format has changed in minor ways, but the basics remain the same.

To win a competition could therefore involve up to 40 three-minute rounds of fighting, each progressively harder as the opposition gets more effective towards the end. It's a very physically and mentally demanding sport. It's also an almost incomprehensible sport to an outsider.

Watching a sword fight in a movie is all about seeing what is going on. Watching a real fencing bout is all about seeing what is being hidden. A fencing point is scored in a split second, and if you, as a spectator, could see it coming, it's almost certain that the opponent would see it too.

High definition and slow-motion replays help to explain what often resembles a cat fight with a wobbly knitting needle, but it's very unsatisfactory. Fencing points are not always pretty, as we expect them to be after seeing sword fights in the movies.

My satisfaction was entirely personal, and based on two pillars that I thought mattered. One was respect from your peers, the other fencers who shared a common sporting ethos, and the second was respect for the philosophy of the sport. What I liked about fencing was that there was no ending to it. Like other martial arts, every opponent is different, and being an expert is no guarantee of success against an awkward beginner.

The enemy in fencing is as much yourself as the opponent. It is what I love the most about the sport. I learnt more than I could have imagined when I started to fence, and in just a couple of years I began to compete seriously. It would prompt me to question my very identity.

It took nearly a full season of competition and training before I started thinking something was not quite right inside my brain. I am not normally a very angry person. I can, on occasion, be a little volatile and I become very passionate about certain things, but destructive anger, seldom. Yet the further I advanced in competition, the more it seemed as if there was a pressure cooker inside my head that wanted to burst. I had never experienced anything like it.

I went back to the drawing board, the same way I learnt to sing again after discovering a different voice inside my body. A bit of research yielded a series of self-help questionnaires and a book of left-brain, right-brain puzzles by Professor Hans Eysenck.

After filling in all the spaces and answering all the puzzles, my conclusion was that I used both sides of my brain equally. I was slap-bang in the middle. It explained why I found it easy to talk to different types of people, but it provided little in the way of advice as to whether or not I might be left-handed, or at least ambidextrous.

The latter characteristic runs in the family. My father and my cousins are all ambidextrous. I fenced right-handed and always had done. I wrote right-handed but wasn't any good at playing racket sports right-handed. I was left-footed and I used my left eye to sight down rifles or look through telescopes. I also favoured my left ear when listening to the telephone.

Cross dominance in hand-eye coordination is not uncommon – it's an excellent set-up for a cricket or baseball batsman. A right-hander with a dominant left eye sees the ball in his peripheral vision a fraction of a second quicker.

There is a theory that in fast-reaction sports the left-hander is innately quicker in plotting a solution, and therefore able to wait longer before making a decision, all of which puts more pressure on the opponent.

I was now in my mid-twenties. I looked at my rather puny left arm. There was a degree of muscle wastage from the nerve damage caused by all that headbanging. My right side was much stronger. Fencing is quite a one-sided sport and even my legs had become lopsided as a result.

I went back to my coach, Ziemek. Could I, perhaps, be left-handed – or at least should I be left-handed?

I put the sword in my left hand. He asked me just to step

forward and back, extend my arm and hit him, not fast, just as smoothly and accurately as I could.

'You are immediately better left-handed,' Ziemek said. Next, he produced a piece of paper and asked me to draw an irregular polygon with my right hand with my eyes closed, which I did.

He put the pen in my left hand and asked me to draw the same shape. With my eyes firmly slut, I drew a mirror image of the shape, almost identical and exactly the same size.

'I think you should be the other way round,' he said.

I started again, but left-handed. I was slow and my coordination painful; the muscle memory was all wrong and had to be reprogrammed. My left arm tired quickly and my neck ached – it was twisted on the side from the headbanging injury. Various small muscles in my forearm had atrophied because of the disc problem. This was the rehab for my body, but it was like a revelation for my brain. The anger was gone. The will to win and the passion remained, but the pressure cooker had disappeared.

The next chance I got, I went to a squash court by myself and took the racket in my left hand. The ball went, unexpectedly, exactly where I wanted it to go. I played with the ball, as opposed to being angry with it. The difference in my head was staggering, as if I had discovered an entire universe of unexpected beauty and movement and, above all, timing. Timing, as in the space between all things, had been unknown to me.

I went back to training, but now left-handed. All of my fellow fencers thought I had completely lost my mind. It was true. I had lost one mind; now I was using another one.

You'll Believe a Drummer Can Fly

I came very close to quitting music after the *Powerslave* tour. I was in no mood for any more backstage politics or solitary confinement in tour buses or gilded cages. I didn't expect others to understand, because I'm sure for many it might seem like the ultimate dream, but I wanted more than the challenge of standing still successfully. When it came time to go back to the grind, I thought we might change radically, just for the hell of it.

It's not good to be in a minority of one in a five-piece band. I was taken to one side and quietly put out of my misery by Martin Birch, who told me that my little 'acoustic' numbers were not the stuff that was required. It was all pretty straightforward, and if you are going to be crushed, better to get it over with and move on.

I'm not one to sulk for longer than five minutes, so I relaxed and thought, *How can I enjoy the next year?*

A small birdie sat on my shoulder and whispered in my (left) ear: 'Why don't you just be the singer and let everyone else get on with it?'

So instead of thinking about the big picture, I just thought about me, myself and I. For a while, it was quite a relief.

We went to Jersey again, this time a different hotel, to write the next album. I did not write any songs, so I went off to Europe to enter some fencing competitions.

I had some pretty odd ideas about stage clothes. There were certainly some *Spinal Tap* moments coming our way, and I wanted to make sure that we were at the forefront of the excitement, however unwittingly.

The album *Somewhere in Time* took a great deal of inspiration from the movie *Blade Runner*. The album sleeve, and even the intro-tape for the show, owed a great deal to the Ridley Scott classic.

'Cyborg' Eddie was our most sophisticated walk-on monster, and the stage set was a fabulously complex creation of aluminium girders and ramps, which rose up with inflatable clawed hands underneath.

The idea was to use a lot of inflatables, but the technology was in its infancy, and so was some of the execution. Half the time the inflatables didn't inflate – not fully, anyway – and often it looked like the great clawed hand was giving the finger to the audience until the other digits managed to pump up the volume.

Eddie's head, the great inflatable version, often took its time to get a second wind, and sometimes it just looked like a baggy bin liner. There were plans for overhead inflatable spaceships and, my favourite, a spacewalking astronaut on an extendable scaffold above the audience.

Alas, the spaceships either didn't fit the venue or health and safety dictated nothing hanging over the crowd, and we just gave up in the end.

At least we had an exploding singer at the end of the first song, only that didn't quite work out either. I had decided, while the balance of my mind was disturbed, to have some stage clothes manufactured, as opposed to stealing them from fancy-dress shops. I remember the instructions I gave to the seamstress.

'What I want is a sort of d'Artagnan outfit, but from outer space. The bottom should look like a strange space lizard, recently killed, then patched together, preferably green and scaly-looking. Got that?'

So now you know.

In keeping with the *Blade Runner* theme, I wanted a leather jacket with a giant, illuminated beating heart, plus rope lights pumping sequenced light around a sort of exoskeleton. I'm sure now it would all be done by CGI, but back then it ended up being designed by our monitor guy, John Thomson.

The jacket weighed around 10 kilograms (about 20 pounds). It was full of copper wire and the power source was a six-volt lead acid battery, plus an on/off switch pinched from a bedside lamp.

The power consumption was such that my beating heart went into cardiac arrest about two minutes before the end of the first song. The entire contraption is now somewhere in the Rock & Roll Hall of Fame, where it is either locked up or being used as a bedside lamp.

My idea was to have a black leather-looking suit that Velcroed from top to bottom at each side. Embedded up the sides of the legs and arms would be flash pots, so that, in mock-*Vitruvian Man* pose, I would dissolve in a puff of smoke at the conclusion of the first song.

So much for fantasy. As soon as I saw the 20-pound pigeon-chested jerkin I was saddled with, we had to compromise. We ended up with one tiny flash pot, highly unreliable, stuck on top of a glove, with a nine-volt battery and a bizarre firing mechanism. It was very unremarkable even when it worked, and when it didn't I was the loneliest quick-change artist in the world as I ran off stage with the device still live and liable to go off at any moment. Road crew dived for cover as I disarmed it before getting rid of my weight belt and illuminated straitjacket.

I grew a beard on tour. In Las Vegas, Rod asked me to shave it off. I shaved half of it off, vertically. There are pictures. I'm not sure what the audience made of it; they probably thought I was off my face.

Mind you, I was very lucky to have got as far as I had on the tour. For a variety of reasons and hazardous situations, I nearly didn't make it.

I was busy fencing with my buddy Justin, and we would train together with shades of *Rocky*, doing sprints up and down the steep hills.

We devised a weekend adventure, which involved trains, planes, ships and two fencing competitions in Belgium and Holland. We would return by overnight sleeper train to Cherbourg, where there was a morning flight back to Jersey, which took all of about 10 minutes, according the schedule.

On the way to France, we missed the ferry, caught the later one across the Channel, and missed the train. We slept on the floor of the ferry terminal, my head in my fencing bag, until we got the 5 a.m. train and fenced all day in Antwerp. We slept in an attic and had a very early start on the next train to Holland, fenced all day and went to Paris. Two bottles of cheap wine and several hamburgers later, we boarded the train to Cherbourg, which, according to my Thomas Cook *European Rail Timetable* (don't leave home without it), only ran on a Sunday night. We soon found out why. There were 600 French sailors on it. We went in one of the couchette compartments and thought better of it. We opted to sleep in the toilets instead. They smelt slightly better.

Snow was on the ground on our arrival as we trudged through the darkness, unwashed and unloved, until we found a café that clearly never shut, and hot coffee revived us.

There is not much demand on a Monday morning in Cherbourg for taxis to the airport. By the time we found one, the plane had gone and the next one was in 10 hours' time.

'Nicko can fly,' I suggested. It was true – Nicko was learning. His instructor was a very jolly fellow called Charlie, and Jersey Aero Club was a very salubrious place to have Sunday lunch and watch the planes go by.

I managed to work out a French payphone and got him at the hotel.

'There's just two of us,' I said.

'Ere ... ooh. I dunno. See, I haven't got my licence yet. Maybe Charlie could do it with me.'

'There you go. You can have a bit of a lesson on the way.'

What could possibly go wrong?

Justin and I waited in the deserted café-bar in Cherbourg airport. No sooner had we arrived than it shut. After two hours, a lone small aeroplane, tossed around by the wind, landed and taxied up to the window. It was, as far as I could tell, the only aircraft in the airport.

This was a first for me. I had never been in a light aircraft before, so my curiosity was overpowering the overall fatigue caused by three days of sleeping on floors, attics and in toilets, and drinking cheap wine in between fencing competitions.

The aircraft in question (I now know) was a Piper Cherokee 140. It was a single-engine, low-wing monoplane, and it had four very small seats. The 140 stood for horsepower. The same aeroplane also came equipped with a 160-, a 180- and even a 200-horsepower motor, but all of them only had four seats. Therein lies a clue as to what happened next.

In flying magazines there are always two regular types of column. One is 'I learnt about flying from that' and the other is 'That worst day'. Pilots love to talk about disasters, partly as a learning process, but mainly to remind them how invincible they secretly are because that sort of thing would never happen to them.

Justin and I showed our passports to the gendarme and we walked over to the plane.

There were only two doors, one for each pilot, and you had to climb on the top of the wing to scramble into the two back seats.

Charlie looked concerned. 'Are they very heavy?' he asked about the two bags we were carrying. My fencing bag, about the size of a golf bag, just like Justin's, was full of wet clothing, a stainless-steel mask, all manner of bits of wire and tools, plus half-a-dozen weapons and spare clothes for a trip away.

'Not really,' I said, trying hard not to expose the groove in my shoulder caused by dragging the wretched thing halfway across Europe.

'Are we okay, Charlie?' asked Nicko.

'Ah, yeah ... should be.' But there was an unconvincing tone, and he was starting to pull so vigorously on his moustache that I thought it might come off.

We clambered aboard and put the bags in the baggage compartment, where they still stuck out between the rear seats. I leaned back; the plane toppled over onto its tail.

'Oh, shit,' Nicko muttered.

'Is it supposed to do that?'

'No. Fuck. It's not.'

Charlie turned and surveyed the scene behind him: two lads in the back, two heavy bags further back, Nicko in the front, tail on the ground, nose wheel dangling in the air, gendarme starting to become interested.

He finally spoke: 'Right, lads. I've got an idea ...'

Straight out of *The Italian Job*, I thought, and appropriate too. The coach, balanced on the precipice, with the gold at one end – we were in exactly the same predicament.

'Everyone lean forward ...'

We did so. Nothing changed.

'Move the bags into the space between the front and back seats ...'

We manhandled the bags until we were trapped behind them.

'Right. Nicko, when I yell "Start the engine" ...'

Charlie ran around to the tail and lifted it off the ground, cradling it while the nose wheel touched terra firma at last.

'Start the engine.'

I watched, fascinated, as Nicko read the instructions. Now, of course, I know it's called a checklist, but it is in fact the instructions on how to start an engine.

There was a series of squelches and squeaks, and a 'boing' noise as he pulled a lever. He tapped several dials, rotated a couple of instruments and filled the cabin with the overwhelming smell of gasoline. After pumping a small plunger into the dash, Nicko stuck his head out of the door and shouted, 'Clear prop!'

This was splendid stuff, and I half expected a squadron scramble. Nicko turned the ignition key and the engine rattled into life. As soon as the prop was spinning, the plane settled on an even keel, and Charlie leapt into the seat yelling, 'I have control!'

We taxied very fast, I thought, and the low cloud scurried rapidly over the runway in the strong gusty winds. We careered onto the runway, and the racket from the engine and prop rose till the windows started to vibrate.

'Everyone lean right forward,' Charlie yelled above the din, his own head pressed firmly against the dashboard.

The runway in Cherbourg, I later discovered, is very long, which is good, because we used all of it to get airborne.

Despite what turned out to be a beneficial headwind on take-off, the wheels barely left the ground at all. The altitude above sea level became clear when we fell, or rather almost fell, off the edge of the cliff that marked the end of the runway.

Below us lay jagged rocks, a grey and angry sea with white horses cresting and crashing, and a low, miserable-looking cloud base to sandwich us.

After about five minutes I worked out what all the instruments were indicating, and 800 feet seemed to be about all we could manage.

'Keep leaning forward,' Charlie urged as another cliff came in sight with a runway attached to the end of it. I noticed that Charlie was quite pale by now, and was sweating – a lot. As we approached the ground I noticed the runway dipped away and rose up in front of us …

'Don't lean back! Keep leaning forward!' Charlie pulled back on the control column, but not very much, and we taxied very fast to park up on a patch of grass.

There was a long sigh.

'Welcome to Jersey,' said Nicko.

Nicko got his pilot's licence and, as you would expect from a drummer with all that coordination, he had a very good pair of hands when it came to flying an aeroplane. Later on, during the US leg of the tour, he flew himself around in a small turbo-prop owned by a commercial pilot who went with him as instructor.

I tagged along on a few of their trips, and I was fascinated by the instruments. So fascinated, in fact, that a copy of *Microsoft Flight Simulator* was my next port of call, which I installed on the suitcase-sized monster that was the Mac Portable, or Mac Luggable, as I termed it. I was already on the slippery slope towards the runway, but first I had to negotiate our last stop in the Bahamas, and a prolonged stay in Amsterdam.

Double Dutch

The Bahamas was relatively brief. The rest of the album would be finished and mixed in Holland, in Hilversum, at Wisseloord Studios.

Marvin still managed to make an appearance, in quite memorable fashion. I was sound asleep but the sun was already up. There was a loud banging from downstairs. Each small house had three bedrooms upstairs, and there was a courtyard at the back with an external door opening out onto the road, across from the studies. The initial banging was Marvin trying to get in. I woke up, the banging ceased, and I started to doze.

Seconds later the sound of splintering window frame, muffled shouts, a woman's voice, a door being kicked in – and the unmistakable sound of Martin in transformation.

He knocked at my door: 'Aha, are you in ...?'

'What is it?'

'You need to come downstairs.'

'It's 7.30 in the morning.'

'Now. You need to come downstairs *now*.'

'Why do I need to come downstairs now?' I had already started putting my pants on, or this would only end in tears, which it possibly would do anyway, but hey.

'It's the most important person ... you will ever meet ... in the whole world ...'

I put my trainers on. 'And who might that be?'

'Just get down here, boy.'

I heard a thumping crash as Marvin collided with the stairs.

Downstairs, Marvin was standing on the furniture again, on one leg, but this time he was covered in earth and his forearm was heavily bleeding.

'Are you alright?'

'AHA! Alright? See …' He pointed to his eye. 'This … the eye of the tiger.'

'Martin, you're bleeding …'

'HA! This … the blood of the samurai.'

'I would get that seen to. Do you want some antiseptic?'

'Death … one blow … Shotokan.' He hopped from one leg to the other. 'For I … am the court jester.'

I sighed. 'I'll make a cup of tea …'

Martin had started out with good intentions several hours before, but had been misled by his own internal Mr Hyde, and finally ran out of people to drink with. After banging on my door at 7 a.m., he had scaled the eight-foot wall and then fallen off into a rose bush, hence the earth, hence the blood.

Undeterred, Marvin had scaled the trellis and kicked in the mosquito mesh, clambered into a roadie's bedroom, and then, imagining that my bedroom lay beyond, kicked the door open to reveal a naked lady in flagrante with another roadie.

'Carry on, dear boy,' was his response.

The doorbell rang and the last piece of the evening's jigsaw revealed itself. I opened the courtyard door and there, immaculately dressed in dressing gown and slippers, was Robert Palmer, clutching a bottle of rum and two glasses.

Martin and Robert went way back to the days when Martin worked with a band called Vinegar Joe. Robert was the singer.

After running out of drinking partners, and having not seen Robert for around 30 years, Marvin knocked on his door at four in the morning.

Unfazed, Robert greeted him with, 'Martin, it's been a long time. Do come in.'

One bottle of rum had already been consumed, and the second was already half-empty, I noted. 'I'll make another cup of tea …'

'This is the most important man you will ever meet,' muttered Marvin, and then he went out on to the balcony, standing on one leg overlooking the sea, but luckily always falling back onto dry land.

I sat down opposite Robert.

'I'm having so much trouble with the album,' he began. 'It's like a mountain and I don't know where to start.'

I sipped my tea. 'Try the steps,' I suggested.

'The steps?'

'Yes, the steps in the side of the mountain. That's what they are for.'

'The steps,' he whispered. 'The steps. Yes, I'll try the steps.' And he wandered out of the door, saying, 'Brilliant. Of course – the steps. Use the steps …'

I finished my tea and left Marvin to his karate exercises.

A couple of hours later, I walked out of the front door to find Marvin standing in the middle of the road, barefoot, still bleeding, and with a manic grin on his face. His hands clutched at the pockets of his shorts, which had been turned inside out.

'Keys, dear boy,' he said, 'can't find the house keys.'

Marvin finally got put to bed, and before long we decamped to a place of even greater temptation, the fleshpots of Amsterdam.

The studio in Hilversum was boring as hell. It was in a complex used mainly for TV and radio, so we had to put up with *The Smurfs* in the next-door studio and the world's most boring cheese sandwiches in the canteen. Hilversum itself is a deathly quiet conservative suburb, and Steve stayed there.

I stayed in Amsterdam, in a loft apartment with a circular staircase and great triangular wooden beams. Downstairs was a nightclub open till dawn, a gay cinema and three red-light window girls. The central station was a 10-minute walk away, and I quickly purchased a stolen bike for 25 guilders. I had a stack of books to read, and I bought a candelabra and would eat in the Italian restaurant next door, carafe of wine, candelabra and book of the month club. Boring it was not, and as I got to know the locals life became yet more illuminating.

I asked Steve why he didn't stay in the centre of Amsterdam.

'Too much dog shit,' he muttered.

Not entirely incorrect, I have to say, and the size of some of the droppings was quite extreme. Not the dogs' fault, and the size of some of the dogs matched the unwanted logs they deposited on the kerb. One such dog was a huge Great Dane that hung out with the equally huge Hells Angel at the neighbouring Café Midnight.

Café Midnight no longer exists, and the gay couple who ran it may or may not have been released from jail by now, but the web that was spun out of one establishment was typical of the underbelly of what, on the surface, was a happy-go-lucky, free-spirited city.

Henrik, shall we call him, was the *capo dei capi* of Hells Angels in the city. Incredibly tall and mild-mannered, his girlfriend worked the bar at the café and she was trouble, but one look at her and it was easy to see why men (and women) fell over every which way.

She had already been responsible for the downfall of a Dutch cabinet minister, and was herself ministering to my very entrepreneurial Hells Angel friend.

'I'm going through hell with the girlfriend,' he told me.

'Sorry to hear that.'

'Let's go for a drink.'

So began a long evening of small beers ending up in a deserted nightclub with the sun rising over the canals.

He explained his business empire and his philanthropic nature: 'We run the chapter like a sort of social-security club.'

'That's nice.'

'*Ja*. For example, one of my guys was dying of cancer. So we all got together and got him something. You know, to make him feel better.'

'What did you get him?'

'A washing machine.'

'A washing machine?'

'*Ja*, exactly. He was in tears. He said nobody had ever bought him a washing machine before. That's the sort of stuff we do. Good, eh? But oh, fuck. I got a big shipment I'm waiting for this month.'

'Washing machines?' I ventured.

'No, drugs.'

'Gosh, how big is the shipment?' I was picturing a couple of plastic bags, or a sack at most.

'A container-full,' he said, as if it was the most normal thing in the world. I looked around the empty nightclub; the windows were all portholes, I realised, for a port city.

'That sounds like a lot of stress, let alone the girlfriend.'

'*Ja*,' he sighed, world-weary entrepreneur that he was. 'You get it wrong you end up in the bottom of the river ...' He had a sip of Heineken. 'You know, last time I was in here a guy tried to shoot me with a Luger. Seven shots.'

'Hmm. You're a big chap. He must have been a rotten shot.'

'*Ja*, *ja*. That's what I told him when I got hold of him.'

I didn't press the line of enquiry further.

'It's been really good to talk,' he said. 'I feel much better.'

Nights like these were surreal windows into the not-so-nice side of Amsterdam. Often I would end up in the late-night club opposite my apartment. There was a very happy hooker who came in after work. She was Australian, and was always delighted to see me.

'Strewth, mate, yer not bad looking. Fancy a freebie?'

I politely declined.

'No, mate, seriously, straight up. I'll blow your mind.'

Probably not the only thing that would get blown, I imagined, but I surprised myself by sticking to beer and conversation. She had a bandage on her arm.

'What happened there?' I asked.

'Jeez, mate. Some fucking guy got out of jail and turned up to work, and then he starts to fucking bite me and draws blood.'

She was a window girl, so walk-in trade was the norm. She was personable and quite good-looking. I was baffled by why she did it.

'Still, the cops are great. They banged him up right away. They take a very dim view of beating up the girls.'

This was a harsh place beneath the fluffy, 'open city' propaganda. No one I met was quite what they seemed: the Liverpudlian scallywag on the run from the British police, happily settled down with a stunning Dutch girl and two children; the Mancunian with a barge full of empty clay pots and vases from Thailand for sale. No clue as to what might have been contained within them during their transit, of course.

There was the happy couple that painted John Lennon's Rolls-Royce and made stage clothes for Led Zeppelin and tried to sell me a piano and introduce me to the new drug ecstasy.

My ecstatic moments did not revolve around drugs. I had found the most bizarre fencing club in a basement. The coach was wonderfully mad and gave lessons outside by the canal on the cobblestones. This basement was so small that fighting was only possible if you fenced across the room diagonally, and even then you ran out of space after three or four steps.

My Australian window girl lived just down the street, and one evening she invited me to her flat, saying, 'There is someone I want you to meet.' Frankly, I didn't want to go, but she was insistent.

'Oh, very well,' I said, 'but just five minutes.'

Up the dingy staircase, one, two, three floors up, twisting around in the old wooden-framed building.

'Who is this person?' I said. 'Is he a fan or what?'

'Shoosh!' Suddenly she looked concerned. A quick glance over her shoulder was, I thought, a trifle melodramatic. 'He's the most wanted man in Holland,' she said.

'I'm sorry?'

'Yeah, mate. He's on the run and just hanging out with me for a few days.'

I entered the small flat and two men were sitting around the kitchen table. They weren't exactly talkative.

'Here's my mate, Bruce,' she said.

I smiled, but not really. 'Thanks. Nice to meet you. Well, I really must be going ...'

I exited very quickly. I don't know if she was dishing out freebies for fugitives as a sort of public service, but I was glad I never indulged.

Amsterdam was like that, unpredictable and sometimes tragic. Like our Liverpool scallywag with the gorgeous Dutch girlfriend. She ended up in a French jail after he persuaded her to drive to France with her children, carrying drugs in boxes of chocolate. He ended up being slit from one side of his stomach to the other in a knife attack. Nice people, drug dealers. You can't persuade me that Robin Hood is out there selling dope, not any more.

As for the girl in Café Midnight, she lost her job when the building was set on fire by the proprietors. Alas for them they didn't do a good job, and returned with more petrol a couple of hours later. The next-door neighbours had already alerted the police because of the smell of gasoline.

Even then bail was jumped, but the miscreants were dumb enough to re-enter Holland, and ended up staying rather longer than they intended. Ten years, to be exact.

Amsterdam is also the only city in Europe where I have had a gun pulled on me, after I remonstrated with a car that almost ran me down outside the American Hotel.

It's not just dog shit that is on the streets of Amsterdam.

So, with a bit more of an education than I got from my A levels, I moved on to be fired from the starting cannon that was the *Somewhere in Time* world tour.

You Cannot Be Serious

The Marquis de Sade wrote famously gross fantasies, though he never got the opportunity to play some of them out. He was firmly locked up for much of the duration of his writing career, where the only material available for composing his scatological hymns was toilet paper.

For very different reasons, on the *Somewhere in Time* tour I found myself shackled in hotel rooms around the globe, and in the spirit of 'What does this button do?' I decided to write a saucy comic novel because, well, I could – and there was plenty of hotel stationery to do it on.

The end result was *The Adventures of Lord Iffy Boatrace*, a hybrid of Tom Sharpe's *Wilt* series and *Carry On Camping*-style innuendo.

The blame for this fledgling writing career must go down to only being runner-up in the English prize at Birkdale preparatory school. Second place was always going to be life's cattle prod, and the shock-treatment was administered by horror writer and Iron Maiden fan Shaun Hutson.

I have read most of Shaun's popular horror fiction. I have also had no choice in the matter, because he gave them to me and everyone else in the band.

I could see the formula in what he did, but also the hand of the artisan in the way he delivered the story. What I enjoyed was the way that the books actually produced a physical reaction. This was not long-winded character development and descriptions of detailed sunsets or locations. This was a universal, gratuitous page-turner with an outrageous death every few pages. Jane Austen, eat your heart out (*and leave the bleeding mess pumping helplessly as the coppery smell of blood filled the room. The walls sprayed as his fist pumped and crushed the organ wrenched from the smashed ribs, which stood upended like broken teeth.* Sorry – couldn't resist a go at a Shaun Hutson homage ...).

Personally, I recommend the passage from *Slugs* where the paraplegic is eaten from the inside out while taking a shit by a spine-consuming slug that crawls out of the toilet and into his anal passage, as opposed to his literary passage.

'How on earth do you write a book?' I asked.

'Well, I just start in the morning, have a cup of tea about eleven, then write till five with a break for lunch,' Shaun replied.

'You mean it's just hard work?'

'Yes, mainly.'

'Well, how long does it take you to write a book?' I enquired.

'About three weeks.'

It took us three months to make an album. *Three weeks must be unbelievably intense*, I thought.

'What do you do to relax?' I asked.

'Twenty-four-hour horror-movie marathons,' he replied. Thank God Shaun Hutson was an author and not a mass murderer. I fear he would have been very efficient.

I started to write, every day. I vanished from view. I no longer appeared at the bar. I was the invisible man on tour. One day, in Finland, there was a knock at the door. I opened it, and there was a member of the crew. I could see he was craning his neck to peer at the paper spread around the room, the curtains drawn and all the lights on.

'The lads are wondering where ... you ... er, what are you doing?'

'I'm writing a story.'

'What sort of story?'

The bar decamped to my room, and for the rest of the tour I had to read every chapter of *The Adventures of Lord Iffy Boatrace* to the road crew as I wrote them.

If I didn't produce a chapter sufficiently quickly to entertain them on a day off, there would be complaints. I had a series of mini-deadlines to keep, and at the end of the tour I had a large sheaf of papers, all belonging to various four- and five-star hotels, which had been conveniently placed for correspondence in my bedroom.

It was my version of the Marquis de Sade's toilet paper.

Astonishingly, Sidgwick & Jackson eventually published the book and promptly commissioned the sequel. Pan Macmillan followed suit by putting both books into paperback and giving me a three-book paperback deal.

The Adventures of Lord Iffy Boatrace took a while to get into print but amazingly sold 30,000 copies, and suddenly I realised that I had a deadline and a sequel to write. My two-fingered typing skills were put severely to the test as I invested in that most ridiculous portable contraption, the original Mac Portable.

With its suitcase-sized case, bicep-building weight and six-volt lead acid battery with enough juice to jumpstart a Fiat Uno, the Mac Portable still managed to run out of power after about two hours. It was possible to extend its life by switching off the backlight, but then, of course, you couldn't see anything at all except in bright sunlight.

It was good for people with colour blindness, being only available with screens in black and white. On a trip anywhere, it was a simple choice: computer or clothes, but not both.

As with everything Mac back in the eighties, it was all about style and nothing to do with practicality. Even while I was staggering up flights of steps with my spine-crippling device, admiring humans would stop me in awe.

'Is *that* a Mac Portable?' they would enquire, as if about to touch a holy relic.

'Yes, it fucking is,' I'd reply. 'Would you like to carry it for me?'

I wrote big chunks of the sequel, *The Missionary Position*, on trains and on tour, and the rest of it while drinking pints of tea at home. I found sleeper trains particularly useful. Nobody bothered you, and you didn't do much sleeping, so bashing away at the keys made sense in the tiny compartments rattling through the night.

So incensed was I at the withdrawal of the Manchester to London sleeper that I included it in the credits on the sleeve. I don't suppose anybody else used it. Sleeper trains have always featured on tour, if at all possible. Before Google I always carried the Thomas Cook *European Rail Timetable*. One evening in Lausanne after a show, the talk in the bar was becoming very tedious, so a quick glance at the *European Rail Timetable* revealed a sleeper train to Venice, which sounded like a good place to wake up. Travelling light, with only a rucksack, suited me just fine. I think I make tour managers nervous. Managers even more so.

The main reason I liked trains was for the time to think the journey offered, in a degree of peace and quiet. Modern trains, alas, are becoming less and less like that, but there is still something theatrical about boarding a train. Its size and speed are momentous, even if its interior is nowadays a bland mix of plastic with coffee-stained cushions, unemptied waste bins and toilets ankle-deep in unfathomable liquids.

Once, in New York, I decided to take the train to New Haven, just up the coast. The local trains were commuter machines, and not terribly interesting, so I opted for Amtrak, from Penn Station, with a proper locomotive and an egg and cheese muffin.

At 2 p.m. we pulled out of the platform, and shortly thereafter we stopped – and we stayed stopped. For two, going on three hours, we remained stationary. Luckily, I had my copy of the *OAG Pocket Flight Guide* with me (never leave home without it), and I discovered a flight to New Haven from La Guardia.

I asked the guard what was going on.

'The lines are down,' he said. 'We are waiting for a diesel train to take us back to Penn Station.'

I was going to miss the show if I didn't catch that plane. 'I have to get off this train. I have to get to New Haven.'

The guard shrugged. 'Gonna be a few hours yet.'

A young lad had overheard the conversation.

'Are you in Iron Maiden?' he asked.

'Yes, I am.'

'I can get you off this train.'

I stopped in my tracks, much like the carriage I was in. 'If you can get me off the train, you're coming with me to the show – backstage, the whole lot.'

We went to the door, and he pulled a couple of levers and it slid to one side with a lazy action, as if to say, 'I'm not really supposed to open this way, but if you must ...'

We jumped onto the tracks, ran down the embankment, scaled a chain-link fence into a US Postal Service depot and ran out onto a suburban street.

I flagged down the first driver I saw: 'How far is La Guardia?'

'Hey man, it's right over there.'

'A hundred bucks if you take me and my friend.'

We got the last two seats on the tiny plane, and I got to the gig 10 minutes before show time.

The *Somewhere in Time* tour came to an end somewhere, and we languished in England again at last.

I was living in the countryside, or the suburban version of it in Buckinghamshire, just outside London. I had a swimming pool because I don't like swimming, a tennis court because I didn't play tennis, a garden because I disliked gardening, and a very long walk to the nearest pub because all I required was a quiet pint without having to drive there and break the law on the way back.

Be careful what you wish for, as the saying goes.

There was a big garage for the bright red BMW I didn't drive, and there was a snooker room, long and wooden-floored, because I didn't play snooker. It was, however, long enough to fence in, so I chucked out the snooker table and turned it into a training room.

Around this time a very colourful Hungarian entered my life and remained in it for the next 25 years, taking me from a place where I didn't know my left from my right to winning the British junior foil championship. Between us, we won the British team championship and represented Great Britain at the European championships. Under the unlikely auspices of Hemel Hempstead Fencing Club.

There were only a dozen of us meeting up two or three times a week in dismal school gymnasiums or community centres. The irascible, eccentric and utterly brilliant coach behind the whole set-up was my Hungarian mentor Zsolt Vadaszffy.

Zsolt had white hair, spoke like Count Dracula and had girls swooning in the aisles despite his being twice their age. He had been one of Hungary's youngest foil prodigies, but his career in sport was curtailed by the arrival of a Russian tank under his window during the Soviet crackdown of the Budapest uprising.

At the age of 16, Zsolt took his passport and walked into Austria. He taught fencing across Europe, and he also ended up as an actor in *The Ipcress File* (evil Bulgarian doctor) and a racing-car driver, before running an import-export business for white goods.

His first and last love was fencing. When we buried him, it was with his fencing glove atop the coffin, and his sword by his side.

Zsolt was almost a second father to my fencing friend Justin, in social as well as sporting terms. Zsolt lived on the other side of the valley from my adapted snooker room. He came round and we started to train. I realised after a while that I had never had a coach who'd taken the time to teach me how to think. When martial artists speak of someone being a 'master', this, I imagine, is what they mean. In fact, a fencing master is beyond a coach; he imparts a philosophy of thought, strategy and movement. It is intensely personal, and it's hard to describe the level of commitment that goes into a one-on-one fencing lesson given at full speed.

At some point in the evolution of the relationship between master and pupil, enlightenment occurs. I mean this literally. It is as if a chain has snapped, and your body and mind have been freed of intention – freed of the tyranny of 'what if?' and the consequent fear of failure.

It happened to me on a few occasions, when, for 20 minutes or so out of our 45-minute lesson, we played only with distance, movement and the feel of the engagement and disengagement of the blades. Consciousness was transferred to the point of a bendy piece of steel, which prodded and conversed with the partner opposite – no longer an opponent, but simply a collaborator in the dance.

No words are exchanged. The actions start and stop, and are resumed according to the language of the blade alone. Afterwards, it's hard to explain to people where you have been, so it's best not to try.

In the beginning, of course, it's not like that. In the beginning it is awkward footwork, unsteady coordination, patient repetition, constant correction and constant frustration until the movements start to automate, and the mind can control the intention without having to worry about the act.

I was lucky that my first teacher at school, John Worsley, taught me well. Not so much on a technical level, as on an intellectual one. He taught as a teacher, not just a coach. Every action was analysed; every action had a motivation, even if it was only 'I want to give up and go home'.

When Bruce Lee wrote his classic *Tao of Jeet Kune Do*, he based his analysis of offensive, defensive and counter-offensive actions on the system developed by Western fencing. It's a very effective and clear analytical tool to pull combat apart – and even tennis matches, for that matter, because any one-on-one sport is, in effect, combat by proxy.

Moonchild

All of this extracurricular activity was bound to be impacted eventually by Iron Maiden, and so began the writing process for our next album, *Seventh Son of a Seventh Son*. It would be one of our best.

Steve was constructing the bones of the album out in Essex at his home, Sheering Hall, which had a replica pub, a real football pitch with home and away dressing rooms and, eventually, a rehearsal room and a recording studio.

Steve and I reignited our songwriting partnership. He mentioned the words 'concept album' and my ears pricked up and my heart began to beat faster. Story, theatre: *Seventh Son of a Seventh Son* had it all.

Except it didn't. Not quite all of it. Somewhere in my dusty collection of mouldy scribblings I have the short story that tells the tale of the seventh son and his family issues and unrequited love that lead him to take a terrible and tragic revenge. We never really consummated the story relationship: my lyrics alluded to the story, whereas Steve's didn't. None of this matters that much in the overall picture because the show, the album cover and the title track were more than epic enough to satisfy the faithful. I would just have liked to have given it a bit more, even to the extent of a graphic novel.

Germany was our destination to record, at the improbable location of the Arabella high-rise building, a hotel in Munich. Musicland Studios was down in the bowels of the building, among the heavily lagged heating and sewer pipes, laundry baskets and kitchen equipment.

It reminded me in many respects of Ian Gillan's Kingsway Studios down in the car-park basement of the Civil Aviation Authority building in Holborn, London. Martin Birch had recorded Deep Purple's *In Rock* down there and, of course, I had later been dragged out of the toilets covered in sick by Ian Gillan.

The studio itself at Musicland was tiny, and the control room cramped, but some great albums had been produced there, everything from Queen to Rainbow's *Rising*. For recreation there was a notorious nightclub called the Sugar Shack, and casualties were frequent and painful.

I discovered the local fencing club, MTV München, and set about training and improving my table-dancing. The Germans were very enamoured of post-training drinking and dancing. I could do a half-decent Cossack dance if plied with enough beer, and the Greek restaurant seemed to enjoy the spectacle.

Wheat beer was a new experience, and it came in brown, blonde and Hefe varieties, the latter being full of yeasty bits more reminiscent of marmite soup. All of them made your head hurt the next day.

We all went a little stir-crazy in Munich. Dave Murray had decided to try a little conjuring in his spare time, of which there was far too much. One famous evening on the sixteenth floor, Marvin appeared when Dave was attempting to make something disappear.

'See that chair,' Marvin growled. 'I can make that disappear.'

So he chucked it off the balcony. This stir-crazy stuff was starting to get quite serious.

I had a plan to save my sanity and, when the opportunity to escape the awful brown and green apartments came, I pottered up the road to what was then the capital of this side of a divided Germany, Bonn.

I rented a small bedsit, bought a second-hand telly and put a mattress on the floor. I would fence full-time at the elite Fechtclub Bonn, a Bundesleistungszentrum. Just rolls off the tongue, doesn't it?

I was one of the oldest guys there, and I still wasn't 30 yet. It was entirely dedicated to producing champions, and everyone thought I was a bit mad, especially as I was still getting to grips with using my left hand. I completely forgot about albums, music and all the rest of it. I had breakfast, went for a walk, went training, then for a beer, watched telly and then to bed.

A young journalist and a photographer from the *Daily Mirror* turned up. I invited them up for a cup of coffee to discuss the article they were going to write – it was obviously all Iron Maiden related. When I went down to the front of the building with the photographer, he asked where the journalist was.

'I left her upstairs,' I replied innocently. He looked at me aghast.

'I wouldn't do that.'

'Really?' I replied. Surely she wouldn't go through any personal stuff, would she?

We retrieved her from my dirty laundry and tins of baked beans. She looked genuinely horrified at where I was living.

'Why do you live like this?' she said.

'What's wrong with it?' I replied indignantly. It was as if having a simple life was an affront to the gods of gossip, which I suppose it is, really.

I learnt a few things about Germans, and one of them is that they love to discuss bodily emanations, especially poo.

I caught a bad cold and was feeling a bit miserable. I had been invited round to a Sunday lunch with Thomas, another fencer. A dozen of us sat around, with me shivering away.

'You are sick,' Thomas announced, and went to a back room. After some rummaging around he came back with a long piece of brown flexible pipe, and what looked like a stirrup pump.

'There, take this,' he proudly offered.

'What is it?' I enquired cautiously, although I had a pretty good idea.

'Well,' he grinned broadly, 'this tube, you put up your ass, and this you fill with water, and in a few moments you will shit like thunder.'

There were murmurs of agreement from around the table.

'Thomas, that's an enema,' I said.

'*Ja*, exactly so.'

'Thomas, what gave you the idea that an enema will make me better?'

'Oh, *ja*, for sure. I use it all the time.' Louder voices of agreement from the guests.

'My mother gave me them from childhood.'

'Your mother?'

Thomas's sister piped up: 'Not just Thomas. We all had them together – the whole family.'

Shit happens, as the saying goes. The family that enemas together, stays together.

Eventually, the band joined me and we rehearsed in nearby Cologne, in a nightclub that was also a gymnasium. I believe the owner was eventually entertained by the German government for a number of years because the powders he was selling certainly weren't Beechams.

I had worked with Derek Riggs on the cover for the album, which had a touch of Salvador Dalí about it, with its slightly surreal procession of candles and a partially disembodied, skeletal Eddie. Next to *Powerslave*, it's my favourite Derek Riggs cover art.

The stage set was enormous, and was based around being elemental, as in ice. The tour was predictably successful, particularly in Europe, where we were hitting the big festivals – famously Donington in the UK.

Sadly, that day was marred by tragedy, with death and injury on account of the appalling muddy conditions underfoot caused by torrential rain. We were spared the details of the terrible event until after the show had finished. Any moment of triumph was short-lived. Nothing is worth the cost of a human life, especially not an entertainment event.

There have been subsequent situations that we have had to manage. A more light-hearted one was when the entire electrical supply at Earls Court decided to weld itself together halfway into the set and all power was lost to sound and lights for a full 40 minutes.

The crew did an amazing job of splicing together high-voltage cables and restoring power while we juggled, pulled faces, played football with the audience and generally kept the plates spinning. These are times when you can be truly proud.

In Rio, at the Olympic Arena, an entire section of barrier collapsed in a heap of jagged aluminium. The barrier was a cheap copy of a successful design, but had been built using substandard materials instead of high-grade metal.

I stood with a translator for half an hour as we persuaded the crowd to leave and come back the next day. That they did so and didn't trash the place is testament to the simple interaction between human beings.

Back in 1988 the *Seventh Son* tour was all-conquering, but equally interesting for me was meeting video director, editor and auteur in general Julian Doyle, who was initially called in to direct 'Can I Play with Madness'. Julian and I went on to direct and storyboard several more ideas and, of course, the Oscar-defying feature film *Chemical Wedding*, starring Simon Callow as the reincarnated Aleister Crowley.

Before Aleister Crowley, though, came Monty Python. Julian was Python's film guru. He reassembled the film *Brazil* from the cutting-room floor, having finished large chunks of it himself because Terry Gilliam was ill. As an editor his credits extended to virtually all the Python films, and he taught at film schools and was his own lighting director and cameraman.

After directing Donald Sutherland and Kate Bush in 'Cloudbusting', Julian was asked to come up with ideas for 'Can I Play with Madness'. He managed to engage Graham Chapman to perform in the video.

Graham was sadly quite ill from throat cancer during filming. He, along with Chris Aylmer from my old band Samson and Steve Gadd, our long-time assistant tour manager and friend, would all perish from the same awful disease.

It would be 26 years before my own diagnosis of the same cancer.

I loved the video and was eager to chat to Julian, because I loved to write and because all of my lyrics were pictorial, at least in my head. When I sang, I saw movies of the story unfolding. All my voice did was tell the tale of the theatre in my mind.

Julian regaled me with tales of *Time Bandits*, Harvey Weinstein and errant Beatles.

'Why don't you do an Eddie movie?' he suggested.

I thought about it, and wrote several treatments, but it was obvious to me that it was neither the time nor the place for an Eddie movie, even if it could have been smuggled past the Maiden gatekeeper Rod Smallwood. It was just not a possibility.

'What about doing a movie about Aleister Crowley?' I asked. 'Nobody's done one.'

Hold that thought.

Slaughtering Daughters

The album and tour of *Seventh Son* put us squarely in arena- and festival-headline territory. I had, by the end of the tour, acquired a wardrobe of fabulously potty trousers, hairy shirts and various masks, including a rather fetching Goat of Mendes number with two-foot-long antlers.

To keep ourselves sane on the road I had my fencing, Adrian had his fishing and Steve had his own football team, often imported for matches. Most of us played, and some of the matches were genuinely momentous, especially for someone like me, who was left-footed and, just for good measure, God had equipped me with another left foot as a spare. Adrian was quite a skilful player, and he had some style. He was deceptively tricky. In many respects his timing was remarkably similar to his guitar-playing. Steve, of course, was principal striker – not by right, but by agreed ability.

I enjoyed midfield. I liked close marking and the frustration generated when the opposition saw their passes thwarted or their strikers denied. It was a tactical style, and actually was not dissimilar to playing flanker in rugby union, which was my most successful position when I played the game from 11 to 16 years old. After that I was getting a little small, or maybe other folk became larger.

Iron Maiden FC opened for an international game between Canada and Greece, and I had to mark the singer from a band called Glass Tiger who was quite useful. Sadly for him, the pitch was in poor condition, and after I chased him around for 45 minutes he twisted his ankle and was stretchered off. I never touched him, ref – honest.

We played the Olympic Stadium in Montreal, as a football team, of course, which was pretty mind-blowing, and finally we played the Estonian side Flora Tallinn in 2000, and achieved notoriety in *The Times* by hospitalising Mart Poom, Derby County's Estonian goalkeeper who was appearing as a guest in the game.

Stretchered off with 'undisclosed injuries to his testicles' was, I believe, the newspaper quotation that tells you all you need to know about the match.

We worked hard and played hard. I would sneak off to train with the Canadian fencing team, or indeed the Japanese team, for that matter. It's the small, hidden worlds that keep you on the straight and narrow on tour. I had seen far too many casualties along the way, and realised that, as I had thought in that hotel corridor on *The Number of the Beast* tour, the music business will drive you nuts if you let it.

Returning home after a tour is a bit like rejoining society after a spell in prison, or being a missionary, or living like a hermit and taking mind-altering quantities of adrenalin every day. It is strange.

I moved back to West London from Buckinghamshire and immediately bought a four-foot long radio-controlled U-boat replica. I still have it, and I came perilously close to buying a real sub.

Why a children's charity would want to purchase a Royal Navy diesel-electric submarine was something I couldn't quite fathom. Purchase it they did, though, and according to the *Daily Mail* they were now keen to unpurchase it.

I came up with a plan to start submarine cruises across the Atlantic for enthusiasts. When they got the straitjacket on me and put me in a padded cell, I finally relented and agreed that there might not be a huge market for such a hands-on experience.

After I had calmed down, I went back to having a few pints of beer by the River Thames and watching ducks and swans go by. This is where Janick Gers and I started to get into double trouble.

I had known Janick from his days in a band called White Spirit, who were contemporaries of Samson. We were both Ian Gillan fans, and Janick clearly had quite a bit of Mr Blackmore infusing his style, in particular the spectacular knee-wobbling lunges that would punctuate his dancing antics. Imagine a whirling dervish with a guitar being suddenly deposited onto a red-hot plate and it may give you some idea of the Geordie guitar jive that resulted.

We had, of course, kept in touch, and we kept bumping into each other as I scaled the height of Iron Maiden success and Janick passed through a series of bands. As we sat having a beer, he seemed resigned, somewhat depressed, about the state of the music industry, saying, 'They're more interested in your fucking haircut than whether you can play guitar.'

Janick was selling his equipment: his old Stratocasters, Marshall cabs and vintage amps. He was doing a sociology degree and thought about teaching, or, well, anything except music. I admired his sincerity, but he was far too good to be wasted on teaching sociology.

In my tiny brain I hatched a plan. I had a bizarre offer, which might just be a solution to his problem.

Ralph Simon of Zomba Music, you may recall, was our bearded, friendly South African music publisher. Once, while temporarily bereft of a home, I was sleeping on a mattress in a vacant room in his Battery Studios. Ralph leapt into action as he apprehended what he assumed was a burglar.

'AHA – got you!' he yelled as he burst into the room.

'Hello, Ralph,' I replied.

'Who is he?' my girlfriend asked, rather more pointedly and covering up various regions that I wasn't already covering up.

Ralph thought this all very rock 'n' roll, and took to calling me 'Mr Libido' in polite conversation, which could sound quite creepy coming from a middle-aged lawyer with an Afrikaans twang to his voice.

Ralph was also a sort of savant when it came to music as well. After the success of 'Run to the Hills' he took me to one side and said, 'You know, what you have is that high-pitched octave that makes the Americans go raving mad.'

'Really?' I replied.

'Yes. Absolutely. You know, Mutt Lange has the same thing.'

Equipped with this insight I muddled through the next few years, until Ralph popped in to the management office one day. This time, I had my clothes on.

'How would you like to do a soundtrack to a movie?' he said.

Having just come off the *Seventh Son* tour I was completely in the space to do a movie soundtrack. Except it wasn't actually a soundtrack to a movie at all. It was one song for *A Nightmare on Elm Street* – number five, I believe, in the franchise.

'There's only a small budget.'

'How much is small?' I enquired.

'Small' was big enough. I phoned Janick.

'You can't sell your gear. You've got to do a track with me, and if you still want to sell it I'll buy it off you and you can use it when you want.'

I had never seen a Freddy Krueger film, so I asked someone in the pub, '*A Nightmare On Elm Street*, what's that all about?'

'Oh, teenage girls go to sleep and get slashed by this scary old dude, but he only gets them in their sleep.'

A love story, then.

The track was wanted almost instantly, so I had to come up with a tune pretty quick. If in doubt, borrow a guitar and play the first thing that sounds good. I have a totally untested theory that every guitar has a tune in it, and this particular one turned up 'Bring Your Daughter to the Slaughter'.

It was only the chorus, and the rest of the song was a sort of AC/DC, Bon Scott-style pastiche with a tongue-in-cheek section of mad monks chanting over tolling bells.

We cranked out the song in Battery Studios in a couple of days. We laughed, giggled and drank beer to celebrate, and in general had a relaxed time making music away from the more intense atmosphere that pervaded the Maiden camp.

The track was too late for the movie, but not too late for CBS Records, who heard it and did backflips. They wanted to give me a solo deal.

Ralph phoned me up: 'Is there any more material like that?'

'Oh yes, loads,' I lied.

Two weeks later I was telling the truth.

Janick's house in Hounslow was right under the flight path of Heathrow Airport. Not just a bit under, but I mean the wheels were almost putting a dent in his roof as they screamed overhead. It meant the next-door neighbours didn't complain about the odd scream emanating from his lounge windows as we wrote the album.

We had to crack on, so I just made a list of staple rock songs. We already had a sort of AC/DC one, we needed a ballad, an anthemic one, a sort of Rolling Stones groove one, a boogie-type thing ... maybe a cover, as well.

Luckily, I had recently done a charity show for the Prince's Trust at Wembley. I was given the Bowie song 'All the Young Dudes' to perform, which of course was a seminal track for Mott the Hoople. I was more surprised than anyone that it seemed a natural fit for my voice, although, to be fair, I don't think we improved on the original.

Then, while having a beer one night, I went for a piss, and there on the wall were the Proustian lines: 'No muff too tuff, we dive at five.' A couple more beers and some further stupidity about the legendary children's TV show *Captain Pugwash*, and 'Dive! Dive! Dive!' was born, or rather submerged. At least I had a four-foot submarine to feature in the video.

The single 'Tattooed Millionaire' was written unexpectedly after talking about Graham Bonnet, the onetime singer in Rainbow with an extraordinary high and raspy voice. And then Janick played what is, for me, the best song on the album.

The TV was on in the background, sound turned down, and Jan played the opening chords to what became 'Born in '58'. I asked what it was.

'Oh, something I had kicking around.'

The instrumental portion was virtually complete. I just added the vocal over the top of it.

EMI Records had given each of us in Maiden a one-off option to make a solo album. Now was the time to exercise that option.

Who should show up to make the video for 'Tattooed Millionaire' but Storm Thorgerson of Hipgnosis – and Pink Floyd – fame. Storm came via a contact of a new manager at Sanctuary, Maiden's management company.

Not quite a yellow submarine, but rather a subterranean submarine upping its periscope into the lurid lifestyles of the rich and infamous was the basic premise of the video. I was very enamoured of the submarine control room and wanted to install it in my attic, complete with periscope, but the men in white coats explained that it all belonged to a prop house. Such a disappointment.

I watched Storm direct, and the cheeky thought occurred to me that he was having far too much fun making all these videos.

'You're just making it up, aren't you?' I whispered to him one day.

'Don't let on, dear boy,' he whispered back at me.

Fault Lines

America turned the page and I re-entered Iron Maiden world, having unwittingly written what would turn out to be our only number 1 single. The reason 'Bring Your Daughter to the Slaughter' isn't on *Tattooed Millionaire* is because it was requisitioned by Steve for the new album, *No Prayer for the Dying*. Of course, it had to be rerecorded.

The idea was mooted that we should somehow go back to our roots. We would record everything at Steve's house and use the Rolling Stones' mobile studio, which all sounded rather grand. There's a line in 'Smoke on the Water' that immortalised the ancient ruin that pulled up outside Steve's Grade II listed manor house.

Honestly, I think we had all fallen under the spell of papal infallibility. Why is the Pope always right? Because he is the Pope, and can never be wrong. Well, what if he actually is wrong?

This is simply a difference of opinion, and the only opinion that matters is, er, the Pope's.

Bands, business leaders, popes and entire countries fall victim to their own circular beliefs. Indeed they become the ultimate victims of their own success. Desperate to avoid uncertainty and surrounded by people who always agree, they cross the line from artistic integrity to artistic stagnation.

Maiden had a double problem, in that it was becoming harder to break out of a core audience without radically changing the sound of the band. The latter was simply not an option. The sound of the band was its identity, unlike other bands who flipped and flopped according to fashion. Maiden's success was based on reinventing the wheel that drove the heavy metal bus. Its dilemma was how to reinvent the wheel with every new album and tour. Maiden had gone way beyond the third-album watershed moment. The big question was: how would the band sustain its trajectory into being legends, and not start a slow parabola into the dustbin of history?

Our problem, in my opinion, was that no one was acknowledging that big question.

Things were, quite frankly, too good to be true.

For the second time in my Iron Maiden career a major schism occurred.

Adrian Smith quit.

Nobody saw it coming, and I don't believe Adrian did either, in the same way that no one intentionally steps into quicksand or plays hopscotch in a minefield. A Roman soldier was famously supposed to fall on his sword to avoid dishonour, but I'm not sure Adrian knew there was a sword lying in wait as he voiced his concerns about the upcoming album one fateful afternoon. He clearly wasn't happy with the current state of affairs, but I don't believe he wanted out; he just wanted to make it better. Conversation turned into accusation and, in the end, it was our own hubris, fuelled by our seemingly untouchable success, that sealed his fate. He was not fired; he simply walked into a lift shaft when there was no lift.

Management, of course, took care of the press fallout in what was quite a surprising story. Maiden's management have always been fanatically devoted to the band at all costs, which is exactly what is required most of the time. Few bands in history have had such a dedicated manager as Rod Smallwood. I once had to give him an award as 'Manager of the Year' at an awards dinner. It was all supposed to be a secret, and it was difficult enough just to get him to turn up. The room was full of his peers plus the great and the good, the bad and the ugly from the music industry.

'I fucking hate these things,' he grumbled. 'Anyway, what the fuck are you doing here?'

I scribbled on a pad under my jacket: notes for my speech.

'What are you fucking writing? I bloody hate this.'

At which point an eager American music executive flashed his instabrite, 1,000-dollar perfect bite at Rod and said, 'Mr Smallwood, it's an honour. I've always been an admirer of your work.'

Any minute now the business card would come out.

'You think I'm in the music business, don't you?' Rod said.

'Why, yes ...'

'I'm not in the music business. I'm in the Iron fucking Maiden business.'

With that retort, the young lion retreated, having been well and truly biffed by the old contender from Huddersfield.

The secret of his success was that he was focused entirely on the band, not on the wellbeing of any other creature on earth, save family. His success in guiding our career was enabled by his partner and our lifelong business manager Andy Taylor. With a first-class degree from Cambridge, where he and Rod met in 1969, Andy has navigated and negotiated Maiden's financial survival and permitted us the creative freedom to play music without looking over our shoulder. But neither Rod nor Andy have ever had any significant input into our musical endeavour. Indeed, there has for many years been a total exclusion zone in the recording studio banning managers, agents, lawyers and record companies from chucking their opinions about. Most of the time I think this is a good thing. Sometimes, though, everyone needs a little guidance, unless, of course, you are the Pope, because then you can always ask God, and he's never wrong, right?

Rod must have had divine guidance, as 'Bring Your Daughter to the Slaughter' was number 1 in the UK after Christmas, much to the chagrin of the BBC and self-styled pop-music gurus. As a service to the nation it knocked the ubiquitous Sir Cliff Richard from the hallowed top slot and propelled us out of the Christmas break with a grin on our faces.

We actually ended up at number 1 for two weeks, and due to a bizarre legal requirement the BBC were obliged to play short extracts of the song through gritted teeth. It's a shame they weren't paying more attention to Jimmy Savile instead of writhing on the hook of a tongue-in-cheek horror-movie soundtrack.

Adrian's surprise departure left some exit wounds, and these could not simply be stitched up by clever PR and careful manipulation of the UK chart system. An essential piece of the Iron Maiden jigsaw was now missing, and the new piece, in the guise of Janick Gers, didn't match the space.

There is no reason why Janick should have sounded like a copy of Adrian at all. His style was clearly different, but we were bereft of the melodic duelling with Dave Murray's more florid style. Dave tended to fuse torrents of notes cascading over the solo sections, whereas Adrian always felt as if his solos were on the edge of a precipice, real cliff-hangers, so that you hung on every note.

Jan's guitar style and sound were more spiky and less processed, but I hoped that his arrival would see a bit more of the Janick that played on *Tattooed Millionaire* start to rub off on the Iron Maiden sound. Caught up in the enthusiasm of a first album, it was too much to expect of him, but our next album, *Fear of the Dark*, was an opportunity to move things on in a world that was changing fast.

* * *

The Aleister Crowley movie was gaining some traction at last. The catalyst was a song I had written called 'Man of Sorrows'. The beastly script that eventually became *Chemical Wedding* was based on a reworking of Somerset Maugham's novel *The Magician*. Maugham had met Crowley, loathed him on sight and created the character of Oliver Haddo, the evil sorcerer trying to create a homunculus or moonchild in his lair in Scotland.

Crowley himself wrote a similar novel, actually called *Moonchild* but with far less of the Hammer Horror plot of Maugham's. Maiden's lyrics are littered with references to Crowley, from 'Revelations' to 'Moonchild' and 'Powerslave'.

Julian Doyle and I had frequent script meetings. One rewrite was done by Jimmy Sangster, who wrote many of the original Hammer movies. I actually liked it, but Julian thought it was horrible and too traditional.

We ploughed on, staying in the period up till 1947, when Crowley died of a heart attack. He was taking enough heroin every day to kill a dozen normal mortals at the time.

I had written a rather dramatic first five minutes that took place at the top of K2, where Crowley led an ill-fated expedition. He was a world-class climber, despite his asthma and drug addiction. That scene, plus the demo track 'Man of Sorrows', saw the film being optioned by Velvel, Walter Yetnikoff's fledgling production company. Walter had been executive producer of *Ruthless People* and now had an appetite for the movies, after CBS Records had been sold to Sony Music for rather more than it was worth.

Walter had three movies he planned to make, and mine was one of them. Money actually changed hands, and I flew out to LA to discuss the script. They were paying the bills so I had no objection to a script doctor coming on board to move things along. In fact, I was interested to see the process, because as far as screenplay writing was concerned, I was making it up as

I went along, except for guidance from a few self-help DIY manuals. Julian was dismissive of structure in a traditional sense. I wasn't so sure, and anyway, this was all a bit of an adventure.

For the next two years the script shuttled across the Atlantic, and I awaited the results of the doctor's surgery. It seemed to take an awfully long time.

In contrast, the latest Iron Maiden album took no time at all.

The rehearsal space in the barn now had a second-hand studio installed in the cramped confines of its roof. I thought the project laudable but flawed in its execution.

The vocals were done and I got on with winning fencing competitions and writing scripts. I was also busy coming up with a third book in the Lord Iffy series, tentatively taking our oddbod laird back to his schooldays.

Looming large was the option to record a follow-up to *Tattooed Millionaire*. Janick was totally absorbed in Maiden by now, and there were various suggestions as to who should be my writing partners. I realised that I didn't know any musicians anymore. In fact, I didn't know much about anything outside of Iron Maiden, so complete had the submergence been for the last 10 years.

Wing Nut

On holiday in Florida, I picked up the phone and dialled. Trial flight lessons, $35. *Microsoft Flight Simulator* wasn't nearly real enough.

17 July 1992 is the first entry in a battered brown logbook that records one take off and one landing at Kissimmee Airfield in Florida. It might just as well have described the journey that Paul undertook to Damascus.

My conversion took place in a Cessna 152, and was caused by half the velocity of the air over the wing squared, multiplied by the coefficient of lift of the airfoil involved. Thus enlightened, my weight was borne heavenwards – or my mass, if you are a Catholic – and, freed of life's drag by the whirling airscrew boring its way through the air, I thrust my way onwards and upwards. In short, I could fly.

I am not a numbers person; I prefer to use words or pictures. Most pilots are probably the other way round, but numbers or words, the emotional response to a first flight I found overwhelming, life-changing and fascinating.

The Cessna 152 is a tiny two-seat, high-wing aircraft, which on the ground appears flimsy in the extreme. Yet here I was, at 1,500 feet above the Florida landscape with a sunset just beginning and the rolling Everglades and lakes criss-crossed by roads and waterways.

It was a meeting of all worlds: poetic, mechanical, logical, daring, experimental, creative, internal and external. In one moment I realised that this confection of aluminium and rivets was keeping me alive. Moreover, in the air I was an interloper and had to respect the ways of the wind, the temperature, the density of the medium in which I hung, suspended only by a difference in pressure, which, although real, might just as well have been an act of faith.

Yet still the conundrum deepened. Where would I go? How would I navigate? How could I predict what failures might occur and when?

From the outside view to the internal turning over of eternal 'what if?' questions, the business of flying was unknowable. If you flew every day for the rest of your life you would never be able to say, 'I've seen it all, know it all and have done it all.'

I took one long, panoramic stare from wing tip to wing tip, and all of these thoughts boiled instantly in my very core. And then my reverie was suddenly shattered. My instructor was quite a serious type, and I think he spotted someone who was about to take flying equally seriously.

'Now, Mr Dickinson, how do you feel about landing it?' he said.

I am sure that most of the landing was him, but no matter, I was eager to hurl myself off the precipice. I was supposedly on holiday in Disney World, but in fact I went flying every single day for the next week.

By day five I had five and a half hours in my little log book, and 22 landings. It said I had taken off, climbed, descended, practised stalls, made steep turns at 45 degrees, flown very slowly and simulated engine failures. My instructor asked me how much longer I was going to be in Florida. I said I had to go back to England and start a tour.

'That's a shame,' he said. 'If you got yourself a medical I'd have soloed you in a couple of days.'

I bet you say that to all the boys, I thought. But somewhere deep down I was kicking myself that I hadn't joined the Air Cadets.

The *Fear of the Dark* tour took over, and the next chance I got to fly was in California, in the midst of the tour. Santa Monica airport, a delightful gem and a haven of aviation joy and *esprit de corps*, was nestled in the lee of the Santa Monica mountains, just behind Venice Beach. Little did I realise that this airport would begin a new chapter in my life, and that I would return to it for years to come.

Justice Aviation, owned by Joe Justice, was the biggest independent flying school and plane-rental business on the field. I just turned up and asked to go flying. My instructor was a physics graduate who had also graduated from Embry-Riddle Aeronautical University, and his dad was a colonel in the US Air Force.

I had long brown hair and wore shorts and goofy T-shirts. He was, I thought, very laid-back for such a strait-laced background, so I made a mental bookmark. To borrow a phrase from Arnie in *The Terminator*: 'I'll be back.'

After the USA we finally made it all too briefly to New Zealand. By now thoroughly bitten by the flying bug, I sought out Ardmore airport and went in search of more knowledge.

'Can I do a spin?' I enquired.

'No, mate. I can't let you do a spin ... but I can do one and you can tell me what you think.'

The nose of the plane went up, the engine note back to idle, one wing dropped so the earth was to my left, and my backside was going the opposite direction. All at once the left-window view said, 'Sky, earth, sky, earth,' and the view through the front windscreen said, 'Earth, upside down, earth getting much bigger, EARTH!' and abruptly the rotation stopped, the wings levelled and the engine note resumed its normal busy grumble. I sat in silence. I was still in silence when I got back to the briefing hut. What was going on here?

'I've never had a blackboard lesson so far,' I said. 'Teach me something.'

What I got was straight out of RAF Central Flying School. Beautifully explained graphs of lift drag and how it related to airspeed and angle of attack. After an hour of that, we went through the spin: how it happened and what happened.

Back in England, I went to Elstree aerodrome and took one more lesson in my unstructured 'try before you buy' learn-to-fly course.

Unlike California and New Zealand, England was green and misty, and aircraft seemed to crawl around in the weeds, forbidden to fly any higher than telegraph poles lest they should collide with stray airliners.

Visual navigation in England was more like orienteering than navigating. My flight simulator on my heavyweight laptop used radio-navigation instruments, and these were all fitted to the Grumman AA-5 that I was learning on.

I noticed the instructor had a map, stopwatch and china-graph pencil and ruler.

'Why don't we take a bearing off a radio beacon?' I asked.

'Good God, you're not allowed to do that. It's not in the syllabus. Stopwatch, paper and pencil, old chap.'

Note to self: must brush up on mental arithmetic.

My next appointment was back in Santa Monica in November 1992. I had a couple of months in the studio to produce what would end up being *Balls to Picasso*, my second solo album, and I decided that I would be in possession of a pilot's licence by the end of it.

I got rather more than I bargained for in both departments.

Many people were under the impression that *Tattooed Millionaire* had been a serious attempt at a solo record, when in fact it was just a bit of fun, well executed and with a lot of record company enthusiasm behind it.

The next record, for me, had to be something much more serious, and what I didn't want was a 'same old, same old' rehash of seventies hard rock. Bands like Soundgarden and Faith No More actually sounded innovative, whereas the 'traditional' metal world often looked like transsexuals in need of a shave.

Maiden had always stood apart from any defining tribe, even though we were endorsed by quite a few. My problem was to establish where I belonged in modern rock music, if indeed I belonged in it at all. I had been steered in the direction of working with a traditional metal band called Skin. This was in the erroneous belief that I wanted to make a sequel to *Tattoo Millionaire* in the same vein. I wasn't happy with the result. As I scratched my head in bemusement at my lack of creative spark, the thought occurred to me that perhaps my time was done. Maybe Maiden was as far as I got in this life. I could take solace in the advice the cannibal who doesn't want to eat his neighbour was given by his hungry friend: 'Oh, stop moaning. Shut up and eat the chips.'

At the end of the *Fear of the Dark* tour I had been on the bus back to Narita airport in Tokyo. We were going home, and it was another self-satisfied success. I had tried to raise my concerns about the sound and production of our albums, about the assumption of perfection and the lack of honest criticism within the band. Everyone looked at me as if I had lost my mind. Maybe I had, or maybe we were on the slow trajectory to a luxurious creative extinction.

Los Angeles would be the origin of my new future. My tapes from the recording sessions with Skin had been sent off to Keith Olsen, a producer of some repute, with the aim of salvaging, reworking, remodelling and generally reconstructing the album.

Keith had his own studio in LA and had reworked David Coverdale's records, turning them into American radio monster hits. The problem was that I preferred David Coverdale produced by Martin Birch. The radio success equalled soulless perfection in my eyes. Nevertheless, I turned up in LA, started to navigate my way round the 10 to the 405 to the 5, and the endless numerical cat's cradle that comprises the freeway system, and arrived on the doorstep of Goodnight LA Studios.

Keith listened to my set of tapes and rough mixes.

'I'm interested because you can actually sing,' he declared. 'You really have a voice.'

Damned by such faint praise, I suggested we scrap all of it and start again. I wasn't in the mood for half measures. I was also paying for it myself. I wanted a dark and emotionally jagged record, in line with my thoughts at the time. One of the albums I referenced was Peter Gabriel's third album, which I regarded, and still do, as a masterpiece.

Keith imported session keyboard players to work with me, plus different drummers, guitarists and backing singers. It was fascinating but artistically barren. The level of technical expertise in all of them was astounding, but they were smooth and effortless. Life is not like that, and nor did I want my own music to be like that.

The icebreaker in all this was Keith's engineer, the rather colourful character that was Shay Baby. He was an ex-US Marine who had done his time in Vietnam and now did his time in the recording studio. As I reworked and waded through musical treacle, trying to find my way through the Grimpen Mire to a Sherlock Holmes moment of revelation, Shay provided me with the compass.

'Come see my buddies Tribe of Gypsies,' he suggested. So I did.

In another revelatory moment, I had my faith in music rekindled by this astonishing combo. The main writer and lead guitarist Roy Z had been a crack addict, and was essentially saved by music from a life of gang violence. The conga player was already an ex-gang member and had done time in jail. The bass player, Eddie, was so cool that even the gangs in the *barrios* gave him respect and agreed a truce around his house. Eddie was a rock. The whole Latino scene in LA was unknown and a mystery to a rich Anglo kid, but my saving grace was that they were all rabid Iron Maiden fans.

If they'd been a man-of-war, I think they would have sunk half the Royal Navy, they were so good. There was love, power, passion and soul, and no money, no managers, no politics. Watching their gig was both inspiring and depressing, because they deserved so much more than half the bands out there.

I went round to Shay's house and met Roy Z, one on one, plus a guitar or two. He was embarrassed to ask if we could write together, assuming that the almighty Bruce Dickinson wouldn't be interested. I was equally convinced that Roy didn't need an old crock like me making suggestions when it was manifestly clear that his band was sensational.

By mid-afternoon we had each other bouncing off the walls. By early evening we needed small buckets of beer to calm down. All it took was Roy playing one guitar riff, which turned out to be the opening to a track called 'Laughing in the Hiding Bush'.

'I thought you might be able to do something with this,' was how the process started.

Back in Goodnight LA Studios, I was halfway through the second incarnation of my solo effort and I realised that the previous day's efforts with Roy Z had made it obsolete overnight. I was going to have to start again. To scrap one album is understandable; to scrap two is careless; to scrap three is just creative payback for 10 years of making music in the same silo.

I was renting a small house in Brentwood, just up the road from where the O.J. Simpson murder occurred. A heaving mass of sinful carnality it certainly was not, at least not on the streets after dark. Indoors perhaps was another matter. LA is a very early town. Maybe the movies and the 5 a.m. make-up starts have rubbed off on the rest of the population, or maybe the stupidly early joggers are just prescription-drug addicts living in plain sight. But in any case, after getting back from the studio in the evening, bed was really the only option.

I was on track to deliver my now third attempt at the album, which I was determined to finish in the UK, with Shay Baby in charge of production and using elements of what I had already recorded in Goodnight LA. Crucially, I would bring over Roy and Tribe of Gypsies to West London and finish new recordings at the Power House Studios in Stamford Brook.

I was also on track to get my pilot's licence before the end of February.

Pilots' licences come in all shapes and sizes, and the USA issues its own, which are recognised by, but are not the same as those of European authorities, and in particular the British.

I was using the US syllabus and the licence would be 'an original issuance' of a US licence. I went on to garner various other US licences up to commercial pilot and flight instructor for single- and multi-engined aircraft. I stopped short of bothering with the Airline Transport Pilot Licence because by that time I had a British airline pilot's licence and was rather busy with a multitude of other activities.

Right now, in California, I was after the most humble of US licences: a single engine landplane (as opposed to seaplane) licence, which would allow me to fly around day or night as long as I stayed nowhere near a cloud and avoided other aircraft, objects and people by use of the Mark-I Human Eyeball, two of which are fitted to this human unit and fully serviceable.

I equipped myself with maps, or 'charts', as my instructor insisted I call them, and a circular computational slide rule from the Second World War, plus pencils, Plexiglas rulers calibrated in nautical miles and a protractor to measure angles.

Ever the master of pragmatism, the US conveniently published all of the questions on their database for the written examination. Ever the model of free enterprise, books were available with the answers to all thousand-or-so questions, along with worked examples of weight and balances, navigational, technical, aerodynamic and regulatory problems.

I imagined people with brains the size of planetariums who didn't go out very much constructing these books, which now, of course, are all available on the internet as interactive instruction programmes.

I spent early evenings and sometimes late evenings with my head down, bashing through the syllabus and practice paper after practice paper. The pass mark in the exam was 80 per cent, and it was conducted by computer, which created a bespoke test for each individual. The inconvenient truth was that it was possible to cram for the test and scrape a pass. It wasn't my intention, but it was nevertheless a possibility.

My strait-laced but laid-back instructor started to quiz me as we progressed through our flying, to simulate the test. The winter weather in Los Angeles can be surprisingly unhelpful. Coastal fog, three-day deluges and mountain-wind effects can all conspire to scupper the most determined schedule. If it rained I did groundschool; if it was foggy I must admit to a fascination since childhood: what daydreams and apparitions could it contain? I would eat breakfast at the Spitfire Grill by the side of the runway and watch the rolling tumbleweed of sea mist curl around the control tower as the airport sat in eerie silence. It was then that ghosts appeared. The ghost of the Douglas Aircraft Company that built the DC-3 right here in Santa Monica.

The airfield was originally known as Clover Field, and aviation started there in 1923. Just offshore lay Catalina Island, with its airport perched atop the fog when it rolled in. Over the mountains to the north was the Mojave Desert, scene of

The Right Stuff and still home to mysterious spooks of its own, including US Air Force base Plant 42 at Palmdale airport, with Lockheed Martin and the infamous Skunkworks.

I loved the desert. When I obtained my licence I would often hire a plane and fly out to near Joshua Tree or Apple Valley. If it was early enough in the morning, the silence after cutting the engine was deafening. My breathing was the loudest sound. The effect on the mind was like dragging a rake across a disordered patch of sand or gravel. The desert seemed to soothe and calm the tempestuous mind that always bounced off the inside of my cranium. It was not inspiration; it was exhalation and nothingness.

I soloed my first three landings at Mojave airport. My instructor said I had been ready 10 days before, but the landing traffic at Santa Monica was always ridiculous, sometimes up to 20 aircraft in the circuit at once. So we delayed until our first cross-country flight, which was to Mojave.

I remember him being very quiet for the whole trip. We landed and the engine was still running as he opened his door on the Cessna 172.

'I'll be in the control tower watching,' he said. 'Three landings and then shut down in front of the tower.'

I was on my own at last. To be honest, it was quite anticlimactic. I would have been far more emotional had I soloed after six or seven hours back in Kissimmee, where they cut the tail off the shirt you were wearing and pinned it to the wall when you went solo.

Conditions were ideal – no wind, enormous runway – so I shut down in front of the tower and completed my checklists. Solo meant I could, after a couple more trips to different airfields with my instructor, fly solo cross-country flights on my own. In fact, it was a requirement, including one solo flight of 240 nautical miles in one day with landings at three different airports.

I was approaching my flight exam. The examiner was booked and I felt confident. My written exam was passed. I just had to complete seven more hours of cross-country solo flying. Saturday afternoon, the skies clear of cloud, was a glorious trip to Palm Springs and back, roasting hot on the ground but a little chilly at 9,500 feet on the way out. One more trip would do it, so I planned to fly to Las Vegas and back on the Sunday with an early start, leaving plenty of time to get back before sunset.

The first time you are really scared in an aeroplane is a memorable event, and I have never forgotten that Sunday. I have had other situations since then when I could have been as scared, or maybe should have been, but this one experience acted like a kind of vaccine for the soul. Be afraid and be scared, but panic will kill you, not fear.

The clear blue sky, the calm wind and runway 03 at Santa Monica airport beckoned. I was the very first person to start his engine that Sunday morning.

The weather in Las Vegas was benign, and I decided to fly along the mountains that topped 8,000 feet before turning north through the Cajon Pass up into high desert, some 3,000 feet above sea level.

The take off was smooth, the sky deserted and I quickly picked up a radar code with a helpful controller who would advise me of any other traffic. Uncle Sam was watching over me.

I climbed to 7,500 feet and it started to get cold as I paralleled the snow-capped peaks, heading out over Ontario airport and towards San Bernardino. Shortly before turning north into the jagged gash that was the Cajon Pass, I felt the tail of the aircraft rock from side to side, then a couple of bumps under the belly, which knocked the nose upward. I levelled the wings using the control column and steadied the tail by exerting more pressure with my feet on the rudder pedals.

'Any reports of turbulence?' I asked Uncle Sam.

'Nope.'

He sounded bored. Not much going on at 8.30 a.m. on a Sunday morning. The bumps continued. This was becoming tedious. I took a quick look on my chart. I would descend 2,000 feet to 5,500, and escape the lumps and bumps that were disturbing my otherwise perfect day.

I thought I would tell the controller – not that he was controlling me – and I did detect a hint of uncertainty in my voice as I announced, 'I'm just descending 5,500 feet to clear this turbulence.'

'Okay.'

Now he really sounded bored. I started a gradual descent and the rocking 'n' rolling stopped. As I approached my chosen altitude I opened the throttle and started a gentle left turn in the Cajon Pass. Below me lay the speckled grey hills and interstate arteries of California, rail and road, climbing the steep incline from sea level to the plateau 3,000 feet above.

At that precise moment a sleeping giant awoke. Invisible but tangible, it seized the back of my aircraft and twisted it like a wet towel, smashing my head from side to side in the cockpit. Next, a giant invisible fist smashed the top of the wing and pressed down, forcing me into my seat as I realised that the altimeter was unwinding rapidly and I was going down.

I raised the nose and applied full power. I looked at the vertical speed indicator: it was pegged at over 1,000 feet per minute down as the vicious brute smashed at the tail upward, downward and sideways. The wings rocked as I fought with the control column to keep them level. My nose was high and I heard the bleep of the stall warning system telling me that any further nose-up and I would lose what little lift I had left to fight the monster crushing the small piece of tin that was my life-support system.

A momentary calculation as I looked ahead at the rising terrain: it was at 3,000 feet; I'd started at 5,500 feet and was going down at 1,000 feet per minute or greater – with full power. My hands were slick and I could feel sweat dripping from my armpits and dribbling down my chest. I could see the headline: 'The fool who thought he could fly'. At this rate I had maybe two minutes to impact …

I forced myself to grip my terror, and I squeezed it really, really hard. I had my fear by the throat in one hand, and with the other I thought to crash the aircraft somewhere survivable, so I'd better start looking below. The whole area was swathed in power lines. Great. Electrocution or decapitation – both best avoided. And then … the evil giant relinquished his grasp, to be replaced by mischievous angels.

My ears popped and I swallowed to clear them as my tiny machine was borne heavenward on invisible wings. The altimeter was rising again and the vertical speed indicator was pegged at over 1,000 feet per minute upward. I pulled the throttle back to idle – to no effect. I was being tossed upward like a feather and I was drifting over to the other side of the V-shaped pass. The entire cycle had lost me 500 feet, and as I approached the top of the ridgeline again, the whole roller-coaster started again. Down I went, full throttle; up I went, throttle at the idle, all the time losing around 500 feet as the ground came up to greet me with each iteration.

Finally, I staggered through the pass and out into the high desert with about 1,500 feet to spare. I still had another two-and-a-half hours of flying before I got to North Las Vegas airport. Somehow, I made it.

I landed in Vegas and bought an omelette and chips. I was so shaken up I thought I might just give up. I was sick to the pit of my stomach, though luckily I am not one to decorate the toilet with good food.

Out of the Frying Pan

'Tears of a Dragon' was the big track on *Balls to Picasso*, and most of it was done at Goodnight LA Studios. Of the various other tracks, most of them sounded emasculated, and that was just a product of the people involved. I didn't feel any closer to a new beginning, except when I worked with Roy Z, who enabled me to be myself as opposed to overthinking who or what I should be. Gradually, the pendulum was swinging back to more conventional rock 'n' roll, but I loved the rhythmic nuances that Roy and the Tribe offered, the sheer groove that was available.

One thing was clear to me. The word 'cathartic' was starting to apply to the entire process, and flying was amplifying my reality. I had written a song called 'Original Sin', which was about the relationship between me and my father. It never made the album, but it's one of the darker songs from the Keith Olsen sessions. I felt quite guilty about the chorus. Maybe it was just me feeling sorry for myself; maybe it was too cruel.

Tell me father where have you been
All these years, in original sin
I saw you each day, we had nothing to say
And now it's too late to begin

Whatever the result of the song – good, bad or indifferent – it was those words that made me wonder what I was doing in Iron Maiden, given the way the albums were going.

I spent my days in a strange mixture of euphoria and uncertainty. One morning the *LA Times* lay strewn around the floor, most of it disposable advertising supplements, and I managed to locate the bits pertaining to actual news and opinion. 'Thought for the Day' was a feature I seldom noticed, but on this day I read it. It was a quote from the writer Henry Miller: 'All growth is a leap in the dark, a spontaneous unpremeditated act without the benefit of experience.'

So at that moment I decided to leave Iron Maiden. You can blame Henry Miller.

You'd imagine that for such a potentially life-changing decision I would have made a plan, but, whether from naivity or just plain enthusiasm, I hadn't.

Rod Smallwood came round to the studio in LA and I played him some of my material.

'I've got some good news and some bad news,' I said.

Rod shifted in his chair and started to look a trifle uncomfortable: 'What's the bad news?'

'Well, the bad news is that I feel I have to leave the band, so I thought I'd tell you first.'

'What's the good news?'

'Well,' I began brightly, 'now you have a whole new solo artist to manage. You'll find another singer for Maiden. It won't be so difficult. There are plenty of them about.'

He didn't look convinced.

'Shall I tell Steve?' I asked.

'No, no. Don't talk to anyone. I'll deal with it all.'

And, of course, he did deal with it, in exactly the way you would expect of one of the best managers on the planet. I still don't know what he told the rest of the band, but I'm sure his mind was already spinning damage limitation and making plans to avoid a rock 'n' roll Chernobyl in the media.

The two live albums released in the wake of my resignation were not the finest in our repertoire, and the second, *A Real Dead One*, seemed almost prophetic in retrospect. Nevertheless, my departure was stage-managed so as not to disturb the delicate equilibrium between perception and reality.

I would do one last tour, followed by a one-off TV special featuring an illusionist called Simon Drake. I happily agreed to be sacrificed in an Iron Maiden at the climax of proceedings, blood gushing out of my mouth as the spikes penetrated my body.

Just to make the point, the cover of the single, 'Hallowed Be Thy Name', featured yours truly being skewered through the chest while being toasted over the fires of hell like a long-haired marshmallow.

Not exactly a flying start to a solo career, but then again people who left Iron Maiden had traditionally fallen quietly into obscurity or been reduced to karaoke-style nostalgia. What happened now was entirely up to me.

Balls to Picasso had limited success. In retrospect it should have been a much harder and heavier album. Much of this could have been achieved if Roy Z had produced it, but out of caution Shay Baby was given the honours. It was a little too early to throw Mr Z into the pot headfirst. I think Maiden fans were variously angry, confused and many other emotions as well over my departure.

As the old military adage goes: 'no battle plan ever survives first contact with the enemy'. The nearest war going on was in Bosnia. I was about to have that first contact.

Into the Fire

The phone rang at home.

'How would you like to do a gig in Sarajevo?'

'Isn't there a proper shooting war going on?'

'Oh yeah, but it's all sorted by the UN. You'll be fully protected. It's all planned out.'

We weren't protected, there was no plan and the bullets were real, but fuck it, we went anyway.

Metallica and Motörhead supposedly turned it down. I'm not surprised. If I had been their manager I would have done too. I didn't exactly tell my manager. In no way did what happened resemble what was supposed to happen. What did occur became one of those events that changed the way I viewed life, death, other human beings – and traffic lights.

I got a band together and we loaded up 500-pounds of equipment onto a 737 and embarked on a military charter flight to Split, in Croatia. The aircraft was half full of soldiers who looked at us with faint disdain. They were paid for putting themselves in harm's way; we were getting paid zero. It was winter in the Balkan mountains. I bought a rucksack. I wore my army boots on stage anyway, plus the old Swiss Army greatcoat I had worn for the video of 'Tears of a Dragon'. Underneath, I had my old smock from my TA days. Lots of pockets, nice and warm, plus a woolly hat. I shoved a bottle of Jameson whiskey in for good measure. I thought a bottle might go down well with our organiser. His name was Major

Martin and he had his own rock show on Radio Z1D, which was a local station still broadcasting in Sarajevo itself.

The plan was to arrive in Split, don flak jackets and blue UN helmets, jump in a Sea King helicopter, fly to Sarajevo, do the gig and come back. Job done.

We got as far as Split. I saw the helmets and jackets piled up in a corner of the arrivals hall. A Colonel Green met us, and no, this was not a game of *Cluedo*.

'Are you chaps the British rock band?' he said.

It was one of the more obvious questions I have ever been asked. I nodded.

'Well, sorry, but you have to go home. Here are your boarding passes.' He brandished out return travel documents. We would be going back on the same aircraft that had brought us.

'What if we don't go?' I asked.

'Next flight is in one week,' replied the colonel. 'In any case, there are no spare helicopters and the weather is bad. Also, the UN have got wind of it and Akashi doesn't want to upset the Serbs.'

Akashi was the UN envoy with a reputation for appeasement.

Colonel Green walked away, obviously busy with more important things than a bunch of crazy long-hairs wanting martyrdom.

Outside were row upon row of white-painted UN trucks and armoured cars. This was a major military base as well as a civilian airport. I was sure we would start getting in someone's way very shortly.

A cameraman from a Reuters news team walked over. They had been hanging around in a corner of the tiny arrivals area.

'I am Bosnian. This is bullshit. We can get you into the city,' he said.

At the risk of invalidating the little or no life insurance that any of us had, I engaged in further enquiry: 'Go on.'

'There is a tunnel. A secret entrance. We can get you in. It's how we resupply the city.'

'Okay,' I said, slowly turning the wheels in my mind. 'How do we do that?'

'I am friend of President Izetbegovic. I call him and get permission,' he declared proudly.

He started putting loose change together and squeezed his body into a tiny phone booth, chatting away intensely for a couple of minutes. Finally, he put the receiver down.

'Well? What did he say?' I asked.

'He's not in right now. He's busy.'

I looked at our small pile of gear, at the ragtag band of faces and a terrified Roland Hyams, a publicist who had thought this was going to be like Glastonbury without the chilled Chablis and yurts.

'We can get into Sarajevo – maybe,' I said. 'There's a tunnel. If we go back, we'll never get there. If we stay, we might get there. Worst case, we stay and drink cheap beer for a week and find somewhere local to do a gig.'

Actually, worst case was being blown to smithereens by a Serb anti-aircraft shell or landmine or getting hit by a sniper's bullet. I put it to the vote, with a promise that if one person dropped out none of us would go, and no one would think less of him as a result. I meant it.

Everyone was up for it, including the guys who were just a tiny bit terrified. They admitted to the fear and voted to go anyway. I took the boarding passes and returned them to Colonel Green.

'Sorry, we are staying. We'll take our chances on getting through the tunnel.'

He took back the passes and thought for a moment.

'Stay right here,' he ordered, and scurried away looking busier than usual. Twenty minutes elapsed before he returned.

'Right,' he started. There was a note in his voice that said he was in charge of something rather than tiptoeing around it. 'You are no longer anything to do with the UN. You are therefore guests of the British Army. As such, we will store your kit in the armoury for now, and I suggest we take you to the officers' mess for a pot of tea.'

The drum kit and guitar amps stacked up against mortars, small arms and magazines would have made a great picture, but we forgot to take one.

By midnight we had been up all day, and had tea and lectures about the war. An RAF intelligence officer stood in front of the big map board and explained exactly what was going on. The situation was not pretty. I still have the set of tactical maps they gave me as a souvenir.

We were into our first can of beer when the door was flung open: 'In the truck, lads. You're going.'

It was T-shirt weather during the day in Split but chilly by night, and it was below freezing where we were going. Come to think of it, where were we going? In what? And driven by whom?

The Serious Road Trip was an NGO (non-governmental organisation) that operated relief convoys in areas the UN deemed too dangerous to contemplate. It famously drove a red London bus into no man's land during the Balkans conflict and ran a clown school for the children of both sides.

The Serious Road Trip was going to take us into the war zone, and we would drive overnight via Mostar and into the mountains, finally ascending the mighty Mount Igman. At the summit, the army would take over. Armoured personnel carriers would meet us at Bosnian Army Checkpoint Bravo One, and from there take us into Sarajevo itself. So much for the plan.

Our vehicle was an open-backed truck – a four-by-four with a canvas hooped top. We loaded the gear in the back and noted the pile of sleeping bags on the planked and metal-framed floor. This would be us for the next 10 hours in near pitch-blackness. Two crates of beer were chucked in for good measure by the chirpy young South African volunteer. He was going with us, as he'd done the run before. The driver was a young architecture student from Edinburgh. We had no escort, protection, helmets or flak jackets, but we had a secret weapon. Who would possibly want to shoot at a vehicle painted like ours?

The truck was bright yellow with rather capable renderings of Asterix the Gaul, Felix the Cat and the Road Runner painted prominently on the sides and rear tailgates. It was the camouflage of imbeciles, and who would want to shoot an imbecile?

We scrambled in the back and made ourselves comfy. Comfort, of course, is relative, and is as much a state of mind as an objective reality. I wedged my backside up against a flight case in the truck, figuring that between the axles was probably less spine-shattering than directly over them. I remembered the bottle of Jameson in my rucksack. I pulled it out. I had been saving it for Major Martin. Not any fucking more, I thought, and I cracked it open, just as Roland Hyams started rolling his first joint with a small piece of cannabis resin.

'Where the hell did you get that?'

'I've had it in the corner of my mouth since England.'

I had several uncharitable thoughts but just let out a very heavy sigh instead. He could easily end up dead, so having got this far he might as well puff away, because it would all be gone by morning. My days of spliffs were long gone, so I passed the whiskey round.

The night passed slowly, sleep was fitful and the cold seeped deeply into our limbs. The world was disappearing behind us through the canvas flap, suffused with a faint red glow from our tail lights, which painted shadows in the thick fog that had now enveloped us. We slowed to a crawl, then stopped. I poked my head out of the back: petrol station. Did people actually stop for petrol in a war? I suppose they did. I decided to sit up front in the cab. We would soon be approaching the base of Mount Igman, the 7,000-foot beast that marked the front line into Sarajevo.

Now we drove into utter blackness; before there had been occasional dim streaks of white light by the roadside. In the distance I could make out the gigantic rock that was Igman. It was easier to see because there was a war going on at the top of it.

Star shells and parachute flares hung in the sky, a firework display presaging death and destruction for those unfortunate souls atop the mountain, which was, of course, where we were headed. As I pondered this, we stopped fairly abruptly, as one does when a man steps out into the road and points an AK-47 at you. There are more friendly ways to hitch a lift, but I suppose in a war zone thumbs have been superseded by bullets and gun barrels.

Our hitcher turned out to be a Bosnian soldier who was fed up with walking and needed a lift to the base of the mountain. He chatted away in Bosnian, and we were almost conversing in sign language when we bade him goodbye. He melted into the darkness and, at around 5.30 a.m., we started the long crawl up the precipitous track to the summit.

'Have you done this before?' I asked our driver.

'Nope. First time.'

I didn't want to distract him. The gravel-and-dirt track twisted viciously and the headlights peered into the darkness beyond the edge. It was almost a sheer drop in places.

'Some of the lads do this without lights,' he offered, matter-of-factly.

I said nothing. He switched off the headlights.

'Tell you what,' I said, 'how about we switch them back on again?'

What a tale those headlights told. In the pre-dawn gloom, we drove through the remnants of the Bosnian army going home. The headlights tracked along the rows of pine trees, and I remember thinking how beautiful this place would have been, and maybe would be again, if ever there was peace. Every few hundred yards was a war drama: two white ambulances with red crosses, windows wound down, bullet holes in the doors, blood streaming down the sides; a dump truck full of combatants carrying plastic bags and wearing half their uniforms wearily returning to what was left of their city.

We were on top of the mountain. The fire fight was over and, like everything in this crazy war, who knew what had happened and who had won? Answer to both questions: nobody.

Finally, we stopped in the snow-covered forest. The track curved away to the left, down a steep incline towards Sarajevo and the front line. Ahead lay a small caravan on wooden piles, smoke coming from a wood-burning stove. A single strand of telephone wire hung across the road and connected the shed to somewhere. We had arrived at Bosnian Army Checkpoint Bravo One.

In front of the caravan was a washing line. The woollens and sheets were frozen stiff. I got down from the truck. I couldn't see any armoured personnel carriers. They were, of course, supposed to be there.

I knocked on the caravan door. Two soldiers, one male, one female, were warming themselves by the stove. I passed them a PR photo of the band and tried to explain our predicament. A shot of whiskey helped – we were all smiles later – but I was none the wiser as to our next plan.

Down below in the valley, Sarajevo was totally obscured by thick, white cloud. Like an inland sea it rolled between the valley sides. The entire vista was Serb-controlled, except for the spot on which I stood. Anti-aircraft guns modified to shoot horizontally ringed the basin, so they could shoot into the city or, for that matter, at the summit where I was standing.

There was no serious attempt to dry the washing hanging on the line. It was a sniper screen. Sarajevo was full of shitty clothes flapping in the breeze to obscure day-to-day activities, lest a Serb sniper should take a dislike to your children.

The sound of a revving engine broke the silence. Around the corner bounced and clattered a battered VW Golf. It pulled up and the occupants got out, high-fived each other and then drove off.

Shortly afterwards, the bread van arrived in similar fashion, delivering one loaf for the people in the caravan. The driver spoke a little German, and with a bit of the sign language that had served us well, he proudly displayed the bullet hole in his front windscreen, exactly where his head should have been.

'He try to fuck me! *Nicht tod*!' exhorted the baker. The butcher and the candlestick maker were nowhere to be seen, but the warming rays of the sun did illuminate our local sniper, flitting in and out of the trees with a bedroll attached to his back and what looked like a hunting rifle with a telescopic sight.

It was the only weapon I'd seen since the AK-47 at the base of the mountain. It turned out that there weren't enough guns to go round, so people waited till somebody died or was wounded, and then their weapon was passed on. Actually, not strictly true: our team in the caravan had one axe, used for chopping wood, and the man had a highly polished hand grenade in his belt.

The sun came up at 8.30. The fog had turned to mist, and Sarajevo started to become visible, like a long rasher of bacon, in the valley below. We had been there for two hours. We were also going to be in plain view of whoever was pointing guns at the track that descended into the city.

That was the good news. The bad news was that our armoured vehicles had been stopped at the base of the hill. The local Bosnian commander had found an NBC camera team in one and threw his toys out of the cot. We would have to drive down the hill ourselves, in full sight of the Serb guns. Surely no one would kill an imbecile? This imbecile begged to differ.

We started round the corner and down the single-track path. As I looked down to my right, I could see the twisted remains of the other vehicles that had been blown off the road. A prickly feeling began at the back of my neck.

In a most bizarre circumstance, we stopped. Coming the other way, up the track, was a Coca-Cola delivery lorry.

There is a Gary Larson cartoon of two deer conversing in a forest. One has a target on his chest. The caption reads: 'Bummer of a birthmark, Hal.' As I stood in the open while our truck backed up into a passing space, I felt exactly like the cartoon critter.

The Coca-Cola lorry passed and we made our way to the bottom of the hill, where white-painted armoured personnel vehicles waited to finally greet us. I met the very enthusiastic Major Martin, and we bade goodbye to our yellow cartoon four-by-four. The gig was the same night, so sleep, food, a press conference and a soundcheck were the order of the day. But first the drive into the shattered city.

The airport perimeter road was the front line. Both sides lay entrenched, yards from each other, as the UN vehicles passed between them in the grey mist. I was given a blue UN helmet and told to keep my head down.

After a few minutes I poked my head out just enough to see the devastation. As we passed rows of semi-demolished houses, children scuttled between them like rats. The war had reduced families to a feral existence, and the city, including the military, was down to three days' supply of food and fuel, and even that was at a minimum level of consumption.

The city that hosted the 1984 Winter Olympics had been smashed beyond recognition. Fronts of buildings were a façade, as the back was blown away, or simply the entire structure was pockmarked with cavities and pebble-dashed with bullets and cannon shells.

In streets strewn with rubble, cars stood like colanders, hundreds of bullet holes ventilating them. I could not for the life of me think what it was about a humble Renault that had provoked what must have been about 200 bullet holes. It was so extraordinary that I took a picture of it.

A river divides the higher and lower sides of Sarajevo as it progresses down the valley. The Serbs controlled the high ground, and the snipers fired into civilians on their way to work.

'Sniper alley' was the name given to the highway that ran from the airport in a straight line to the city. Every time you drove up and down this road you rolled the dice. We rolled it several times, the locals rolled it twice a day or more.

We arrived at the UN Headquarters, the former Olympic Village. The road crew got billeted in the bit with concrete sandbags instead of windows. The band got the penthouse suite, of course, which had iron bunk beds with old mattresses and the ubiquitous sniper tape covering the windows. Breakfast was a cheese roll and a beer, plus I donated what was left of the whiskey to Major Martin. He popped it in his desk drawer before proudly pointing to a dinner-plate sized cavity on the wall behind his desk, just above his head.

'Fifty-calibre shell,' he grinned. 'Bastards haven't got me yet.'

Don't waste time before drinking that whiskey, I thought.

The spirit of the Blitz was alive and well in Sarajevo. The night was already falling when we woke up, with the cold starting to gnaw at our bones. We headed for the press conference. The Brits had managed to put together something resembling canapés – Ritz crackers with ketchup – and I sat with the local bands who would support us. There was no electricity, and the generators to power the gig would only be switched on moments before in order to save fuel.

The guitarist next to me spoke some English.

'How do you rehearse with no power?' I asked.

He cut me a glance as if to say, 'What sort of a ridiculous question is that?'

'We rehearse,' he began proudly, 'with our spirit.'

Put firmly in my place, I nodded. 'I believe you do,' I muttered.

The Bosnian Cultural Centre has probably been remodelled as you read this, but when I visited in 2015 it was identical to the place we played in 1994. The corner of the building back then had been rather impressively melted by an anti-aircraft rocket, but most of it was below ground.

Word had got out about the concert, and because the Serbs were in the habit of mortaring public gatherings, schools had been closed and kids made their way home furtively, lest they became a target. Queuing round the block in Sarajevo was not just tiresome – it was life-threatening.

There were rumours that wealthy 'nationalists' paid money to go on assassination vacations in the war zone. The head of the UN fire service claimed that he had a Serb hitman gunning for him back home in Connecticut. Like most things in this zone of lunacy, it was best taken with a pinch of salt. Our jolly fireman was the local CIA rep.

The perversion of normal behaviour and the corruption of innocence was brought home to me when we visited an orphanage, which, sadly, was a work in progress, as fathers were being killed on an ongoing basis.

At first we saw the infants, tightly swaddled like small mummies in an impossibly hot room. One male nurse in a lab coat was metaphorically spinning plates, trying to keep them quiet; their expressions were like masks, devoid of emotion, bereft of human touch. I made the fatal error of picking one up and feeling the warm pulse of humanity in my arms. First its dark eyes fixed on my face, then the hands started to open: a gurgle, a smile and a finger seized with the force that only a newborn can muster. The tears that flowed were of confusion, joy, anger and sorrow. What kind of a world was this innocent going to inherit? Chaos ensued rapidly. One gurgling infant led to the others awakening from their suspended animation, like a room of clocks all striking midnight at different times.

Panic-stricken, our plate-spinning, lab-coated jailer rushed from cot to cot, desperately trying to put his charges back into the dead zone. Now the whole ward was anarchy: babies standing up, laughing, giggling, quite literally throwing things out of their cot. I had never thought of myself as a baby anarchist before, but I had a massive grin on the side of my face as we left the room. As Doc McCoy said in *Star Trek*, 'It's life, Jim ...'

The bigger kids played outside, in the exposed cellars and broken staircases. The lack of adults meant that the 'big boys' looked after the tribe in what looked uncomfortably like it might have been a scene from *Lord of the Flies* by William Golding.

We had a pair of drumsticks, an acoustic guitar and yours truly, so we started busking with Alex Elena, our Italian drummer, tapping away at the soot-blackened wall. It was a slightly awkward moment, as we realised that many of these children had never seen a guitar, let alone touched one. They were spellbound.

'Hey,' Alex shouted, 'everyone clap, c'mon.' And he started enthusiastically putting his hands together.

In a moment still burned in my brain, one of the older children leapt up and clapped his hands – 'rat-tat-tat' – at the nearest group of kids. They fell down dead. The clapping was the sound of death – of machine guns and snipers. And so the next group fell down too, until all the small children lay with

Giving the finger to the masses on the *Somewhere Back In Time* tour.

Yogic flying.

Left: Brownbeard. Backstage and bonkers.

Below: That's me wearing the mask (I'm the one on the left).

Above: The band, management and our very own Buddha! Left to right: Steve Harris, Nicko McBrain, me, Rod Smallwood, Janick Gers, Dave Murray and Andy Taylor.

Left: Good taste in guitarists. Bad taste in beer. Me and Janick Gers.

. . . But I did.

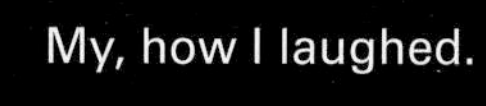

My, how I laughed.

The new band. Left to right: Eddie Casillas, Adrian Smith, me, Dave Ingraham and Roy Z.

Left: Trevor (right) and another tragic day in Sarajevo.

Below: A gun that didn't like Renaults.

Right: No man's land. The last bloke that did that got shot.

Left: Back home for Christmas.

Back in the game.

Above: Astraeus Airlines try to get the flaps to work. **Right:** I'm too fat to get out of the window.

Spot the one who's not been drinking all night.

Shoot the Fokker.

Beer is the key.

Halfway through cancer treatment. I'm already worried about the moustache.

An unorthodox stance and bat to knock cancer for six.

their limbs flailed out, frozen at the point of death. We stopped playing, dumbstruck. The kids got up and fell about laughing. It brought home to me how such a small thing as clapping can be twisted and subverted by the grim realities of a war zone.

Down at the show, I was amazed to see a modern PA system had been set up. Our sound engineer, Jed, from Ireland, was scratching his head in wonderment: 'Where the fuck they got this from, I don't know, but it's good kit. It all works.'

I soon found out. The hall was rammed, and the heat from the bodies was cooking the air. This wasn't a war zone: this was freedom; this was rock 'n' roll – time to remember joy. The soundcheck was fine, and with 10 minutes till stage time I was summoned by Major Martin.

'We have a problem,' he stated.

I met the problem upstairs. It was the group of bandits who had purloined/provided/hijacked the PA. They wanted money or they would take it away. There were six of them, all Bosnians, an interpreter and Major Martin, whose hand was starting to twitch around the butt of his sidearm.

'I have paid you 500 dollars,' the major said.

Cue the bandits mumbling.

'They want another 500,' said the interpreter. 'They say they are professionals.'

'I will pay them out of the T-shirt money,' Major Martin offered in exasperation.

Another round of bandit mumbling. No deal.

'Let's have another coffee,' I suggested, and smiled at them. 'Why don't they want to help their own people? I am not getting paid for this.'

The interpreter relayed. More mumbling and a little bit of discussion ensued. The coffees arrived, thick shots, like black mud.

'They say they are professionals.'

'Okay. Tell them I am a professional too and I promise they will be paid.'

This went down well. The ringleader gave me a bear hug, and I thought we had resolved the issue. Not quite. In stepped a blue pullover with a man called Trevor wearing it.

Trevor was, I later found out, assigned to be our personal security. He was not best pleased when Major Martin took us on an unguarded tour round the war zone in a Land Rover, and he was definitely not best pleased now. Trevor claimed to be an off-duty fireman from Glasgow. If you want to see Trevor in reality, there is an appalling, iconic picture of the shooting of a young mother and her five-year-old child captured by a news photographer. The child lies in the street in a pool of blood, and Trevor is one of two soldiers leaping out of a UN vehicle to try to save the boy's life and protect the other innocents at the scene.

Trevor had heart and soul, two Heckler & Koch submachine guns and a sidearm, and he was standing right beside me, pointing angrily at the bandit ringleader.

'You,' he spat, 'I will personally deal with, if any harm comes to any of these bands.'

Trevor was probably a rotten fireman, but I suspect he was a very good shot.

The bandits erupted in a flurry of 'poor me' gestures and loud groaning. The interpreter was about to translate.

'DO NOT translate what he said!' I said. 'Tell them … tell them Trevor is concerned that the building will be damaged if we don't go on stage soon, and someone might get hurt.'

Care and maintenance of soft furnishings in a war zone was an ironic bluff, but it bought time.

'What the fuck is going on?' I hissed.

'These fuckers here threatened to break the legs of the support bands if they don't pay protection money for using the PA,' Trevor said.

'Trev, once we've done this gig, I don't care what happens to these bozos.'

The gig was immense, intense and probably the biggest show in the world at that moment for the audience and for us. That the world didn't really know didn't matter.

Back in the sniper-taped barracks we drank beers with the small, mainly British, UN contingent, plus a few Norwegians who all spoke with Scottish accents. Go figure.

I asked a young Parachute Regiment officer what it was like being under siege.

'Fucking boring,' he said. 'Frankly, I'd like to go on up the hill and kill the fuckers. They are cowards.'

Former US President Jimmy Carter was coming to town in a matter of weeks to negotiate the peace deal, so our friend never got his wish.

We, of course, still had to get out. There had been two Sea King helicopters available over the border in Croatia, but one had been shot down the day before. The story was that General Sir Michael Rose was on board and that five 7.62 rounds had been fired through the fuel tanks and main rotor blades by what was described as 'probably a drug dealer who panicked'.

The real story was somewhat more serious. Twenty years later, while doing a charity simulator session on a 747 for Help for Heroes, I met the engineer who fixed the shot-down chopper.

'Oh,' he laughed. 'No. The Serbs targeted it with 50-calibre anti-aircraft fire to try to kill him and screw the peace talks.'

The only remaining helicopter was flying us out, *Apocalypse Now*-style, with belt-fed machine guns pointing out of the sides. We travelled in Land Rovers back across no man's land on the airport perimeter road. We would have to pass a Serb checkpoint run by a devotee of the Rosa Klebb school of etiquette, known locally as 'the bitch from hell'.

On the way, lying in a ditch, was a burned-out Soviet main battle tank. In one of my more stupid acts of bravado, I stopped the Land Rover, got out in the middle of no man's land and took what would now be called a selfie.

'Fair play,' the army driver commented. 'Last bloke who did that got shot.'

We were under instruction not to look too closely at the bitch from hell's face. From a distance, she looked quite attractive but, close up, heavy make-up concealed scarring of the sort that comes when you kiss hand grenades.

According to Trevor, she is no longer on this earth, having been taken out by an allied air strike. She was implicated in the murder and torture of numerous families. We pulled up alongside her at the checkpoint.

Don't look at the face of the Gorgon, I thought. And I immediately peered closely at the damage.

She seemed taken aback.

'Where have you come from?' she asked.

'Sarajevo.'

'Why were you there?'

'Hey, we had a gig. We're a rock band.'

'Sarajevo is a dangerous place. Never come back.'

She handed back the passports, and we drove the short distance to the base where we loaded ourselves aboard the chopper. The other one was having its rotor blades changed in the field next door.

I was sent upfront and given a headset.

'You fly, don't you?' asked one of the pilots.

It was the outgoing squadron chief trainer, flying with the incoming squadron chief trainer. Two trainers flying together. This could get interesting.

We lifted off, and after about two minutes: 'Would you like to see what happens when we go operational?'

I felt sure that what I liked wasn't going to alter anything.

'Mmm. Very interesting,' I said.

One trainer turned to the other trainer: 'No pussies in the navy.'

The other shot back: 'NO pussies in the navy, aye sir. Going down.'

For the next 15 minutes I was very quiet as the Sea King was flung round valleys and mountains, power lines and trees. The shadow of the rotors seemed to be almost cutting the grass on the mountainsides.

Finally, the airport of Split came into view, with a beautiful sunset. There was a party with the navy that night, to celebrate the shot-down pilots' incredible bit of flying that had saved the general's life and probably the peace process with it.

Next day, with almost the worst hangover in the world, we boarded an RAF C-130 Hercules for the four-and-a-half-hour slog back to Lyneham.

The train back to London was surreal. What passes for normality seemed like a dream, a veneer of certainty over a pit of hell that bubbled yards away from all of us, if we did but know it. Christmas was approaching, and it was a poignant reminder that some people would be spending the festive season without the indulgences deemed essential on the advertising hoardings.

As I stepped out on the platform at Paddington, late at night, I decided to take a walk in the chilly London air. I tried to collect my thoughts of the previous five days. I couldn't. The first image that struck me in the street was the absurd number of traffic lights. I sat on a bench and watched them change: red, green, amber, and all the time people measured their obedience, refusing to cross on a red light or drive on an amber. Pedestrians would wait for a green light even though the nearest vehicle was miles away. I sat for maybe 15 minutes watching a spectacle I now regarded as highly ridiculous, then picked up my rucksack and caught the tube to West London. I found a corner in what was then a smoky pub, pulled out a pen and paper with my pint, and started to write some words.

'Inertia' was the song about Bosnia on the next album I would do – a very different album, with a very different attitude and a very different haircut.

Radio Pirate

The gods of media had thrown me a bone, offering me a job on Radio 1, which was a live show on the biggest pure 'music' station in the UK.

The BBC was, and probably still is, riddled with focus groups and Machiavellian politics to rival the Borgias. Whichever pair of faulty bifocals had the vision to bring me along to the party, I never found out, but it probably had to do with the Silver Sony Radio Award from 1994 that is pinned to my wall.

I scripted and presented two documentaries for Radio 1, which – shock-horror – received the thumbs up from both critics and audiences. I can only assume that, having left Maiden, I was seen as being a more neutral character. In any case, I presented a series of live Radio 1 shows, broadcast from London and then Manchester.

It was the beginning of a 15-year radio career, encompassing Radio 1 and 2, a couple of small digital independents, plus an eight-year stint at BBC 6 Music, where I was on air for six hours a week.

I worked with my own independent producer, Ian Callaghan, to produce a series of semi-documentaries for Radio 2 called *Masters of Rock*. I say semi-documentaries because they were, in fact, a weekly Radio 2 rock show. We were basically producing a Trojan Horse to tempt the BBC into finally admitting that Radio 2 needed a rock show.

It was a fascinating time during which I had a succession of interesting interviewees and some very bizarre situations. I developed a show for 6 Music called *Freak Zone*. Initially, I had been asked to add a further three-hour rock show, but I protested that there wasn't enough quality new music to sustain six hours a week. Better to condense to three hours and keep the show tight.

With my playlist firmly in place, *Freak Zone* became a haven for writers, eccentrics, purveyors of Brazilian beatnik horror 'music' and unusual guests who you would never suspect might have, er, suspect taste in music. The snooker player Steve Davis, for example, is a massive fan of French jazz-rock combo Magma.

The battle at 6 Music was always the tiny budget, and as usual at the BBC it was mismanaged, as some DJs were grossly overpaid for performing on what was a digital-only station with a very small but loyal audience. It was, in fact, not much larger than an FM college radio station, but the big bosses had delusions of grandeur with taxpayers' money and built lavish studios costing millions. A commercial station could have achieved the same results out of two broom cupboards at a fraction of the waste.

Being on the other side of the microphone was instructive and amusing. I interviewed Peter Green, the legendary Fleetwood Mac guitarist, at great length on *Freak Zone*. He'd famously had a major mental health problem, which had disabled him for many years, but was now back playing.

We spent ages talking about penknives and his extensive collection. I never touched on the subject of music until he mentioned it himself, and then an avalanche of stories tumbled out, including the fact that he'd never wanted to play guitar and only took it up because his brother couldn't play a Christmas gift very well.

I caught a very frail Peter Grant shortly before his death. He was in reflective mood, and not at all the monster people portrayed him as during his seventies heyday. I always regretted deadlines in interviews. I hated the pressure of time. People need space to breathe and relax. That is when the truth is spoken, and you find that it's not the cardboard cut-out character that people expect.

It wasn't all London studios, however. I did get to travel, and it was as gamekeeper turned poacher when I ended up in Los Angeles to do a story on the launch of a new album by the nun-devouring son of Satan, the cardinal of carnality, the great and powerful Blackie Lawless (pay no attention to the man behind the curtain).

Blackie and his former band WASP had been managed by Rod Smallwood. In Maiden we viewed this all with some bemusement. However, Blackie and the gang proved that you can't keep a good manager down, and they had a fair bit of success.

'Animal (Fuck Like a Beast)' was their apogee, and Blackie sported a bloodied chainsaw extending from his crotch, plus a firework, which may or may not have malfunctioned to create a new recipe of 'Blackened Chicken in Jockstrap'.

Those halcyon days had passed. Rod had moved on and Blackie was making a comeback, and I was there to witness the moment on behalf of the BBC. Blackie had created an album titled *Kill.Fuck.Die.*, a monument to existentialism if ever there was one, abbreviated to KFD, which sounded awfully close to a brand of fried chicken.

Being backstage, not on stage was odd, but it gave me a little chuckle. It was fun to people-watch, especially when you knew what they should all be doing. Something was disturbing the force and Blackie was not happy, though. In the depths of the dressing room in a theatre by the side of the Capitol Records Building, someone had pulled his porker.

He was missing a band member – a pig, to be exact. He was, it was rumoured, about to sacrifice the animal live on stage, but a stagehand reported the plot to the LAPD who turned up with the animal welfare people and removed the bacon.

'So,' I switched on the tape. 'The pigs stole the pig?'

Blackie bristled with indignation.

'I lived with that pig,' he said. 'He rehearsed with us every day. He slept in my house.'

The ultimate fate of the pig is not recorded, but sadly it was probably only a stay of execution before pork chops beckoned.

I sat outside after Blackie's gig, watching the la-la land scene unfold. I too was bemused. I was weary of the LA circus. The energy in this Hollywood place is lost, I thought. It was exhausted, empty and clueless. I was glad I had cut my hair off.

After Sarajevo I had taken a look at the publicity photos and noticed that the band all looked terrific apart from the odd-looking fellow with the lank hair who didn't look like Jesus anymore. That was me. My hair was for the chop.

Taking inspiration from the aeronautical genius Clarence 'Kelly' Johnson, I decided to name the next album *Skunkworks* and also to develop a band of the same name. The record company were horrified. They'd hoped to trade on the Bruce Dickinson name with its Iron Maiden, traditional heavy-metal connotations. They wanted to worship the statue; I wanted to blow it up.

Thanks to our Sarajevo experience I thought the band had been blooded sufficiently to make a plan. I pulled out my favourite Soundgarden and Alice in Chains albums and made contact with legendary Seattle producer Jack Endino. I got back in touch with Storm Thorgerson.

'Storm, I want to do an album cover based around a Lockheed SR-71 Blackbird and the design philosophy of Kelly Johnson's Skunkworks.'

How could he possibly refuse? It was exactly the sort of project Storm loved.

Great Linford Manor is a rambling old farmhouse studio in Milton Keynes. We moved in, jammed and regressed to the seventies. Jack Endino is a wonderful man with an extraordinary manner. With a gait like a benevolent spider and an air of mad-professorial uncertainty, his eyebrows alone could keep a room in thrall. His voice was a low rumbling drawl, which meant the word 'pain' could extend for several minutes before disappearing over the horizon.

This was one coherent band, although the amount of ganja being smoked probably stretched the credibility of the word 'coherent'. All the musicians were several years younger than me, so I left them to it. They had more brain cells to lose than me.

Skunkworks was finally released to shock and horror. Not only had I cut my hair (shock-horror) but I had the temerity to vary the sound of my output even more than the last album.

I received hate mail in profuse quantities. I was quite pleased. I could never make a record to satisfy the bigots, so best we parted company and they could forget about me. In a sense *Skunkworks* was a version of what Bowie tried to do with Tin Machine. It didn't work for him and, ultimately, it wouldn't work for me either, but it set a lot of things straight and taught me in one year what I had forgotten during 10 years of Iron Maiden.

Skunkworks is an interesting record and I think it's a good one. Its one big Achilles heel is what Chinese medical practitioners would call 'lack of joy'. It is a dark, angry, sometimes magnificent but brooding album. It is one gigantic index finger elevated and pointed at the world.

We toured Latin America, which was chaotic but hugely uplifting, and we toured Europe, supporting traditional metal band Helloween, which was massively depressing. It was the wrong music for the wrong tour. I needed a free-thinking rock audience, not a conservative metal ghetto.

Edison and the Light Bulb Moment

Aviation and music had already started to coalesce in a sort of unstructured huddle, mainly because I enjoyed doing both, but also because the one – music – gave a purpose for the other. The very first incarnation of Iron Maiden's *Ed Force One*, for example, took place on the brief *Skunkworks* tour of clubs in the USA.

We rented an eight-seater Piper Navajo. She was a tired old girl, and if there weren't holes in the floor, maybe there should have been. Still, we rented the aircraft and packed ourselves and a few pieces of kit in the back. Everything else we needed, we hired at the destination. It was exactly the model for the Iron Maiden tour to come.

I don't know what the landing fee was for a 747 at JFK airport in 2017, but for a lowly Navajo back then it was 16 dollars. The small general-aviation terminal rolled out a red carpet, and then rolled it back up again once they caught sight of us.

'Do you have a limo?'

I shook my head. 'Do you have any luggage trolleys?'

He shook his head.

We found some supermarket trolleys in a small lot nearby. We stacked up our equipment and pushed it all the way round to the British Airways terminal, which was locked and deserted at 4.30 in the morning.

Pre-9/11 there were no cops, no pre-recorded announcements and no paranoia about bombs or terrorists or any such things. We were, of course, flying back in the cheap seats. That didn't matter. I sat on the kerb by my supermarket trolley as the sun came up. Concorde was parked, silent and gleaming, the dew twinkling on her white delta wings.

I cracked a bottle of Fuller's ESB and savoured the moment. There was Concorde; here was me. I was a pilot and a musician with a bottle of my favourite beer from a homeland far away. It doesn't get better than this, I thought.

Sadly, Skunkworks as a project petered out as the gulf between expectation and actuality became clear. An artistic crevasse had started to open as new material became available. Al Dickson, the guitarist, had a prodigious output. He was, and still is, one of the most talented musicians I have ever played with, bar none. Frankly, though, I was fed up of bouncing around from genre to genre, and visiting sub-genres. To make an analogy with a restaurant, at some point you need to have a style or signature dish. So far, I had managed a lot of starters, in a variety of styles, but that was no way to have people coming back for more. The band were going their own way, and I wasn't going with them. I decided to end the project. In fact, I almost decided to throw in the towel and stack shelves, become a pilot, try a bit of acting – anything except music, which was a pain in the arse.

Feeling sorry for myself is not my natural state, and I sat at home one night staring at the walls, pondering the life of a tube driver. The Metropolitan line seemed quite interesting: long trips, nice views, open countryside. The phone rang. It was 11.30 p.m.

It was Roy Z: 'Hi, dude. What are you up to? How's it going?'

'Oh, not much right now. I canned the whole Skunkworks thing.'

It's a shocking cliché, but people really do play music down a telephone and ask for an opinion.

'Hey dude, listen to this,' Roy said, and then he did exactly that.

It was the opening riff to what would become 'Accident of Birth', the title track of my fourth solo album, and it was an epiphany. After about a minute I had scribbled down some words.

Journey back to the dark side, back into the womb, back to where the spirits move like vapour from the tomb ...

'Roy, play it again.'

Welcome home, it's been too long, we've missed you. Welcome home, we've opened up the gates. Welcome home to an accident of birth.

I breathed out a long sigh of relief. Roy was busy playing me another track, equally as good: 'Roy, stop right there. I'll see you tomorrow.'

I spent a week in Los Angeles, out in the Valley in Roy's tiny demo studio at the back of his kitchen. I came back with over half an album almost completed, rough mixes, vocals and guitars over a drum machine, which was generic but very skilfully programmed by Roy.

The record company were ecstatic. They thought it was the finished product. I patiently explained that the actual album would have real drums, not ones from Legoland.

'What? They're not real drums?'

'No, and the rest of it is only knocked together. I've got to go out and finish it.'

So finish it we did, in a tiny studio in Burbank, California, which from the front resembled an empty shop front. It was a bit like the Del Floria's tailor shop, which was the secret entrance to the headquarters of U.N.C.L.E., or Maxwell Smart's phone booth.

In the alley round the back was the small office, stacks of books about aliens and Nikola Tesla, and a fish tank. The back door to the studio was always left ajar, and people just dropped by with presents of beer or Mexican food, and they all stayed to listen to what was going on. This was open house in Burbank.

And then there was the return of Adrian Smith. I had phoned him and asked if he wanted in on the album. He could do what he liked – solos, some writing, whatever he felt comfortable with.

In many respects *Accident of Birth* was the album Iron Maiden never made. The first song we did, called 'Wicker Man', was recorded as a B-side before it ever surfaced in Iron Maiden as a totally different song with the same name.

Maiden, meanwhile, had recruited Blaze Bayley, a thoroughly decent chap with a career so far built around his success in a band called Wolfsbane.

As I communed in the back of a converted shop, the full weight of the EMI and Maiden press machine commenced the carpet-bombing of the world's media. Blaze gave a somewhat wry-sounding interview, and I felt a huge degree of sympathy when he said that he felt like 'Dorothy in *The Wizard of Oz*, trying to find a way home'.

I knew that same feeling. Back in London I painted two house bricks yellow, gift-wrapped them and sent them to him, wishing him good luck. I'm not sure anyone quite understood the connection.

I made a point of not listening to the Maiden albums with Blaze. For one thing, it wasn't my band anymore, and for another it only begged the question, 'What do you think of Blaze?' which was a pointless exercise.

Accident of Birth was shaping up well. We had enough metal fans through the studio doors to know that we were heading in exactly the right direction.

With Adrian on board, I decided to go for broke and see if Derek Riggs, the original Maiden cover artist, was available. I always had a good relationship with Derek, even though his personality was somewhat mercurial and had caused the falling-out with Rod.

With memories of being skewered on a stick and spit-roasted at my Iron Maiden exit, I decided to have a bit of fun and create a character of my own. I had met some of the puppeteers from the TV show *Spitting Image*, and I would create a character, get Derek to do the artwork and then *Spitting Image* could build me a puppet that I could use on stage or in videos. Thus was born the spawn of Mr Punch, 'Edison'.

In line with the album title, Edison is bursting, *Alien*-style, out of the stomach of a suitably unimpressed gentleman. Mr Punch was updated for the nu-metal century. Metal teeth, bloodshot eyes and broken light bulbs instead of bells on his cap, because, well, who invented light bulbs? His traditional swizzle stick now looked like a baseball bat embedded with spikes.

I have always fancied a metal Punch and Judy show – as if I would ever have time.

The album went down well. The critics loved it, having been impressed with the integrity, if not necessarily the content of *Skunkworks*. It was as if I had done my penance in the wilderness, and my star was rising again.

Rod Smallwood was furious.

'It's fucking Eddie's son,' he frothed. 'It's taking the piss.'

'No, it's not!' I protested. 'Edison, he invented the light bulb. It's just a bright idea.'

I took the bright idea out on tour, this time with the Tribe of Gypsies as the band, plus Adrian Smith on guitar, minus the Latin percussion section.

We toured the US, Europe and Latin America. The latter was its usual frantic self, and we recorded a live album, despite some spectacular cock-ups. Our engineer, the wonderfully dry Stan Katayama, had carefully advanced all the equipment requirements and, being a devotee of detail, was satisfied.

When we got to Brazil, we discovered all was not as it should be.

'Ah, this is a different desk,' he noted.

'Yes. It is a better one. Brand-new Yamaha Digital,' said the smiling Brazilian.

'But I wanted the analogue desk.'

'Yes, but we changed it. This one is new!'

'Ah ...'

The manual for programming the desk was extensive, and Stan had four hours to figure out how it worked. He did it. We soundchecked and did the show. It was a great show. Stan came backstage, looking crestfallen.

'There was a problem ...' he began.

'Oh.'

'With the microphone inputs ...'

'Oh, which one?'

'All of them.'

'All of them?'

'Except bass drum. We have bass drum for the first five songs.'

'That's it?'

Stan nodded gravely. I had the distinct impression he might commit hara-kiri with a mic stand. He explained, 'Everything was okay before dinner. Then it happened. No sound. I cannot explain it.'

'What did you do?'

'I was very angry. But I knew not to shout at Brazilians. I have been told that if you do, they walk away. So I asked nicely.'

Admirable self-control, I thought. Luckily, we had another night to save our live recording.

In America I went to Addison, Texas, and rented a small Piper Seminole to keep my flying skills bubbling. I flew up to Minneapolis then down through Ohio, and finished in Raleigh,

North Carolina, doing gigs as I went. Most of it was solo instrument flying, and the night approach to Raleigh–Durham, was the first time I was on my own in weather that was genuinely 'on the deck' heavy fog.

I had taken off after finishing the previous show. I had towelled down, taken a big mug of coffee and packed the post-gig spare ribs in tin foil for a bite to eat when I arrived in Raleigh, three hours away.

It was a beautiful still night. The twin propellers hummed away outside my headset and the aircraft, which had no autopilot, was stable, enabling me to gaze at the stars and the crescent moon. The weather forecast was clear, but in the valleys as I approached the East Coast, I noticed white patches of ground mist and fog. In flying, anticipation is almost everything. I asked for an update on the airport. It was looking worse by the minute, with visibility dropping and cloud lowering. Out came the map and a torch, then a few bits of arithmetic to calculate where I would go if I didn't make it in at Raleigh, and then more checking up, to see if the weather was suitable at any of my alternatives. The fog wasn't forecast, which locals will tell you is common at certain times of the year.

In fact, Raleigh seemed to have its own weather system dumped on top of the airport. All around was gin clear, and I noted two small airports that were options if I couldn't see the runway at 200 feet above the ground.

I descended into the milky soup. The air was warm and moist, the props sounded muffled, the red flashing beacons on my tail diffracted and pulsed in the mist, pumping red light into the cockpit in a seductive lightshow. I felt as though I was back in the womb, and even the throbbing harmonic of the twin propellers sounded like a heartbeat.

This, I thought, is how people die.

The distractions were overwhelming, and all my concentration had to focus on the six instruments on the panel in front of me. They were reality and they were the only things keeping me alive as I tracked the instrument landing system, hand-flying the aircraft, my scan increasing in speed and intensity as the ground approached invisibly. Altitude, airspeed, vertical speed, left or right connection, altitude ... airspeed, altitude ... power ... checklist ...

Out of nowhere, I realised how tired I was. I pushed on through that barrier; I could not afford to be tired. I looked out the windscreen and back to the instruments: approaching 200 feet ... and suddenly a faint, white glow and then the blinding brutality of the strobing approach lights. The slate-grey runway, wet rubber – and I was down.

I sat for a few moments after exiting the runway and tried to figure out where I was on the airport. Taxiing to the small ramp, the airport was still quiet at 2.30 a.m. The lineman called a yellow cab for me as I took my spare ribs off to a motel. Locking up the aircraft, I heard the rumble of a big jet approaching. I was still close to the runway so I waited. The rumble turned into a roar, and I heard the beast go around and vanish into the fog. I figured I might actually be turning into a real pilot.

Brain Swap

Being a pilot was one thing, but writing and producing a movie was more problematical. Julian Doyle and I had been spending some quality drinking time together. After nearly 10 years of frustration, we decided to have a crack at raising some money and doing the Crowley film ourselves, which meant low budget, no frills. The early Python movies were done in exactly that way, and Julian was responsible for much of the filmmaking prowess that gave them a look that punched way above their financial weight.

The problem with a biography of Crowley was that he had no particular centre. Although a fascinating eccentric and narcissistic visionary, his life was a series of episodes. One of the biggest issues was his death, in 1947.

'We can't afford period,' Julian declared.

'Well, he did die in 1947. It's a bit difficult to avoid.'

'Well, we can't afford it.'

My two-fingered typing skills had produced by now over 800 pages of rewrites. I sighed.

We sat in silence and the light bulb switched on in my brain: 'Unless ... we bring him back?'

'Interesting.'

'Yep. Let's bring Crowley back into the present day and see what he makes of it all.'

'How do we do that?'

I thought back to a classic sci-fi B movie called *Donovan's Brain*.

'Brain-swap machine,' I declared.

'Huh?'

'Well, a device, a mechanism. Maybe a ceremony? Someone, somehow, thinks they have become Aleister Crowley.'

'Like a kind of alchemy?'

'A chemical wedding, as in Christian Rosenkreuz.'

Now we were both excited. Julian recommended that I watch a film by Jacques Tourneur starring Dana Andrews, *Night of the Demon*. It had a thinly veiled Aleister Crowley as the sinister magician.

My 800 pages went into the metaphorical dustbin and I started again. I only kept the first five pages, which took place close to the summit of K2. We had attracted quite a few potential investors with the opening scene of the movie.

'The mountain scene is great, but we can't afford locations,' Julian stated cheerfully.

I groaned inwardly, but somehow I had always known this would end up getting the chop.

'Why don't we flip the movie on its head? Let's start with Crowley's death,' I suggested.

So the new shape of the film slowly started to emerge. Before going anywhere near making it, I stole the rather excellent name of it for my new album. It was *The Chemical Wedding*.

Merck Mercuriadis, my day-to-day manager, gave me his thoughts on the next album: *Accident of Birth* had got me back on track; now it was time to go places.

Accident, though, was still rooted deeply in the traditional mould of metal. Metal itself had moved on, and I wanted to embrace it while still being true to my own direction and integrity. *The Chemical Wedding*, I thought, needed a theme as epic as some of the riffs flowing from the frets of Roy Z and Adrian

Smith's guitars. Enter the artwork and poetic world of William Blake.

I started to read the excellent biography of Blake by Peter Ackroyd. I think it is one of the best of his books, the other being *London: The Biography*. I got the feeling that Ackroyd was almost channelling the spirit of Blake to rise from the pages and speak directly to the reader. I certainly went to bed with the strangest dreams, and I started to wonder if I had in some way fallen under the spell of the difficult, curmudgeonly but otherworldly Blake. Now was the time to hurl myself into the cauldron of creation that was *The Chemical Wedding*.

Most of the album was heavily influenced by Blake – not just in a literal sense, but in a spiritual one. Blake was almost certainly an alchemist or member of a group relating to the occult or magical philosophy. At the same time, I was struck by his two characters 'Los' and 'Urizen'. Los (or Sol backwards) was creative and doomed forever to have his head buried in a bucket of fire, symbolising the torture of the endlessly creative soul. Urizen was the cold repository of logic, chained to a rock, dismal and brooding.

To me they seemed like characters in Blake's subconscious, acting out the drama in his soul, expressed as art and poetry. I had some inkling of what it felt like to love the creativity but be held back by the grim realities of the commercial and the fear of change. I could relate to Blake.

I rented a small apartment in Santa Monica and filled the walls with Blake prints. I thought I might drive myself slightly mad with designing the words to the album. I was stepping in and out of a drug-free dream state.

Back in the studio, Roy was busy brushing up on his mandolin playing. I had decided to rewrite Blake's poem 'Jerusalem' more as the pagan-alchemical verse I thought represented its true meaning, rather than the hymn. Blake, I think, would have been horrified at the jingoistic interpretation put on his anti-materialistic message.

I had already used tarot-card imagery in Maiden songs – in particular 'Revelations', with the Hanged Man – but working with Blake meant that the Fool, the Tower and the Lovers could all make appearances on *The Chemical Wedding*.

The cover art was a Blake painting, *The Ghost of a Flea*. The Blake Society gave permission for its use, and by the time the album was released the University of East Anglia's English department invited me to give a seminar about William Blake. Go figure.

I was delighted to accept, although I think the lecturer in charge thought I was slightly mad.

When the time came to take *The Chemical Wedding* on tour, I had a problem. Roy Z was not available. His health was sometimes fragile on tour; not only that, but the success of the record and its fantastic critical reception meant that his star as a record producer was on the rise.

There were not too many players around who would fit the bill as his replacement. We hatched a plan. Roy would find a friend and teach him how to play the tunes. So enter the slightly bizarre world of the 'Guru'.

Adrian's guitar contribution was his own unique style, but I needed a foil to his looping, shifting solos. In short, I needed Roy Z's identical twin guitar brother, but they were in short supply.

Roy's suggestion was to train someone and that someone was going to be a local LA musician called Richard Carrete.

At first I didn't think it would work. The first couple of rehearsals didn't click right off the bat, and I had the awful sinking feeling that my lifeboat didn't have any oars or a sail, for that matter. Panic is rarely a solution to anything, so quiet relaxation and patience were the key. Richard was probably so nervous it was a wonder he could function at all. Like many Americans he had never left the country; now he was being offered the chance to go on tour in Europe with one of his childhood idols.

I'm not sure how the name 'Guru' came about for Richard, but it's probably banter from one of the late evenings with too many Negro Modelos crippling our livers. Guru he became, though, complete with leather trench coat and *Easy Rider*-style sunglasses.

Guru had his fair share of misfortune. A dog had recently eaten his car, and his Japanese girlfriend had deserted him with the words, 'Your existence bother me.'

In the case of the car, the dog in question was a Molossus, a gigantic, dangerous dog that Guru had agreed to look after while a friend was away. The dog took a liking to his car, specifically the interior, which he destroyed and ate.

In the case of the girlfriend, Guru explained that he had rolled her up in a carpet. We sat around as he recounted the tale, staring into our beers.

'Why? Was it a sort of Genghis Khan-fetish thing?'

I never found out, but Guru settled down and we re-invaded Scandinavia and had a rather splendid time.

The Chemical Wedding album and tour cemented the pathway created by *Accident of Birth*, and suddenly I really did have a purpose, a meaning and a real career as a solo artist. I was aware that over in Maidenworld things were not quite so chirpy.

It was hard for the band to adjust to their dwindling audience, particularly in the USA. It was not as if I was benefiting from their discomfort, though; my fate was now securely in my own hands.

Bob Dylan knew which way the wind blew. There were only a few options open to Maiden, and one of them was to ask me to rejoin.

There was a part of me that was reluctant to throw in the towel on my solo career. I had come so far, and in the company of fine musicians and really decent human beings. I had learnt so much: about music, about songwriting, about singing and my voice itself. I would have learnt none of this had I stayed in the Maiden fold and ploughed a similar furrow with a trusty old tractor.

When the phone call eventually came, I watched with wry amusement the diplomatic tap dance go on behind the scenes before the big meeting between me and Steve Harris. This was all done with the customary paranoia about the media and the stipulation that we should not be seen speaking before the press release was drafted.

Before the meeting, indeed after the first phone call, I called in Roy and the band.

'They've asked me to rejoin Maiden. What do you think?' I asked.

'Dude, that's really cool. You have to do it.'

I was astonished. They were signing off, back to their day jobs, in effect – apart from perhaps Roy.

'Realistically I can't support a proper solo career and be in Maiden. I know the demands that will be made on my time. We will have to go our separate ways,' I said.

People who don't understand Iron Maiden won't comprehend the impact it has had on so many people's lives. Maiden has represented a personal affirmation of self-worth for millions of people down the years. Above and beyond pop music, fashion and the detritus and useless decadence of 'reality' celebrity, Maiden was hard work and tangible, substantive and complex, but also visceral and aggressive.

I watched the faces of my bandmates in the room. I think it was Eddie Casillas who spoke. Eddie was the carpenter who never formed a gang. Eddie had the safe house where no gang members fought. Eddie was a rock, and played bass like one.

'Dude, you have to go back. The world needs Iron Maiden.'

I would never have given myself the title of 'pocket Pied Piper', but it seemed that I was expected to lead a new Iron Maiden tribe into the next millennium.

I had some ideas stored up to throw into the mix. Not concrete plans, but, better than that, visions brought on by the last few years in the wilderness.

There is nothing like adversity to bring out the best in an individual, and I had gone through my own rebirth. Rejoining Maiden would be restarting the music of the spheres. If the universe had been frozen for a few years, I felt we could walk through the walls of ice and into a world of fire and passion.

I met Steve in a bar in Brighton, some anonymous location near a marina. The sort of place that neither of us would be seen dead in normally. Rod tiptoed around, waiting for any fireworks, and I found the whole process faintly amusing. Behind the sight of two blokes in their late forties chatting in a deserted bar lay the hopes of millions of fans.

Steve asked me why I wanted to come back. I said because I think that together we could do great things again.

'Fair enough,' he replied.

There was also the question about how to handle Adrian's rejoining, to which Steve replied, without hesitation, 'I always wanted three guitarists anyway.'

I knew that we could be so much more now than we could ever have been before. We'd stared into oblivion and one way or another determined that it was better to burn out and quit than fade away.

Rejoining Maiden lit the blue touch paper for an incendiary future, and I relished the challenge.

Feet Wet in the Goose

Rejoining Iron Maiden meant that any chance of an airline job was fading rapidly. There would, however, be a financial windfall from my return. So I decided to buy an aircraft. What was the point of having a wallet full of professional pilot licences on two continents if I was stuck on the ground?

Next door to the flight school at Justice Aviation in Santa Monica was a guy called Ken Krueger, who sold aircraft. I had my mind set on something with two engines and six seats, very similar to the aircraft I had flown in Europe during my flight training.

Sitting out on the ramp was a selection of Ken's aircraft for sale. One of them caught my eye. It was pretty big and looked very impressive – a Cessna 421 Golden Eagle. I had heard that their engines were a handful to operate and their reliability was questionable. In earshot was Duke Morton, an ex-Air America pilot, who had flown the plane.

'Nothing wrong with that aircraft. I flew her for years. Never crashed. She's a good ship.'

'What about the engines?'

'The rumours are a load of garbage. You just have to handle them correctly.'

The plane had belonged to Arnold Schwarzenegger's lawyer. He was selling it because he had purchased a King Air turboprop. I went to take a look. She was pressurised and went to 30,000 feet if you had the courage and didn't mind a nosebleed. Club seating and a toilet (well, a bucket) and she carried six people in the back and two upfront.

As with all things aviation, it was a learning curve. Figuring out how to handle the 421 with its relatively complex systems was stage one. Fortunately, I borrowed Joe Justice, head of the flight school, to babysit me on my first few flights, and then launched around the USA on an Iron Maiden tour.

Musically, without trying to sound blasé, rejoining Maiden was like slipping on your favourite pair of hiking boots. The groove was still there, worn in place by the years past. What was different, though, was the renewed sparkle and energy. The confidence I had as a result of my solo work and the growth in emotional range in my voice just added more firepower.

I fired up the aircraft, nicknamed the 'Bruce Goose'. The plan was to fly direct from California to Bangor, Maine, and pick up survival suits and life rafts, then up to Goose Bay, in Canada, before refuelling in Narsarsuaq, Greenland, and thence to Iceland, where we would have a snooze. Iron Maiden's security guy, Jim Silvia, was to be my companion on the flight. Jim was quite a character, having been a New York detective and having worked for the DEA and FBI. He was also a private pilot and quite fancied an adventure.

After Iceland, we'd fly to the tip of Scotland at Wick, then Luton, and on to Paris–Le Bourget, ready for tea and medals plus the continuation of the Iron Maiden tour. The maintenance, predictably, was late and overran by a week.

'She needs a flight test,' stated the engineer.

'Well, I'll fly to Bangor, and if I have to come back she's failed.'

He shrugged.

'Oh, and the autopilot doesn't work.'

'What?'

'Yeah, sorry. The new radios don't work with it, and it seems that the whole unit is not working at all now.'

'Oh well, I'll just take her as is and fix it in Europe.'

Bangor had 600 metres visibility in fog. The weather was on the deck. I flew the approach, landed manually, picked up the life rafts and we took off for Goose.

'Well, I guess the new nav kit works okay,' I commented as we topped the cloud layer into a glorious dawn up in northern Canada.

Some time around 10.30 a.m. we landed, refuelled, topped up with coffee and launched towards Greenland.

Hand-flying the aircraft across the Atlantic sounds daunting, but actually she was very stable and the handling was such that long stretches with no autopilot were not onerous.

Narsarsuaq is a notorious and historic airfield. At one end is a glacier surrounded by jagged mountains. During the Second World War and the Cold War it was a very important US base, known as Bluie West 1, and many a pilot lost his life on the terrain or ran out of fuel searching for the runway in low cloud or fog.

I was lucky, for the skies were clear and blue, and I climbed to 21,000 feet for the crossing, trimmed the aircraft so she was flying almost hands-free and marvelled at the miracle of GPS. I had a precise position, a moving map, an exact ground speed and estimated time of arrival at my fingertips.

Second World War aircraft would have been unpressurised and freezing cold, with a navigator hunched over his plotting charts, giving his best guess as to where they might just have been, and therefore where they might end up hours later.

The art of navigation inspired the Maiden song 'Ghost of the Navigator' on *Brave New World*.

We were just over halfway to Greenland when Jim returned to the cockpit.

'What's that red light?' he asked.

Most aircraft have a fire light in clear view, and a loud bell to draw your attention to it should you not notice burning-red coals assaulting your eyeballs. Because the Cessna was designed to a less rigorous standard, the engine fire light had no audible warning, and the previous owner had moved it to below the instrument panel by the pilot's right foot.

'Shit, how long has that been on?' I wondered aloud.

I looked at the left engine out of the window. There was no sign of fire, but that didn't mean there wasn't one under the cowling. The Cessna 421 had a history of turbo-charger exhaust fires and, in certain circumstances, it was possible for an uncontained fire to melt the fuel feed lines behind the engine firewall. This would lead to the burning fuel being ducted into the spar, which held the wings on, and the sight of a wing falling off a burning aircraft was not a pleasant movie playing in my head.

I checked the gauges, fuel flow and exhaust gas temperature – all normal.

'Jim, go down the back and see what's coming out of the back of the engine.'

Jim peered out through the passenger window: 'There's a load of black shit coming out.'

I shut the engine down.

The engine fire light stayed cherry red after the propeller stopped turning. The prop was feathered-edge on to the airstream to reduce drag. In the back of my mind was always the possibility that this was a spurious warning, especially after the aircraft was fresh out of the hands of the mechanics.

But there was still that light on, and I only had one fire extinguisher.

'Never a better time to fire this bottle, Jim.'

I slowed the aircraft up to increase the effectiveness of the extinguisher, and pressed the button to release the fire-suppressant.

The fire light went out.

Now I was really baffled. Maybe there really had been a fire? I waited for the wing to fall off. It didn't.

With only one engine, we slowly lost altitude for the next couple of hours, before stabilising at 7,000 feet. I put out a Mayday distress call, which was picked up by a kindly Aer Lingus pilot high above us, and relayed to the authorities. I never got to say thank you in person, so this small dedication will have to do.

The vast expanse of ocean suddenly became very vast indeed. Jim pointed at a fleet of ships in the distance.

'Ships,' Jim observed. 'We could always ditch next to a ship.'

Half an hour later, we realised that the ships were in fact icebergs.

The GPS guided us to the runway and, low on fuel, we landed in Greenland. Just as I was about to touch down, I noticed the engine fire light flicker momentarily. As I'd half-suspected, this was probably a spurious warning.

I shut down in the still, sunny chill of a Greenland early evening, and then decowled the left engine. Clearly there had not been a fire.

In the morning, frosty and bright, blue-purple-tinged mountains greeted me as I took a stroll. The beauty was marred by the sadness of the place. Up in the foothills were the remains of a US Military psychiatric hospital – just the foundations of the huts that comprised a substantial complex during the Cold War. It was a holding pool for soldiers who had cracked up under combat stress. They were hidden from view, in a way that we would now regard as shameful. They were deemed to be a threat to national morale, and so were hidden away in Greenland. Also hidden was an enormous munitions storage facility burrowed into the mountain that ran alongside the runway. The tiny private museum on site was, unfortunately, shut.

My own problems were partially solved by a grinning Greenland Air engineer.

'Ho, ho, ho ... FIRE. Ho, ho, ho ... FIRE.'

He fiddled under the engine cowl and the fire light lit up on his command.

'Very funny,' I grumbled 'What was it?'

'Loose wire.' He grinned. 'It's not loose anymore.'

Story of my life, I thought as I took off and pointed the plane at Paris. All of this transportation, of course, was in support of my comeback tour, a brisk reintroduction of yours truly to a delighted fanbase. The main event to come was the new album, which I suggested might be called *Brave New World*, after the Aldous Huxley novel. Steve had a house in Faro, Portugal, and we all decamped to holiday villas and apartments in a tourist colony to live together and write.

Faro in summer is lovely, but in winter it's damp and miserable. Janick and I shivered under piles of overcoats at night.

Golf was on the agenda, mainly because it was almost free, and also because other than drinking in the deserted local pub, life outside of songwriting was desperately boring.

Nicko is very good at golf. Nick Faldo took drumming lessons from him in the hope of winning the Ryder Cup (he lost). At the nearby driving range and putting green, I tried. Left-handed, right-handed, this iron, that iron – golf does not cause my pulse to race. I'm with Mark Twain on this one, a good walk spoilt. I did try, though, and I accept it is a very challenging and skilful sport. I used to caddy for my father when he played in Sheffield. Near-vertical slopes and gale-force winds, plus none of that namby-pamby electric invalid-carriage nonsense meant that being a caddy at least meant real pain and suffering. I only did it because I had wet dreams about the buck-toothed clubhouse barmaid until I got up close and realised that she really ought to take a lawnmower to her forearms.

Nicko was good enough to play on exalted turf, with exalted people. Martin Birch, for example, is, I believe, a fine golfer.

The course at Wentworth has a hidden horror thanks to the pair of them. Nicko often had a trouser problem on some courses, with his choice of decorative leg-covering frowned upon by the relevant committee. Usually trousers were available on loan for just such crises. I am not sure whether on this occasion Nicko was wearing his own or someone else's trousers, but his underpants were definitely his own.

Martin was addressing the ball, which is not to say he was writing a letter to it. Addressing the ball is a roundabout way of saying: 'I am looking at that blasted ball, and I am wondering how I am going to hit the wretched thing and not make a fool of myself.'

Martin raised his club to strike the ball, at which point Nicko broke wind with such violence and flapping of trouser material that it caused Mr Birch to send the ball to the wrong address.

In the middle of Wentworth's hallowed green, Nicko McBrain had pooed his pants.

'Fuck me, Mart. I think I've followed through.'

'Bury it,' Martin suggested.

'Let that be a lesson to you, Goldfinger,' as Sean Connery might have said. 'I can see why they call your manservant Odd Jobby.'

To Fly, To Swerve

We were energised as a band. I stuck my neck out with some comments about Metallica in the press. Lots of controversy resulted. Frankly, we needed to be outsiders again. Maiden had to be not just the comeback kid, but the unapologetic version. A touch of arrogance? Well, yes, actually. But I'll take a little bit of Muhammad Ali over sitting there like a happy dumpling any day of the week. It also meant that when you stood up and said 'I am the greatest' you had better deliver on the promise.

The return to Rock in Rio gave us that moment, and this time we were headlining.

I don't suppose you could describe 250,000 people as being more intimate than the 300,000-plus we played to in 1984, but it was certainly more organised.

The build-up was pressure, more pressure and expectation. There was a massive live TV audience and a one-chance live-recording opportunity. I had locked myself in my hotel room for two days in the dark, just resting and rehearsing in my mind.

When we hit the stage I felt like a greyhound being released from its trap. The heat and humidity were exhausting, but the adrenalin surge just kept coming – to the point that I thought either my heart would burst or my legs would fold under me. I ran and jumped and sang, and jumped again until nausea started to seize the pit of my stomach and then – it was over. Cold beers had no effect, I was so wired. It took four hours to begin to calm down.

Maiden had nailed it. *Brave New World* was not just an album title, it was now our very existence. 'The Wicker Man' had, of course, been the first single, but not the 'The Wicker Man' of my solo album. The stage set featured a replica of the burning Man from *The Wicker Man* movie.

At the climax of the show I was supposed to be dragged into the Wicker Man by vestal virgins in diaphanous drapes. In practice we used anybody from the catering girls to girlfriends, and most of the time they were covered by an old sheet.

I was lucky to survive intact in Norway. The female stagehands were somewhat robust and took their sacrificial duty rather too seriously. I emerged with bite marks and scratches, which looked like I'd had an argument with a barbed-wire fence.

Returning home, I used my time to sign up for a Multi Crew course – effectively a bridge into the world of airline flying. I spent two weeks at Heathrow in the classroom and 20 hours in a simulator, learning the basics of flying as part of a team. The flying I had done on the Cessna was terrific experience, but much of it was single pilot. Airliners and a single-pilot mentality don't mix. I learnt a lot; I liked being part of a team.

The Cessna now lived in Santa Monica. After the European section of the *Brave New World* tour had concluded, we'd returned to the States. I had flown it back across the Atlantic, this time via a more northerly route, to start the tour in Toronto. When I returned to California, a local doctor in Santa Monica bought a half share. I reasoned it would be cheaper to keep it there and, anyway, I was busy enough.

I still had one last solo album to deliver, so I combined a trip to Los Angeles to write with Roy with a mission to sell the last piece of the Cessna. The doctor was keen to overhaul the engines and get a new interior – virtually a new plane – and he wanted an autopilot, so I agreed to pay for one if he bought the aircraft.

When I arrived back in the UK a friend asked me to sit in on a simulator assessment he was undergoing. I would be the 'sandbag' – the dead weight acting as co-pilot and helping him operate the systems on the 737 simulator.

The guy in the back was the chief pilot of the airline. I was on best behaviour. I flew the flight test profile to give my buddy a rest.

'Where did you learn to fly like that?' the instructor asked. I explained that I had been flying around the USA, Europe and the Atlantic without an autopilot for a couple of years.

'You'll be giving me your CV next,' he joked.

'Funny you should ask ...' I pulled out the envelope.

We chatted a bit, and I was put in his in-tray as 'potential first officer'.

I got a part-time job doing sightseeing flights out of High Wycombe and I volunteered for a few charity days. At home one evening at the beginning of June 2000, the phone rang. It was the chief pilot from the simulator.

'What are you doing on Monday?' he asked. I got the impression from his tone that he was going to tell me. 'Boeing 757 course. 8 a.m. Monday start. Full-time. Can you do it?'

'Yes, absolutely. I can do it.'

I put the phone down. I had absolutely no idea how I was going to do it, but I would worry about that on Monday.

I duly turned up at British Airways Cranebank Flight Training centre, or Braincrank, as it was not so affectionately known. I was out of my comfort zone, a fish out of water. My life has been a continual succession of 'out of the frying pan, into the fire' moments. Deep down, I think I probably enjoy it. You are never so alive as when learning something new and overcoming adversity.

Up till now I had been in the luxurious world of the voluntary airline pilot or commercial pilot. Now I was in the 'take no prisoners' commercial world. As another pilot author has observed, the commercial type rating is like trying to drink from a fire hose.

My eventual employer would be British World Airlines – one of the UK's longest-lasting independent airlines. Their job was outsourcing. Other airlines needed spare capacity in the summer, enter BWA. Summers were therefore busy and winters desperate, because aeroplanes sat idle on the ground, but costs didn't have the decency to follow suit.

Their idea in acquiring a medium-haul 757 was to break this cycle and achieve year-round demand with an aircraft that could fly the Atlantic just as soon as operate a shuttle service an hour down the road.

Training pilots to fly their new machine was contracted out to British Airways and, in fact, I was earmarked to fly with British Airways as a co-pilot for 20 'sectors' to accelerate my 'line' training.

'Line' training is supervised flying with real passengers. It happens after ground exams have been passed about aircraft systems and performance, which takes three weeks of hard grind. Next is another 15 sessions in a simulator and a final check.

Not done yet: a week of security training, emergency equipment training, putting out fires training, jumping down slides, opening doors and, finally, bobbing around in a swimming pool in a life raft.

The Boeing 757 is a beautiful brute. Beautiful because of its elegant, swan-like nose. It sits high on its landing gear, looking almost like a bird of prey coming in to land. A brute because the benevolent madman who designed it put two engines in with 40,000 pounds of thrust each.

Think of it as half the power of a jumbo jet strapped on to a quarter of the weight. A lightweight 757 is climbing off the runway with a vertical speed of 60 miles an hour – in excess of 6,000-feet-per-minute ratio of climb.

My first empty take-off at Shannon Airport was overwhelming. The outside world is so much more real than the simulator. The plane was so light its take-off speed was very slow, and I felt more like I was in a lift than an airliner.

Base training completed, uniform obtained, hair cut short, and equipped with that most ludicrous item, a pilot's hat, I showed up for my first day at work with passengers.

On 28 July 2001 I flew from Heathrow to Frankfurt and back, and then Heathrow to Munich, where I night-stopped. There was only casualty. On only my second landing, at 200 feet going into London, the windscreen was suddenly full of this large white gull, coming directly at me. At the last moment it veered over the windscreen and there was a loud thump as it splattered on top of the cockpit.

'Was that a bird strike?' I muttered as we approached touchdown.

'Mmm,' was the response.

At Munich I waited, in uniform, by the bus stop for the crew bus to take me to the hotel. Out of the corner of my eye I spotted an Iron Maiden fan, and he spotted me. Bedecked from head to foot in badges, cut-off biker denim and Maiden shirt, he made a bee-line for me.

He stared at me and said, 'Excuse me ... but is this the bus stop for Munich?'

'Er, no. Next one up.'

He turned and walked away. He never knew – nobody knew, except me – that I was an airline pilot. Unbelievable.

Black September

Maiden world was in a state of relaxed hiatus. The dust had settled after my rejoining, and my Muhammad Ali 'We are the greatest'-style wind-ups in the press had, by and large, been grudgingly acknowledged. Nobody likes a clever dick, all of which goes with the territory of being lead singer.

The crucial statement as far as I was concerned was the one I had made regarding *Brave New World*. I declared our intention to deliver an album that would set us back on the path to an adventurous future, not a piece of nostalgia or thin pastiche of former glories. There were plenty of cynics who didn't believe me, and we proved them all wrong.

The summer and autumn of 2001 saw me hopping from Janick's house to Adrian's, and scribbling lyrics and melodies to what would end up being tracks on the new *Dance of Death* album. My interest in the occult had led to a trip to the ruined fortress of Montségur in France. Climbing to this castle in the clouds was jaw-dropping in itself, but wandering inside its quite small remaining walls led to my imagination running riot. *Game of Thrones* is nothing compared to the slaughter that took place in Montségur, and the extinction of Catharism that precipitated it.

While wandering through the countryside, Rennes-le-Château and the Arthurian forest of Brocéliande also got paid a visit. My experience with *Chemical Wedding* and my love affair with Blake all added resonance to my peripatetic adventures.

All of this I did in between my flying roster. It was astonishing to experience what might be termed a 'proper' job. Unlike music, airline work had strict rules governing how hard you could work, like the railways. When the flight was done and paperwork completed, the door was closed. People simply went home and relaxed. What a concept. I began to enjoy my new-found sloth. 'Sorry, I can't do that; I am on standby' became my excuse for turning down most things.

I was released from flying with British Airways after 16 flights, and joined British World Airlines. The headquarters were at Southend, but the aircraft was based at Stansted.

I started flying their one 757 and, in a small break, Iron Maiden asked me to go to New York to do some press. It was just a couple of days and an interview with MTV in the morning before my flight back to London later in the day. I never made the interview and I never made the flight, because that fateful day was 11 September 2001 – the day the skies stood still.

I had my 757 technical manual with me, good little student that I was, so as to make use of the long chunks of dead time waiting around. I sat with it on my lap on the roof of my hotel, where there was a small sundeck and indoor pool.

A little old lady emerged from the lift and quizzed the pool attendant: 'Have you heard anything about a plane crashing into the World Trade Center?'

I looked up. I thought to ask something but then didn't. Probably a light aircraft, I mused. There were plenty of small planes that criss-crossed the city, all with single engines. London didn't allow them unless they were Spitfires over Buckingham Palace for the Queen. It wasn't the first time that a plane had collided with a building in the city. In the 1940s the Empire State Building had an air-force bomber embedded in its upper storeys. I went back to my 757 manual.

More people emerged from the elevator, and now quite a crowd was outside on the sundeck, peering in the direction of Greenwich Village – the hotel was just south of Central Park.

'What sort of aircraft was it?' I asked one of them.

'An airliner.'

I put down my manual. Airliners don't just fly into tall buildings on clear September mornings. I went onto the sundeck. There was nothing to see. Then I heard the air-ripping sound of military jets: a pair of them, flying low. This, I thought, is not good, and maybe standing on a roof is not smart.

Down in my room, I turned on the TV. One tower was down, the other ablaze. My mobile rang. It was Merck Mercuriadis.

'Have you seen what's going on?' he asked.

I phoned down to reception: 'I'd like to extend my stay.'

Nobody in New York City was going anywhere soon.

The aftermath was like a slow, surreal dream. The awful carnage at Ground Zero contrasting with the calm and peaceful central New York; thousands of people simply walking around in the sunshine, interspersed with constant sirens. On 8th Avenue, I watched as fire trucks raced back to the scene. The firemen were entirely brown and grey with the toxic filth from the building. In the gutter lay a child's cuddly bear, covered in dust and resting in a pool of water that had leaked from the fire hoses on the truck. Its beaded eyes looked out as if to say, 'All of my innocence is now lost.'

The bars in New York were full. The TV news showed replay after replay, while every few minutes another 'suspect package' was discovered.

Next day, I wandered the streets and tried to give blood, but in vain. The queue was round the block, but sadly all the blood in the world couldn't bring the victims back. We were all sent away with bits of paper saying we would be contacted if needed.

The city was like a ghost town. An eerie pall of white smoke and fumes was creeping up from Ground Zero. The wind had changed, and the aerial dust and God knows what else it contained stung my lungs. 'Healthier inside' was my reaction.

New York was in lockdown, and the airport was in meltdown as normal activity slowly tried to assert itself; there were thousands of people camped in and around the terminals at JFK. It was like watching newsreel footage of the evacuation of Saigon, except this was twenty-first century America. After five days of being stranded I finally made it back.

The September 11 attacks changed everything. The world became paranoid, common sense went out the window and politicians eager to make gestures clashed with pilots who thought many of the security measures just window dressing. A classic was an early confrontation over the liquids policy. On one flight, the captain I was working with was incensed at having his bottle of water confiscated.

'If I want to make a mess,' he thundered, 'I have 34 tons of kerosene at 600 miles an hour to make a mess with.'

But it did him no good. I nearly came to grief with two tins of baked beans. Security pulled them out.

'What are these?'

The clue is in the label.

'There's liquid in there,' she challenged.

'Tomato sauce, yes,' I replied.

'Well, is there more than 100 mils?' she demanded.

Thankfully, a supervisor intervened. With an impish grin he inspected the cans.

'Ah,' he stated. 'These, you see, are Marks & Spencer baked beans.' He turned to my accuser. 'Not much liquid in Marks & Spencer beans – mostly beans.'

Best of all was Captain Clusterfuck. Not his real name – but close. Captain Clusterfuck had thought to take a jumbo-sized marzipan fruitcake through aircrew security at Gatwick. As the cake went through the X-ray machine, sirens erupted, red lights flashed and the X-ray machine operator turned pale. The fruitcake showed up as high explosive, and the problem was the marzipan. Gelignite smells like almonds.

The world changed for ever and one of the casualties was my first airline. British World went bust shortly before Christmas 2001. At least I was a fully qualified, line-trained Boeing 757 pilot. Not much use in a world where the aviation industry was on its knees. At least I wouldn't have to try to make excuses to my airline about working on a new Iron Maiden album now.

A Close Shave

It was decided that 2002 would be a year of rest and recuperation for the band. Maiden had been battered but had come through more intact than ever. As usual, my idea of rest and recuperation was to nibble away at a couple of new projects.

Back in the mists of time I have no clear recollection of who suggested the idea of a metal version of The Three Tenors. The idea was interesting. Managers and, in particular, agents were salivating at the prospect of selling out venues with me plus two other alleged legends warbling away. Nice idea, but the devil, as always, was in the detail.

I wanted Ronnie Dio from Black Sabbath and Rainbow and Rob Halford from Judas Priest alongside me, and I think probably everyone else on the planet would have done, too. Rod Smallwood was vehemently against Ronnie. I suspect it was because he didn't see eye to eye with Ronnie's manager, Wendy Dio. In any case, Rod suggested Geoff Tate, Queensrÿche's singer, to complete the triumvirate.

I went to LA to try to write an album with Roy Z for the project. Even with Geoff Tate on board, the album was difficult. I wanted any record to use all three voices to their strengths, but also to combine in unexpected ways. It was a tall order in a short timespan.

The song that Roy and I came up with was called 'Tyranny of Souls', and it borrowed from the three witches in *Macbeth*. Each witch corresponds to a voice, and I wrote the melody, the phrasing and lyric to reflect what I considered to be the essence of my fellow tenors. In the demo of the song I even did a little imitation of their styles to give them a clue as to the intentions of the project. 'Tyranny of Souls' was only one song. I would need several more if I was to make an album of material that did the three of us justice. I had a stage format and presentation that allied with the demo song, but it would take a lot more thought and design to keep an audience entertained for two hours. It wasn't simply a question of bolting vocal girders together to form the Sistine Chapel.

Pressure from management made me look long and hard at the idea. If there wasn't time to do it right, better not to do it at all, was my attitude.

A meeting with Geoff Tate sealed the fate of the project. We didn't see eye to eye about almost everything. I never wanted him in the first place. I always would have picked Ronnie Dio.

'Tyranny of Souls' was thus recycled as the title track on my new, and last, solo studio album, the rest of which didn't yet exist. I wouldn't be writing it for a while. I had just been headhunted for a start-up airline, out of the ashes of British World Airlines.

In mid-February I was moving the furniture into Richard Branson's old office building, from where he coordinated his balloon adventures. The desks and chairs were from a skip, including a very nice boardroom table that British Airways had declared substandard.

The airline was called Astraeus, and it rose, phoenix-like, from the ashes of British World Airlines and the remnants of Go, the BA subsidiary. It was the start of the best airline experience ever.

Even while Maiden world appeared to be snoozing to the eyes of outsiders, in reality it was always busy. Even when ticking over, Maiden is a huge responsibility to manage, and we had taken on the challenge of Clive Burr and his struggle with multiple sclerosis. In March 2002 we played the first of a series of benefit shows at Brixton Academy. Clive's chirpy irreverence was still intact, even as he struggled to find any kind of equilibrium with his condition. One day he would be walking around, the next he would be in a wheelchair. There was no clear pathway for the disease, except that it was ultimately incurable with present levels of technology.

Clive was a big Second World War history buff, and we chatted about aircraft and the fact that I was shortly about to start a course to learn to fly a 737.

May saw me down in Gatwick, huddled over a computer-based training programme that may well have been a pirated copy of Lufthansa software. The clue was in the awful jokes inserted every 40 minutes: 'So, now you know everything about ze 737 air-conditioning system – so you are a cool guy.'

The hoops to jump through were the same as with British Airways, so after groundschool, simulator and base training, I entered the on-the-job training, which was abbreviated on account of my experience as a first officer on a 757. I had quite an interesting experience on my first day at work.

It was Gatwick to Faro, a full flight with 148 passengers on a very old and beaten-up 737-300. After British World went bust, Astraeus had inherited their two rather long-in-the-tooth 737-300s. It was a glorious day and, from 150 miles out, Faro gave us a radar vector for a 12-mile visual final. Basically, the sky was ours. I descended, turned right towards the runway and started to slow down. I could see the threshold.

'Visual, disconnecting autopilot.'

The aural alarm of the autopilot being disconnected was silenced by a second push of the button. My eyes were firmly out of the window, judging the final approach visually.

'Flaps, one,' I commanded.

The captain's hand positioned the flap lever to one.

'Speed, one-ninety.'

The training captain rotated the speed knob to read 190. I reduced thrust.

'Flaps, five. Speed, one-eighty.'

I glanced down at the airspeed. She wasn't slowing down very much. Shit.

'Gear down. Flaps, 15. Speed, one-fifty.'

The racket of the gear dropping into the airflow sounded comforting, but we were 1,200 feet above the ground and still not slowing down.

'I'll give you a hand,' the training captain said, and he reached for the speedbrake and pulled it all the way out. The speedbrake is two barn doors on each wing that raise into the slipstream, destroying lift and increasing drag. We slowed down a bit, but not nearly enough.

At 800 feet the aircraft shuddered and the control wheel juddered violently as the stick shaker activated. We were on the point of stalling, and Mr Boeing wants you to know so he installed a system to rattle your nerves should you approach a stall. This is the stick shaker system, which does exactly that.

I glanced down. The flap lever was at 15, but the flap gauge told a different story. No flaps had deployed. No wonder we hadn't slowed down. I was looking out the window; the training captain was probably monitoring my flying. But the fact remained that we were on the point of stalling at 800 feet with 148 passengers.

'Going around,' I declared, but this was a rather different situation. I reverted, under stress, to the 757 and firewalled the throttles.

'Shit. Don't do that – the engines will melt!' said the training captain.

The 737 had no automatic protections like the 757. In any case, I started a very shallow left turn out towards the ocean as the speed increased. With the airspeed at a more sensible 210 knots we entered the hold offshore at 2,000 feet. We would have only 20 minutes to sort this out before fuel became critical. As it happened, all the efforts to get any flaps or slats to deploy were useless. After 10 minutes the only option was a landing with no flaps and no slats at Faro.

'I think you'd better do this one,' I said to the captain, before checking the performance tables to see if we would stop or go off the end of the runway.

We were within two or three miles per hour of the maximum tyre speed as we touched down at over 200 miles per hour. To Boeing's eternal credit, the 737 stopped with 150 feet to spare and we disgorged our passengers. We never found out how the problem arose. The local Portuguese engineers wanted to take the wing apart there and then. We decided to phone home, *E.T.*-style, and call our own engineers.

Their advice was blunt: 'Switch the aircraft off. Wait 15 minutes, then switch it back on again.'

So we did, and it worked. The Portuguese engineers went away grumpy.

That summer, I flew all over the place: Funchal, Innsbruck and Sharm El Sheikh, plus all the usual holiday spots – Greek islands, Alicante, Málaga and Palma de Mallorca.

I had such a torrid time on the 737 groundschool course that I offered to write a study guide for new pilots. Having written it, I was then co-opted into the training department and packed off to Amsterdam to run groundschool courses and debrief exams. I was supposed to be a wild and crazy drug-fuelled rock star, but here I was in a simulator teaching company-standard operating procedures. Go figure.

I really enjoyed it. I remembered how hard I'd found it on occasions when I first started training, and I was determined to encourage others not to give up when the going got tough, as it inevitably did at some point.

I was still fencing, but not with any degree of expectation of the success I'd had 10 years before. I was 43 years old and still in pretty good shape, but I was starting to pick up injuries – and they lasted longer. The foil is a mobile weapon, heavy on the legs. I was lucky that my legs were well-maintained by hurtling around on stage with Maiden. In the heat of competition, though, the springs became a bit creaky just that little bit sooner than the opposition's, to my intense annoyance and their benefit.

I flew 300 hours in the 737 during the summer and autumn of 2002. By now, Astraeus had added a pair of new-generation 737 aircraft to the fleet, and in the space of a year we had four aircraft.

Some of those aircraft were old, and equipment failures often meant that pilots had to actually hand-fly them. One day I turned up for work, where Gatwick to Athens and back was the mission, except the plane was broken and all its autopilots were not working. I expected to be back in my bed at home watching late-night TV around 1 a.m. In fact, that was the time I eventually took off. We hand-flew the aircraft to Athens and back overnight, finally landing at 9 a.m. I was so tired I could hardly see the white lines on the road driving home. I pulled over and slept for three hours. Character-building stuff.

By contrast, going on tour with Iron Maiden was like going on holiday. The looming Give Me Ed Till I'm Dead tour was a great escape to warm up the vocal pipes before the official *Dance of Death* album tour, which would spill into 2004.

The album, of course, was already in the can. We had recorded in the urban bohemia that was Notting Hill in West London. The studios, now called SARM West, had quite a history. Jimi Hendrix had lived in an apartment upstairs, and a huge sunken bath had been installed at the request of Bob Marley, who clearly enjoyed a good soak with his smoke. The whole album, for me, was not quite as good as *Brave New World*. It was as if we had a little creative hangover and were trying just that little bit too hard to top the previous effort.

The one exception, in my opinion, was Adrian's solo composition 'Paschendale'.

It was jaw-dropping lyrically, musically and emotionally. It gave us a set piece to recreate on stage. I set about doing that with barbed wire, dummy bodies and portable searchlights to rake the audience.

The cover was also controversial. A partially finished version was presented as a work in progress, but Steve loved it and was not to be shifted. Personally, I still find it embarrassing. We had such a tradition of extraordinary and iconic covers that I couldn't help feeling that maybe the artist should have had a little more say, seeing as the visual was his essential medium. The artist was so mortified that he withdrew his name from the album credits. I didn't blame him.

I was flying the pants off the 737 for Astraeus right up to the Give Me Ed Till I'm Dead tour. Looking back now at the schedule, it was gruelling and the pressure was on, because we were now headlining arenas at a minimum, with outdoor shows accounting for almost a quarter of the total gigs. The idea was to set up the *Dance of Death* album with what was essentially a greatest-hits tour.

The Give Me Ed Till I'm Dead tour was the not-so-subtle double entendre that lasted for over 50 shows and three months across two continents. Give Me Ed rolled straight into the *Dance of Death* tour, I resumed flying the 737 and put in another 100 hours in between the 40 European shows. All the 'heavy iron' flying was well and good, but I yearned for something more interesting and romantic. I bought a share in a German biplane, a Bücker Jungmann.

Dating back to before the Second World War, the Jungmann was a primary trainer for the Luftwaffe. It was open cockpit, fabric and wood, and operated from grass runways. Better still, it spun beautifully, and in the right hands (not mine) it was a graceful aerobatic aircraft. Not only that, but I swear that it improved my jet landings. It was a reconnection with the elements.

Dance of Death blitzed the world again in January 2004: Latin and North America, then Japan. We played the Universal Amphitheatre in Los Angeles for two nights. The crowd was surprisingly boisterous for such a plush venue, and I went flying, but not in the way I normally intended.

Trips, slips and falls are part of the risks associated with leaping around stages, juggling microphones and guitars. Over the years I have fallen over in front of thousands of people and usually got back up relatively unscathed. Janick was not so lucky at a show in Mannheim, Germany. He fell head first into a steel girder, tumbling several feet to the ground. I was horrified – I thought he was dead. His body lay at the foot of the stage, his limbs arranged unnaturally by his loss of consciousness, his head covered in blood. He was not moving, and I couldn't see if he was even breathing. It happened in a heartbeat – one slip and he was gone. It took Janick several weeks – months, in fact – to recover fully. My demise was equally sudden, and was indirectly attributable to Janick's birthday celebrations.

In the early days, birthdays were things to be celebrated, especially when we were not so old as to be candidates for radiocarbon dating, or counting tree rings. Celebrations normally ended up with paper plates of shaving foam being splattered over the hapless band member.

Latterly, we'd learnt that shaving foam tasted pretty disgusting and stung like hell, so we relented and used whipped cream instead. A couple of the excess whipped-cream-pie plates were placed on top of the catwalks at the rear of the stage, just adjacent to the front corner of Nicko's drum riser. The wood that comprised the floor of the catwalk was painted matt black. The cream soaked into the wooden boards and remained invisible, but it was slippery like an oil slick. I was in the habit of running up to the edge and making great drama of my emergency stop – except, on this occasion, I didn't stop. My head went from 12 feet above the stage to impact in a fraction of a second. It happened so fast that the band didn't notice; so fast, I was disappointed to discover, that my plummet wasn't even captured on video. Where was a handy bootlegger when you needed one?

Like most accidents, things go in slow motion until impact. After that it hurts. As I tried to slide to a stop, I went head first towards the drum kit.

Make a plan, I thought, protect ribs at all costs – tuck and roll. But I had a bass drum and a set of aluminium steps to fall over before I actually struck the stage itself. I stretched out my left arm, which was not holding the microphone. I would try to bounce off the bass drum then forward-roll onto the stage.

I had figured without the cymbal stands, and the gap between my little finger and ring finger caught on the spigot sticking out from a crash cymbal. It wrenched my left arm behind me, ripping my chest muscles and twisting my back so I went backwards into the kit. I was still holding the mic after I rolled and stood up. I carried on, but the pain was intense. The next night was the same, and then we all flew to Japan. I was a pathetic mess.

At the first show in Japan, my back gave way and I spent the next four weeks hobbling around – the first week of it with the aid of a stick.

I was supposed to return to LA to finish the vocals on the *Tyranny of Souls* album. Roy had sent me various backing tracks, and I wrote the lyrics while limping around the streets wearing headphones.

I duly arrived back in LA and set up a bed by the side of the microphone in Roy's home studio. I could manage about five minutes of singing before I had to have a lie down. I was not a happy bunny, but remarkably the album sounded amazing. It was released with little in the way of fanfare, but it has garnered a steady following over the years.

The Spruce Bruce

My aviating had led to an approach from a TV company who wanted to make a show for the Discovery Channel. The title was *Flying Heavy Metal*.

I had made music videos and was still busy juggling the script of *Chemical Wedding*, but TV documentaries were uncharted territory. Like everything else, it was a learning curve, and a steep but enjoyable one.

The initial idea was quite unstructured, and mainly based on the idea of me wandering around and flying planes. I am not a fan of celebrity-based shows. I wanted a proper structure and a story. The style of presentation could allude to the celebrity angle, but the content had to be rock solid underneath. Ricochet, the production company, wanted three months to film five half-hour episodes; I told them I could do it in a third of that time, including two weeks in the USA.

As a result, the schedule was pretty tight, with long shooting days, but the results were fantastic. There was always a degree of tension over the script, which was dumbed down and which I frequently ignored, rewriting it on the hoof.

Most of the best bits of the interviews I did never made it into the series, otherwise we would have been making 10 one-hour shows, and then we really would have been filming for three months.

Typical was the session where I flew the prototype Airbus A320. Because it was full of experimental equipment I could legally fly it with a test pilot on board. Consequently, I could do things that most Airbus pilots have only done in a simulator, tail sliding over the Pyrenees, engines at idle being just one of them. The Airbus has all kinds of protections built into its normal flight controls to prevent mishandling, and one is that the aircraft control system will not permit a bank angle in excess of 60 degrees.

The director had the camera pointed at me from the back, and GoPro cameras were capturing my face. He was wedged out of sight, lying on the flight-deck floor behind my seat.

'Can you say, "Sixty degrees and the Airbus says roll no more"?' he shouted as I rolled the aircraft on its side.

'Okay,' I replied, and said the line.

'Oh, just again – the sun was a bit weird on your face.'

The test pilot leaned over and whispered gently in my ear, 'Don't hold it at 60 for too long, old boy. The laws of physics still apply.'

Later, in the USA, I was due to fly the Boeing 727. The aircraft was an empty freighter. The director of the film was very clear: 'Now, listen. You're not insured to take off and land.'

'Okay.'

The captain jumped in the seat, and there was a flight engineer on board, which was a first. We started the engines and taxied into position on the runway, deserted in the middle of the Everglades.

'You're a 757 guy, huh?' the captain asked.

'Yep.'

'Helluva plane. Used to fly them myself.' He thought for a moment and then said, 'Standard Boeing calls and procedures – you have control.'

To my surprise, a hairy hand grasped the three thrust levers and pushed them forward to set take-off thrust. It was the flight engineer – and it was his job. The plane started to move;

my hands were on the control column, feet on the rudder pedals.

'What are you doing?' squealed the director.

'Taking off.'

'But you're not insured,' he panted.

'No, but I am,' grinned the captain as I pulled back on the controls and the sublime Boeing creation elegantly streaked into the warm Florida air.

Early 2005 saw the show air, and it was a great success, achieving surprisingly good ratings among female viewers, to the delight of the network.

I did one more show for TV, although I was offered most of the series if I wanted. Sky were producing a series of shows entitled *Inside* ... followed by the subject matter. One was *Inside Wayne Rooney*, for example. The producer had commissioned *Flying Heavy Metal* and had moved on from the Discovery Channel. We had lunch and discussed my involvement, all of which made me feel terribly grown up.

'I don't really have the time. I know how long these things take. Look, what's the most potty one you have?' I asked.

'*Inside Spontaneous Human Combustion*.'

'Brilliant. Completely bonkers. Can I do just that one?'

Documentaries are fun because they turn knowledge into entertainment, but I have turned down over 20 series since. I simply don't have the time.

What Could Possibly Go Wrong?

Summer of 2005 was a US tour followed by a brief festival tour of Europe. It was about seven weeks long in total, and afterwards the writing urge was stronger than ever. Steve and I were starting to converge, and I began to get the same sort of goosebumps I'd had before the *Seventh Son* album. If we just took our time on this occasion and didn't do everything in an unholy rush, the next album felt good.

We allowed ourselves plenty of time, and therefore used hardly any of it. In fact, it was difficult to keep up with the number of ideas coming thick and fast. The album was on the verge of becoming a double, but we held ourselves in check, lest we bit off a bit more than the audience could swallow.

It was clear that there was a theme running through the album. I had reprised a song from *Skunkworks*, 'Strange Death in Paradise', and repurposed the idea for Maiden with 'Brighter than a Thousand Suns'. The song was about the atom bomb and, of course, we were all children of the Cold War. The themes of war and conflict were plentiful on the record. I suggested the title *A Matter of Life and Death*, after the classic Powell and Pressburger epic, which is one of my all-time favourite films.

The title had the advantage of being not exclusively about war; it is, in fact, a love story, where love redeems all. It therefore could cover a multitude of song topics without being specific to any of them. It was, in a word, enigmatic.

The cover was anything but: skeletal-zombie mercenaries riding shotgun on a militarised-Eddie-stencilled main battle tank. We met with Rod.

'We want a tank on stage, and a fucking big gun.'

This was *Boy's Own* adventure stuff. Nuance went out the window. This was the apocalypse, end of story. We recorded in SARM in Notting Hill again, and took no prisoners. Large chunks of the album are first takes. When we listened back to it, we decided to play the whole thing live.

In many ways, that decision set in stone a process we had started with *Brave New World*. The world of media had become so shallow, so short term, that it had effectively disowned us. There was, therefore, no point in pandering to ancient history either, unless of course you wanted to write a song about Alexander the Great. Which, of course, we had.

To the outside world, it looked like madness to play a whole album of new material. To us, though, it was essential in order to lay down a marker with what was an increasingly young fan base. There were kids whose first Iron Maiden record was *Brave New World*, not *The Number of the Beast*. They were the future and they were the people to carry the torch for the band. It was for them that we played that album. It was a gamble, but we rolled the dice anyway.

Mainstream media and Maiden had always been unreliable bedfellows, and now we effectively kicked them into the long grass. Anything in the future would be on our terms, as the internet was becoming increasingly useful, a trend that has, by and large, continued.

The airline was now at nine aircraft and would shortly grow to 11, with five 757s, five 737s and an Airbus A320. Even as a small airline, we had over 500 employees, and there was always a need for captains. We had a lot of over-55, ex-British Airways guys, but the supply had dried up, and soon pilots would no longer retire at 55 but work, like everyone else, till 65. Most pilots wanted to, anyway.

Unlike the big behemoth airlines with hundreds of crew and Byzantine seniority rules, we were small and operated on a pragmatic promotion system based on demand and merit. As an experienced first officer, I had been assessed as suitable for command training, the first of several hoops to jump through before becoming a captain.

The bulk of my training came after our short A Matter of the Beast tour, and a good job too, because becoming a commander requires your full attention.

I flew to Hurghada in Egypt, Uralsk in Kazakhstan, Mykonos and various other points in between. The time rapidly approached for my check flight. All boxes ticked and all quizzes answered, I turned up to fly to the tricky little airfield of Calvi, in Corsica.

What could possibly go wrong?

Well, initially nothing. It was a sunny day and the winds were light. Calvi is a one-way-in, one-way-out airfield, on account of the bloody great mountain at the end of the runway. It's a captain-only landing, so I flew it on the basis that I would end up as a captain or not at the end of the day.

The landing was fine; we disgorged the passengers and I started on the flight paperwork. Then I noticed two official-looking chaps staring at me from outside the cockpit window. I wound it open.

'Ramp check,' one shouted.

A 'ramp check' is a sort of mini-inspection by the authorities – in this case the French DGAC – to ensure safe operational standards. I welcomed them aboard, made them a cup of coffee and they started pulling apart our documentation: flight plans, navigational logs – all standard stuff. And, of course, there were no problems.

'I just need to see your licence and medical.'

So I showed them. All in order.

'And the other pilot. Where is he?'

Well, the other pilot, my check pilot, had visited the toilets at the rear. I paid a visit. He cracked open the toilet door.

'They want to see your licence,' I said.

'I haven't got it,' he hissed.

'What?'

'It's in my other jacket, in Redhill.'

'Can't someone get hold of it?'

'No. I'm the only person with keys.'

'Shit.'

I went back to the cockpit. I made another coffee for them. Maybe I could persuade them to go away.

'Ah,' I said, 'we are just starting to board. Is there anything else you would like to see?'

'No,' they replied. 'Just the other pilot with his licence.'

'Ah.' I owned up to the problem.

They laughed. 'This is not the first time this has happened. Simply fax us a copy and you can be on your way.'

Before electronic records, our operations department kept copies of licence details in a filing cabinet. I phoned Gatwick.

'Oh, sorry,' they said. 'We don't have keys to the cabinet and it's a bank holiday weekend. The only person who has the keys is away.'

This was turning into a farce.

'Look. You'll have to break into the cabinet. I don't care how you do it.'

My check pilot finally appeared, suitably apologetic, but there was no moving the officials. We sat and waited. The aircraft was fuelled up and ready. I could sense the problems already arising with the passengers. I would have to say something over the PA.

The phone rang; it was operations: 'Okay, the fire brigade are coming.'

'What?'

'Yes. They have a big axe and they are going to chop the cabinet open.'

The image of Crawley Fire Brigade wreaking destruction in our small ops room to obtain a photocopy raised an internal chuckle.

An hour later, the document arrived and we finally took off for Gatwick. As we approached 41,000 feet the left-hand engine overheat light came on. We nursed it back to Gatwick at reduced power till it seemed to operate normally at lower altitudes.

Back at Gatwick, check passed, I pondered the day's experience.

'What could possibly go wrong?' Anything. And if it can, it will.

Bruce Air

It was 10 July 2007. I was a Boeing 757 captain. I would never have believed it possible when I sat in that tiny Cessna 152 in Kissimmee back in 1992. How the world turns.

The world was turning in the film department as well. Finally, we had a trickle of funding, and we had found our star in classical actor Simon Callow, who had wanted to play Crowley for years. A special-effects company contributed a sort of benefit in kind (but no cash), and we ended up with a budget of half a million pounds to make the feature. Along the way I had to make a presentation to a bunch of 'high net-worth' individuals about the movie, in the hope of raising cash. It was a thoroughly depressing experience. There was a banker with a convoluted tax scheme, pie charts, graphs and the phrase 'even if it tanks, you make money'.

Great. That really set the stage for my presentation on what the film was all about, and what artistic effect they could achieve for their money. For the most part, they fiddled with their phones or laptops, then left. Feeling grumpy, I spied one enthusiastic soul still drinking coffee and, shock horror, actually smiling.

'Hi. Are you going to put some money into the film?' I said.

'Oh no, certainly not,' he smiled back.

'Well, if it's not a rude question, why are you still here? The coffee is lousy.'

'Mmm. You see, I have a project I need to raise money for, and I heard about this tax scheme, so I thought I would tag along and try to copy it.'

This was the most interesting man I had met all day.

'What's your project?' I asked.

'Oh, I'm Roger Munk and I build airships.'

I had seen this man before. He was a visionary who had recreated the modern airship, before advocating, in a Discovery Channel documentary, a revolutionary hybrid vehicle – combining hovercraft, airship and aeroplane – that would travel point to point with large payloads for a fraction of the fuel cost and inconvenience of using airports then trucks or railways. I was enthused.

'Come up and see me sometime,' he said. He gave me his card. The address was the hangar at Cardington where the R101 airship had been built. I had the plastic kit when I lived in Worksop. Nothing in childhood is ever wasted. I would go to see him, but not yet.

First, I had my other crazy plan to attend to – a round-the-world tour in a 757 with the band, crew and equipment on board. The legendary *Ed Force One* was in preparation.

The basic idea for the whole scenario had already been rehearsed on the *Skunkworks* tour, but the justification of a tour costing millions required more than just the basis that 'this might be fun'. Although, frankly, in the spirit of rock 'n' roll, what more justification is needed?

Fundamentally, the case for *Ed Force One* depended on two strands coming together. First, we as a band had a requirement to tour all the odd and out-of-the-way places in the world. On the internet we were being hounded by thousands of fans who were demanding to see us. Second, we needed a big, cheap aeroplane.

Ed Force One worked out because of the vagaries of the aviation industry. Rock's peak touring time in the biggest southern-hemisphere markets is late summer, in other words February and March. This is exactly the northern-hemisphere winter period during which a European airline such as Astraeus would chew its arm off to have an aircraft on a two-month contract. There was a cheap deal to be done.

A perfect storm came together: an airline that needed to do a deal, a band that needed access to markets to satisfy its fans and an income versus expenditure that meant the price was right. After crunching the numbers, it made unexpected business sense. We only intended to go round the world once, but ended up doing it three times in rapid succession, such was the success of the concept. Like most things, the devil was in the detail.

The 757 had to be extensively modified, and the rear of it, where passengers normally sat, was turned into a cargo compartment. The airline had to negotiate various hurdles before the final form and shape of the structure was agreed. A bulkhead was installed between passengers and cargo – in fact, it was the old flight-deck door, obsolete since 9/11. In the cargo compartment a steel floor reinforcement was installed plus a cargo liner around the roof and side walls, which involved removing the rear toilets and galley.

To meet European regulations, smoke detectors monitored whether the drum kit might spontaneously combust and, even if it did, cameras were fitted so the flight deck could observe the event.

Last but by no means least, giant cuboid bags were constructed, which were designed to be fireproof, and these engulfed the equipment strapped to the reinforced-steel floor plates.

The fire testing of the bags was farcical. Petrol bombs were hurled inside them, and they were promptly extinguished due to lack of oxygen. After several more attempts to provoke disaster, the authorities gave up and issued a safety certificate.

After two hours of trying to set fire to the bags, the surface of them was barely warm to the touch.

We did have one exceptional problem, however. There was a severe lack of storage space on the aircraft for food and water. The enormous rear galley had been removed and was off-limits during flight. Nevertheless, the storage space was available, so we asked the Civil Aviation Authority the question: 'Can we use the rear galley space for stores?'

'No.'

'Why not?'

'Fire hazard.'

'What about storing water?'

'No.'

'Why not?'

'Fire hazard.'

There are some things that are just not worth arguing about.

The back story to *Ed Force One* actually began in Paris. When I was flying the 737 I came up with the idea of flying a bunch of Maiden fans to a show and back. Predictably, I called the concept 'Bruce Air'.

I chartered the aircraft myself, and put together a team to administer tickets, a rather splendid goody bag unique to the experience and a chaperone to supervise ground transportation and overnight hotels, if required. There were trips to Paris, Milan, Prague and Trondheim, to name but a few.

The Paris trip stands out – if only for having the most number of sick bags I have ever had to deal with on an aircraft.

When we took off from Le Bourget there was no realisation of just how serious the weather would be at Gatwick. A freak line of thunderstorms was moving swiftly towards the airport. The turbulence was excessive, and it was barely possible to read the flight instruments. The normal headwind at Gatwick had sheared to a 50-knot tailwind. A poor Flybe turboprop was on final approach when the controller told him the bad news. The pilot didn't seem so happy, but then again our passengers weren't delirious with joy either. The aircraft was battered at the storm's edge. I was weaving in and out of nasty red lumps showing on the radar screen.

A squall line of extremely violent storms had suddenly appeared from the south-west and, as we transited it, the cabin was tossed around like a log flume in an amusement park. The punters were not amused.

Gatwick was shut, and everything was grounded. Wind shear is a very hazardous weather phenomenon that can bring down airliners. It is a sudden and often powerful change of wind direction, so much so that the wings of an aircraft lose lift. A lone British Airways aircraft took off underneath us. He radioed to the tower: 'For your information, at 1,000 feet we had zero rate of climb, with full power.'

Normally, the rate of climb would be 2,000–3,000 feet per minute, with reduced power, so this indicated an extremely hazardous situation. We waited another 20 minutes for the storm to pass, and then landed. An array of passengers slumped off the plane, faces either white or green, having accounted for at least 25 very full sick bags.

'Bruce Air' as a mini-charter-excursion project continued for a while, until I broached the subject of *Ed Force One* with Rod. To my amazement he thought it was a very exciting idea. It tied in so many different strands. It was win-win both for the airline and Iron Maiden. And it was not just a way for me to keep flying; it was something that genuinely seemed to seize the imagination of the whole world.

On *Ed Force One* we carried three pilots at all times, which included me. This was not just for crew rest, but insurance against sickness. For good measure, all of our pilots were captains.

The very first stop was India, and we refuelled on the way to Mumbai at Baku in Azerbaijan. The only crisis thus far was running out of beer.

Mumbai was charming, and we stayed in an excellent hotel – so far, so good. From Mumbai we were to fly to Perth, with a refuel stop just west of Singapore. I was being rested – I had just done a show – so I checked in with everyone else. In a T-shirt and shorts, sitting in row one, I declined the glass of white wine in favour of coffee, white, one sugar.

Alan Haile, the captain for the day, was his usual chirpy self. I stuck my head in on the flight deck for five minutes then left them to it. Two hours into the flight, I got a tap on the shoulder from our senior cabin-crew member: 'Could you pop in the cockpit?'

It was not an anti-aircraft missile or an engine failure that might cause us to land prematurely. Captain Haile was looking anything but hearty. He was slowly turning grey. We went through his breakfast menu: he had been sunk by the Mumbai sausage. I stayed around.

At first he protested: 'No, no. I'm fine.'

I waited.

'Actually, I'm not fine,' and he jumped out of his seat and retired to the toilet – and then to the back of the aircraft. I didn't see him again for three days.

This is why we have three pilots, I thought as I strapped in.

It was a long night. We refuelled at Banda Aceh, and I had never seen so many ships in all my life as we flew over Singapore on the way in. Refuelling was protracted, as we argued about who would pay the bill (it was supposed to be prepaid), until someone found the fax under a pile of papers in a chaotic-looking office.

We landed at Perth just as the sun was rising on a glorious day. The Aussies had never seen a 757 before and had no towbar for it, so we parked up in the middle of nowhere.

Unloading was unique to this machine, as was loading it. We had to explain the routine to the ground handlers and emphasise the need to be careful not to wreck the main doors at the rear. Every piece of equipment had to fit through those doors, and a ham-fisted handler could easily damage the seals or door slides – which would have grounded the aircraft.

The sun was well up in the heavens by the time the plane was empty. The other captain and I had been abandoned. The transport had gone and everyone was asleep. Great. Luckily, the local customs officer was a cheery soul.

'Hey guys,' he said. 'I'll get them to open up the VIP suite for ya. At least we can shut the plane up.'

Ahh. Aussie hospitality at its best – or so I thought.

The VIP suite had some comfy sofas and a well-stocked bar. Frankly, we both deserved a beer. Thank you, Mr Victoria Bitter. As we sat back, dog-tired, and savoured our beer, what sounded like a character created by Barry Humphries boomed down the corridor: 'No spirits – only beer. And no bloody musicians!'

A very hostile-looking host of the VIP suite appeared at the door, eyes squinting at us. He peered closely at me – trainers, shorts, but I was wearing a hi-vis jacket.

'You. You're not a bloody musician, are you?'

'Me? Heavens, no. Both pilots.'

'Yeah, well, I bloody don't like 'em. I had that bloody Sting in here once. Some eco bollocks to do with the Prime Minister. Anyway, no bloody spirits.'

Welcome back to Australia.

We didn't so much romp around Australia as tour its extensive toilet facilities. The pernicious Indian bug laid low almost everyone in various stages of incapacitation. Steve has always had a sensitive tummy and suffered more than most of us, but the dressing room on occasion looked like a dysentery triage outpost.

The schedule was punishing on these tours. It had to be in order to justify the costs, but the results were outstanding. In essence, we were doing gigs with the same regularity as in

Europe, except that instead of London to Antwerp overnight, we were doing Tokyo to Los Angeles. Jet lag was extreme, and it troubled Adrian in particular. Because we were going the 'wrong' way round the world, we 'lost' time continually.

I planned it that way for two reasons. Firstly, we needed to be awake at 9 p.m. local time every night, with our bodies ready to jump around and perform. Going the 'right' way round the world means that by 9 p.m. your body is saying, 'It's two in the morning – go to sleep!'

The disadvantage of my plan was that opportunities for sightseeing and a social life were curtailed. It was impossible to go to bed until dawn, and hence you didn't wake up till 4 p.m. My attitude was that we were there to work and to perform at our peak. If we had to find a pub at 4 a.m. to socialise then so be it.

We were also, of course, flying with the prevailing winds behind us, which saved quite a bit of aircraft time and fuel.

Ed Force One was probably the most photographed plane in the world in 2008. Everywhere we went there were TV helicopters live on the national news, and if the US President himself had arrived, I don't think the reaction could have been greater.

As we landed back in Stansted, the plans for the continuation of the tour in 2009 were already underway.

Alchemy

The *Chemical Wedding* movie reared its head again. I met with the sales agents. They were a thoroughly disreputable bunch when it came to representing what the film was about.

They were attempting to piggyback everything on Iron Maiden, which was, of course, a non-starter. More than that, what really got my Goat of Mendes in a lather was their treatment of Lucy Cudden, our female lead. Lucy is a talented actress who worked extremely hard in the movie. The Hollywood salesmen proudly showed me the poster they were using to pitch the movie. It showed a Photoshopped *Game of Thrones*-style buxom warrior with a great mane of ringlets.

'Who is that? She's not in the movie.'

'Er ... no.'

'Well, why is she on this poster instead of the lead actress?'

'Well, er, the tits – the *breasts* – are just so much more prominent. And, well, that's the stuff that sells.'

While I struggled to avoid thumping this twerp, the movie was actually in the process of setting up. Bushey, north of London, was the location, and the crew set to in earnest. The movie opened on the day of Aleister Crowley's death, and the mortified Mr Crowley was played with admirable menace by John Shrapnel, a gravel-voiced stage actor.

Everything was cut to the bone. Exterior shots were expensive and kept to a minimum. Most of the shoot was done at a disused Masonic school, which already doubled for various locations in several TV series. I recognised it because we had shot a video there for 'Abduction', from *Tyranny of Souls*, when we availed ourselves of the autopsy set one evening. Julian Doyle directed that too.

I had two or three cameo moments in the film. In fact, most of the crew ended up in it at one stage or another. I played the dodgy landlord of Mr Crowley's flat, complete with comedy bad back. I discover him, dead, from an overdose of heroin. My only two words in the movie: 'He's dead.'

Take five, enter the room, kneel by the body, feel the pulse, check for breathing … at which point the corpse made a remarkable recovery: 'Fucking hell, get on with it or I really will be dead.'

Apart from me, the shoot was quick. Simon Callow was extraordinary. His preparation was word perfect, and every take was useable. When I hear about the professionalism of actors, Simon is a benchmark.

Once wrapped, we had to screen it and market it.

'Why don't we do the Cannes Film Festival?'

Every objection was made, including the lack of hotel rooms, hideously expensive flights and, of course, the fact that we weren't invited. All true. So far, so good, so what?

'Let's just rent a cinema in Cannes, fly down in the Iron Maiden plane with a bunch of journalists and cameras, and pretend that we have been invited.'

Which is exactly what happened. A day trip to Cannes, watch a movie, do a load of press, have our interviews on the promenade like movie stars, then fly home to bed. No hotels, no permission, and it all worked out cheaper than flying commercial.

Flying commercial was what I returned to in between the *Ed Force One* tours, interspersed with radio shows. I flew trips to Lourdes from Dublin, scheduled flights to Tel Aviv from Heathrow and, just to be even-handed, went to live in Jeddah,

Saudi Arabia, in order to service the annual Hajj, the pilgrimage to Mecca.

To spice up the mix further, Astraeus also became the national carrier of Ghana, so I flew the 757 on its daily trip to the capital, Accra.

Ghana is a terrific place: friendly, good food, but like many African countries, there are always small caveats. The government was not terribly disposed to paying on time. In response, the Iron Maiden aircraft was dispatched to Accra. No one would get on it. Eddie on the tail terrified the locals, who thought the aircraft had bad ju-ju. To make matters worse, passengers also refused to board the Virgin plane next door, on the grounds that the ju-ju might be contagious. The money turned up more rapidly, and we agreed to provide a more modestly decorated aeroplane in future.

The same problem was not true at RAF Brize Norton, where we had a 757 based permanently to transport troops. I made several trips to Akrotiri, Al Minhad and Thumrait. One in particular was memorable. We flew out to pick up the RAF regiment from Cyprus. They had been 'decompressing' for some days after a harrowing deployment in Afghanistan, where they had lost several personnel on the tour of duty. The padre insisted on visiting the cockpit and giving us all RAF service Bibles. I thumbed through it. It was exactly the same as the small volume carried by my godfather in the Second World War.

The passengers were, as always with the military, outstanding: quiet and unassuming, but always ready to take the piss at the drop of a hat. They were being returned to a world that could not possibly comprehend what they had been through.

Our destination was unusual. It was not Brize Norton, but the small runway at RAF Wittering, near Peterborough. In the middle of a grass field by the runway, there was a ski-jump developed for the Royal Navy. 'Home of the Harrier' said the caption on the side of the wooden structure.

Lining the side of the runway were all the kids and wives and partners of the personnel on board – probably the loved ones of those we did not bring back, too. Children held up homemade banners reading 'Daddy, you are always my hero'. I could hardly taxi the aircraft. Julie, my co-pilot, was looking the other way, out of the side window. Her eyes were welling up with tears, and so were mine. She was trying to hide it, but I had to avoid hitting anything, and I could barely see through the tears flooding my eyes and flowing down my cheeks. I applied the brakes, composed myself and wiped the liquid away.

'Clear left, clear on the right?' I asked.

Julie looked over at me and nodded. We said nothing, but we both knew how each other felt.

Bitter Experience

A new year, 2010, was beckoning, and a new album and, beyond that, a mammoth greatest-hits tour designated Maiden England, which would keep the band on the road until 2014.

Compass Point Studios in the Bahamas had been booked for early 2010 to record, and we wrote and rehearsed in a studio in Paris. Some of the material was ready to go, some was written in rehearsals. 'Coming Home' was specifically written about the headspace that pilots inhabit in their strange internal world. It was an attempt to touch the outside world with what is normally only an internal moment of reflection.

The Final Frontier was both a delicious wind-up (as in our last album) and a reference for Trekkies everywhere. Space was the theme for the cover, and the idea of comic-book-cover-style single artwork was my idea, but executed far better than I could have imagined.

I was never 100 per cent convinced about the space monster Eddie, but we did do a spectacular animated video. By and large, we were now avoiding being in videos if we could possibly manage it. The best thing about space monster Eddie was his evil eyes, and they were very scary indeed.

'El Dorado' was an attack on the banks and wheeler-dealers who had brought down the world economy, along with a side-swipe at the rest of us for being so naive as to believe their bullshit. We finally got a Grammy for that track, having been nominated in previous years.

Recording in the Bahamas was a little strange. It was not the place it had been in 1983. Most of the charm had been replaced by American concrete. In my hotel I could have been in Florida, Vegas or anywhere else in the USA for that matter. My favourite hangout was a daiquiri shack by the side of the road. I suspect that the sideline of the owners may have been related to the acrid weed smoke coming from the car park, along with the comings and goings of enterprising young ladies.

The daiquiris, though, were spectacular, and there was a splendid Bahamian soul-food stall next door. During recording of the album, the awful earthquake hit in Haiti and I ended up entertaining a crew from Astraeus in the daiquiri shack, which was unexpected. The Icelandic owner of the company had decreed that Iceland Express (his own brand) must send aid to Haiti, and thus a 737 full of supplies had been dispatched.

I rented a scooter and rode to and from Compass Point every day. The studio was run down and it was obvious that it was nearing the end of its life. The couple who ran it knew it too, and ours was the last album they made – quite literally *The Final Frontier*.

We had to bring in large amounts of equipment to record, and we ended up barely using any of the existing studio kit. The jack-plug patch bay on the desk, for example, was so badly corroded that it was barely usable. It was a sad but symbolic way of consigning the eighties to ancient history.

The album was mixed in Malibu, in producer Kevin Shirley's upstairs mixing suite, and that's where I did most of my vocals. It simply wasn't worth wasting time doing them in the Bahamas.

As 2010 turned in to 2011, it was the return of the 757, complete with *The Final Frontier* paint job. It was our longest and, we thought, our last gasp of a round-the-world aircraft tour. Jakarta, Seoul and Belém in Brazil were new destinations

– humid and toasty. Our opening show in Moscow was the polar opposite – and we nearly didn't make it at all.

The previous day I had flown the aircraft out of maintenance at Southend and into Stansted to be loaded up. On the way, we did an air-to-air photoshoot over the North Sea. The camera ship was a Jet Provost vintage military trainer, and it had severe difficulty keeping station with the airliner, even with us at minimum speed and our flaps deployed.

The next day, the aircraft developed a problem with its bleed air valve in one engine. Predictably, like loose wires in fire-detection systems and other gremlins, problems always arose when leaving maintenance. We only had a short time to fix the problem. We delayed the flight by over four hours. We even had a new piece of piping manufactured onsite, but it didn't fix the problem. Ian Day, our tour manager, told me that if there was no change, we would have to charter two aircraft, the cost of which would be borne by the airline. It was half a million pounds.

No pressure, then, as the captain in charge, representing both Maiden and the airline. One good reason for not being issued with a uniform hat is that there is no provision for wearing two at the same time.

After we dragged the aircraft out for the fourth engine test run, I called in the engineer: 'Take a long, hard look at that gauge.'

'Well, I think I see an improvement.'

'Sign the fucking tech log, then, and let's go, before the aeroplane changes its mind.'

Moscow was a blizzard, with thick ice on the runways. We flew from the winter fury and two-foot-long icicles into the tropical heat of Singapore with a sense of relief.

We thought we'd have a fuel stop and a short break in Bali. As we were going there, we arranged a gig. The venue was surrounded by cliffs, including a small one backstage. I decided to climb it 20 minutes before the show. I was about 15 feet up the vertical face when the rock started to crumble. Silly boy. The rock was porous and liable to turn to dust beneath your fingers.

I had two choices: fall off and try to cling to the wall, or just fall off away from the wall. Fifteen feet doesn't sound a lot, but believe me, falling down a cheese grater in a T-shirt and shorts is not an option. I pushed off the wall and, to my great surprise, hit the ground immediately.

I was sure I had broken my foot. I hobbled through the gig, and later, in Melbourne, I had my foot X-rayed. It appeared to be okay. To this day my right foot aches after shows. Oh, well. Do the crime, do the time.

The Final Frontier was reached back in Stansted on 19 April 2011. We had been gone nearly 11 weeks.

Jet lag was insufficient to stop the Maiden juggernaut recommencing a tour by truck and bus, starting 28 May and finishing up at the final *Final Frontier* shows at the O2 in London on 5 and 6 August – the day before my fifty-third birthday. It was a 35-date fourth leg of the tour and, frankly, I think we were all feeling a little fried at the end of it. Unlike the *Powerslave* tour, we acknowledged it to ourselves, and I had a particularly robust evening with Rod Smallwood.

There was no question, I said, of anyone walking away, but if we did not manage our bodies as we got older, our bodies might just do the walking on our behalf. Not only that, but we were having – and should be having – the time of our lives on tour. I had no intention of retiring unless I had to. I made the suggestion that 'little and often' was a better strategy than trying to reconquer the world every year. We would last longer and be more effective, and the world wouldn't get fed up of us being in its face every five minutes.

There was, of course, another greatest-hits tour planned, and we had almost an entire year to recover. I went back to flying, but not for much longer. The airline that I was employed by and which had borne Iron Maiden round the world on its silver wings was about to go bust.

The writing had been on the wall for some time. Astraeus had been losing money since day one. The Icelandic owner had insisted on using our aircraft at bargain-basement rates – good for his Icelandic travel company, bad for our profitability. To make matters worse, two-thirds of our fleet was sent to Iceland for the summer – except the Icelandic summer only lasts four months. The rest of our competitors were putting their fleets out on six-month contracts at market rates.

The winters were always a problem. Only two aircraft were needed in Iceland. The other nine cost half a million a month each to park up, unused.

It was a death sentence for over 500 employees at Astraeus, and the end of one of the best experiences of my life in working almost 10 years with the company.

There were plenty of other things to occupy my attention in 2012. The last of our three greatest-hits tours was commencing shortly, and it was one of my favourite eras, covering the *Seventh Son* album in all its epic glory.

We emerged into the Floridian sunlight to rehearse for our Maiden England tour, 100 dates starting with some of the biggest US and Canada shows we had done in ages.

Even on tour, aviation kept popping up in unexpected places. A visit to Boeing in Seattle meant meeting my namesake, Bruce Dickinson, the manager of the 747 and 767 projects. I flew the 787 simulator, and the instructor watched me fly a few landings before he asked, 'Would you like to see what she'll do?'

At eight miles out, with the autopilot engaged, full flaps and gear down, plus a 46-knot crosswind, we failed an engine. I sat back and watched as the autopilot adjusted and performed a perfect landing, stopping itself in the middle of the runway. He was right; it was impressive.

The chief test pilot for the 747 was seated in the back impassively.

'Well, go fly the 747-800 next,' he stated. 'Bear in mind, for this aeroplane, the pilot needs to show up,' he added dryly.

Little did I know that a few years later this experience would stand me in very good stead.

The US tour was a spectacular success. Our days of tour buses were long gone. We were chartering planes to take us around, and even starting to adopt American practices such as basing ourselves in one place and commuting to shows. It made sense and it made days off useable. In America it was so easy to accomplish. I chilled out as a passenger and discovered the joys of backseat driving.

We had several months' break between the end of the USA leg of the tour and the beginning of the European one. Tours were increasingly becoming summer affairs, as there would inevitably be an element of outdoor festivities involved at some point. None of us objected. We had done plenty of winter tours in the USA and Europe, and summer, late spring and early autumn seemed infinitely preferable to the snow and ice. Winter was for hibernation or making albums.

Even though *Ed Force One* was history, history itself had us in its gunsights. I couldn't believe it when Rod phoned me to tell me he had arranged for a Spitfire to open the show at Donington – as in a real Spitfire from the Battle of Britain Memorial Flight. The idea was that it would fly over the top of the stage moments before we started our own intro tape for 'Aces High'.

We had a helicopter on hand to film it. Our camera guy wasn't quite *au fait* with the language of air displays, so I did a bit of mediation. I spoke to the Spitfire pilot beforehand.

'What height are you cleared to?' I asked.

'Two hundred feet.'

'And what do you propose to do?'

'Well, come in low over the back of the stage, make one pass around the crowd and then exit back over the top of the stage.'

I was visualising it, and a large internal grin started to develop.

'I suppose,' I began, 'that there is always a possibility that, through optical illusion, the aircraft may seem to be much lower than that.'

'Yes, that's quite common.'

I'm saying nothing further save that the roadies hit the deck on the final pass. It was a heart-stopping moment, and Donington's collective jaw dropped. Grown men fought back tears. It was a Griffon-engine Spitfire, which has a distinctive growl, as opposed to the whistling howl of the supercharger on a Merlin engine. No one will ever forget that moment. It upstaged everything.

The Maiden England tour part two lasted the summer of 2013, and at the end we returned to the USA for a brief spell. After that came Latin America and the beginning of the last leg of the Maiden England tour. The pace of work and projects intensified as, like red London buses, you wait all day for one to come along, then 10 turn up at once.

For a year or so, I had been farmed out to do corporate speeches. At first I was deeply suspicious. My initial gig was to 200 travel agents at a conference in Malta. I had absolutely no idea what to do, and I rambled back and forth for 45 minutes and then shuffled off into a corner. There were a few more bookings until, one day, in Sweden, the light-bulb moment happened and IBM's global conference gave me a standing ovation.

Like music, speaking is a combination of content and performance. It's not a lecture; it's not telling jokes. Actually, it's another theatre of the mind, just without guitars and without Eddie. The whole speaking-circuit scene was a complete unknown to me, but it is a huge worldwide industry. I suppose that, as the world turns politically correct shades of beige, there will always be a demand for oddballs who scream for a living and fly airliners. The one thing I don't do, however, is talk to people after they have had their dinner. It's rude to give them indigestion.

Pilots, of course, are quite social creatures, and I met the head of training for Air Atlanta Icelandic, Arnor, a 747 operator, who was curious about the screaming airline pilot. Having a coffee, I popped a question: 'Your 747s. How many do you have?'

'Ooh, I think about 15 of them.'

'You wouldn't happen to have a spare?'

Arnor thought for a moment. 'I believe we do.'

'You don't fancy an Iron Maiden world tour, do you?'

The next red bus to come along had writing on the side of it. There was a proposal to develop a Maiden beer. The two big ale drinkers in the band were Nicko and me – but Nicko lived in Florida.

The harsh reality was that some hapless fool would have to drink sensibly and creatively to come up with what would become a beer called Trooper. It was a thankless task, but someone had to do it.

The world of brewing comes with its own pitfalls, and it turns out that some breweries seek the same high standards that we do. Before we could do anything, the brewer wanted to make sure I was serious.

I thought my auditioning days were over until my taste buds were placed in the firing line, when I met the prospective brewers, Robinsons of Stockport. I was put through a blind taste-test of 10 different brews, some of which I had name-checked as personal favourites, and the rest of which were their choices.

To my surprise I identified half a dozen of the beers. Without wasting any more time, Martyn Weeks, their master brewer, set about my nose with hop teas and my mouth with crunchy malt grains and, by the end of the afternoon, we had come to a bare-bones sketch of what our new liquid would be. One thing we agreed on was that the bottle experience should try to be as close to a cask experience as was possible. This meant a beer heavy on flavour yet low on carbonation and acidity. It was to be an everyman beer – something you could live with and return to over time, like an old friend. There are plenty of extreme beers in the marketplace, most of them short-lived. Robinsons and I wanted to create a classic, and I believe we did.

Martyn made two test brews, and the great day came up at the brewery. Two half-pint glasses, versions A and B, direct from the tank. It was the second version, by a country mile, that got the nod of approval. Trooper was born. As I write this, 18 million pints of the stuff have been drunk worldwide.

We were looking forward to the next album. To my delight we were going back to Guillaume Tell Studio in Paris, the scene of the *Brave New World* order. The summer tour of 2014 would set the band up in the right frame of mind for the new record.

In 1914 people said the war would all be over by Christmas. By 1917 aviation, born with the Wright brothers, had been advanced exponentially by the demands of warfare. At first as reconnaissance aircraft, and then as bombers and fighters, the modern air force was created. Of all the legendary pilots in that war, none was more infamous that the Red Baron, Manfred von Richthofen. Most of his victories were not scored in the red-painted Fokker Dr.I that he was killed in – probably by a bullet from the ground. His death, though, did cement the legend in aviation folklore of the fearsome Fokker triplane.

At the end of 2013 I bought one. I had talked myself out of the purchase on a regular basis: I didn't have time, where would I keep it, and any number of other excuses. The aircraft itself was for sale due to a personal tragedy. The builder of the full-sized replica was John Day. He was a master craftsman, and had also built a beautiful Nieuport 17 and a spectacular Fokker E.III. He flew the latter aircraft in a display team dedicated to recreating the sights and sounds of early air combat, the Great War Display Team.

When flying the Fokker Eindecker in a team practice in 2013 the aircraft crashed and John was killed. His widow put the triplane up for sale. After stalling for a month or so, I turned up on a freezing, rain-sodden winter's day at Popham airfield in Hampshire. The aircraft was in storage and the engine inhibited.

Slowly, Gordon Brander, the Display Team manager, and I pulled off the tarpaulin, and I almost gasped at the aircraft. Despite being a replica, every tiny detail was as real as could be. John had made no concession to modernity. Here was combat, red in tooth and claw. The triplane is a big machine. I mounted the cockpit. I say mounted because you get in and out of a triplane like a horse. The massive prop stood at the vertical, and in front of me, menacingly, were the two synchronised machine guns that made the triplane a deadly adversary in a dogfight.

A chill went up my spine. The aircraft was primal.

'I'll buy it.'

Once the weather improved we could ready the aircraft for a ferry flight to restore her to operational status. I had a home for her in the same hangar as the Bücker Jungmann, and also Gordon's own Sopwith triplane. Quite a cool hangar, it must be said.

To get me up to operational status as a display pilot would take some hard work, but there was a busy season in 2014 because of the commemoration of the start of the First World War. The team was much in demand.

I flew the Bücker Jungmann around to obtain my display licence. In effect, I was performing dummy runs with hedges and trees simulating crowd lines, with my instructor, Dan Griffiths, observing me from the front seat. There was an element of groundschool to pass, and a flight test.

Dan is a highly experienced test pilot. In fact, he was, for a while, the chief test pilot of the UK Civil Aviation Authority. Luckily, he also flew the Fokker triplane, so there was quite a chance of some knowledge transfer, but no chance of a dummy run on the aircraft itself.

The Fokker only has one seat. The first time you fly it is, well, the first and hopefully not the last time you land it. On 9 April 2014, according to my logbook, I became a triplane pilot. I made a couple of bunny hops down the runway with the wheels just leaving the ground and then back to a full stop. Old aircraft always operated into wind and, especially with a triplane, any crosswind is strictly verboten. A wooden skid on the tail and the lack of effective brakes ensured that the machine would always operate on grass.

Forward vision on the ground was virtually zero; the massive wings blotted out the horizon. It was like taxiing a combination of a venetian blind and a bookcase.

Simply starting the Fokker was hazardous. The massive wooden prop would kill you in an instant, and there was no starter fitted, other than a human being to swing the propeller. In the cockpit – by far the safest place to be – there was a complex ballet requiring four hands and both knees, plus a great deal of shouting.

Sometimes the aircraft would start almost spontaneously, especially from cold. On a hot day it could take 20 minutes of hard work, always conscious that a mistake could be fatal.

After my hops down the grass runway at White Waltham, I taxied back to the start. The wind was light, straight down the field. Gordon looked at me from the sidelines. I gave a shrug. Now or never, I thought. I put my thumbs up and pointed down the runway. Game on.

As I opened up to full throttle the tail rose in a few yards, and suddenly the world came into view between the camouflage and duck-egg blue of the wing fabric. My aircraft was not a red triplane; it was painted in the authentic colours of Lieutenant Johannes Janzen. He survived the war and, to my delight, Corgi made a metal model triplane, which is a replica of my replica, complete with the same paint job.

In the air the triplane was in its element. I can do no more than quote the Red Baron himself, when he was asked how it was to fly the Fokker: 'She can climb like a monkey and manoeuvre like the devil.'

My three landings that day in benign conditions were really quite reasonable. Beginner's luck. I already had a crazy idea of what the Great War Display Team could do for rock 'n' roll. Why not a dogfight at a festival to honour the combatants of the First World War?

Our final show at Knebworth was the obvious location, but first I had to join the team and learn the delicate art of chasing 100-year-old aircraft around at 50 feet above the ground without crashing.

Two days of team practice put me as Fokker One in the nine-aircraft display. I finished off the 15 minutes of simulated combat by chasing the Sopwith triplane up, down and along the crowd line until we performed a head-on pass; I hit the smoke button and spluttered off wounded, but returned as we flew a final fly-past salute.

None of this is supposed to be dangerous to the crowd, and very stringent rules exist to ensure that this is the case. While danger is minimised to the public during the course of the action, it is never far away for pilots when chasing each other close to the ground.

Far and away the greatest hazard is getting close up and personal with the tail of an aircraft, and flying into the disturbed air and propeller wash. The primitive flying controls and aerofoils used on the wings make for a double whammy. Not only will the aircraft suddenly and without warning drop a wingtip towards the ground, but the pilot has to be quick and use absolutely every flight control in whatever axis it takes to keep from turning into a smoking ruin.

At altitude it is merely uncomfortable, but being thrown on your side at 50 feet above the ground in front of 25,000 people at the Duxford air show certainly warrants your full attention.

To Ride the Storm

After the summer I wanted to clear the decks for what was to be a very important Iron Maiden album. Steve was unhappy about writing in a rehearsal studio. He had a point. Anyone could stand outside with a digital recorder and bootleg the album before we had even recorded it. Instead, we went direct to the recording studio and rehearsed, wrote and recorded in the same place. It was one of the best decisions we ever made.

I had broached the possibility of a jumbo jet for a world tour. Rod was jumping with excitement about it. The tour would start in February 2015. The album itself had so much going on that it quickly became a double album. Digital recording in my case meant trying to get my digits to play the piano. I had two aviation songs on the album: one was 'Death or Glory' – about the Red Baron and life and death on the front line in the air war – and the other was 'Empire of the Clouds', my two-fingered piano-based epic.

I sat at home with a very modest electric piano I had won in a charity raffle and started doodling, coming up with some small sequences and an atmospheric intro. The plan was to write a Great War aerial warfare epic, and a piano intro was the opener. 'Death or Glory', though, said it all in a much shorter span.

I have at home a few artefacts that I purchased at an auction of airship memorabilia. At the auction, anything German was going for ridiculous prices: crockery, bits of aluminium from crashed Zeppelins, all going for crazy money. What interested me was the British aviation heritage. Two items in particular I found fascinating. One was a pocket watch of one of the few survivors of the R101, the British airship that tragically crashed on its maiden voyage, killing most of those on board; the other was a tankard from the R101 – possibly a promotional item. It was a leather-embossed case with a pewter mug inside. Faded in the brown leather could be seen the airship itself, complete with its registration G-FAAW.

Around the rim of the pewter was inscribed: 'Welcome aboard from the airship crew'.

Late one night, after coming in from the pub, I sat playing the intro over and over. On my bookshelf I had several rare airship volumes; one of them, *To Ride the Storm*, is a classic analysis of the R101 accident.

I closed my eyes and, instead of seeing a row of First World War aircraft at dawn, with mist hanging in the trees and frost turning to dew on their air frames, I saw a great silver cigar hanging in the sky.

I could handle the pewter tankard and the watch. They were a tangible link back to the fateful day of the crash, and they drove me to the piano – a concert grand this time – in the studio, till long after the rest of the band had gone home. 'Empire of the Clouds' grew into the story of the R101, the greatest flying machine the world had ever seen, truly so big that the entire *Titanic* would have fitted inside.

It was a story of human error, hubris, compassion, heroism and sheer bad luck. The rest of the album was no less ambitious, and unless a song was obviously brief, we saw no reason to compromise on the grounds that people had short attention spans. Iron Maiden fans are quite used to engaging their brains.

By the time Kevin Shirley, our producer, arrived, we already had two or three songs ready to go, and the rest were works in progress. Once we got stuck into the business of tracking, we worked fast. Maiden is a curious mix of old-school playing – all of it for real – while using new technology simply to represent what we do naturally.

Basically, digital hard drives enabled us to capture every sound – good, bad or indifferent – that we played. Because of the internal geography of the studio, it was easy to cluster in a circle around the drums. The building's previous incarnation as a cinema from the thirties made for a drum room par excellence. The nooks and crannies in the walls contained guitar speakers, each in isolation. Each musician had his own headphone mix, controlled by a tiny personal mixing desk right by his side.

The whole monitor set-up belonged to Kevin, and it was the key to getting the results out of us.

On 6 October we started, ironically with 'The Great Unknown', and on 25 November we finally put 'Empire of the Clouds' to bed at the mixing stage.

On 12 December I was diagnosed with head and neck cancer and the world stopped dead in its tracks.

Fuck Cancer

Six weeks previously I had come to the same conclusion via self-diagnosis on the internet. I knew something was wrong in my body. I was sweating a bit at night – maybe it was the sheets in the hotel.

There were occasional flecks of blood when I cleaned my teeth – maybe I was brushing too hard.

I felt as if I was about to catch a cold, but I didn't – hey, it was November and there were lots of bugs going round.

Lastly, one of the glands in my neck was swollen – see excuse above – except there was an odd smell coming from the back of my throat, like rotten cheese. It was quite disgusting.

I plugged the symptoms into search engines and, given my age, came up with a diagnosis of squamous cell carcinoma, probably related to HPV infection. This I then ignored. I had an album to do, I was singing well and I was having a great time. The last thing we needed was a Google hypochondriac.

Nevertheless, the lump in my neck got bigger and my sweaty episodes were now sometimes in the daytime as well. As the last note rang out on the finished mixes of the album, I asked someone at the studio to call a doctor.

The French doctor was sharp, and even with his limited English his advice was clear: 'You must have a CT scan on your head and neck; you must have a chest X-ray; and here are some antibiotics in the unlikely event that it is an infection.'

I decided to do everything back in England.

My doctor in England felt the lump. 'Are you losing weight?' she asked.

'Ha, ha. I wish.'

'They all say that,' she replied grimly, and sent me downstairs for an ultrasound after taking an armful of blood for testing. The ultrasound guy probed around; his assistant was a bit of a Maiden fan.

'How are you with needles?' he asked. 'I want to poke your lump and take a few cells out.'

This was Monday 8 December. On Wednesday the blood results came back, all good, but I sensed – I *knew* – there was something else.

On Friday I had three missed calls from the doctor.

'You have squamous cells in your biopsy, which are cancerous.'

That evening, I was in front of the head and neck, and ear, nose and throat specialist. A year and a half previously, I'd had a full ENT check-up. I was right as rain.

It was a gigantic room on Harley Street with a huge desk – and a very eminent-looking doctor. She opened her folder.

'I have here a letter stating that you have head and neck cancer,' she stated bluntly. I was momentarily taken aback at the starkness of the approach. I decided to return service.

'Okay. So what is it? Where is it? Why is it? And how do we get rid of it?' I countered. I think she rather liked the approach.

'Well, you are taking it rather well.'

'I could roll around and chew the carpet if it makes you feel better, but let's get on with it.'

'Do you have any plans for the next few days?'

'As of now, my only plan is to get rid of this, and my only goal is to achieve it. If that doesn't work then I'll have to think of a new plan.'

Monday was an MRI scan of my head and neck with a dye that made the cancer visible and also made you want to pee yourself. Next was a chest X-ray, and after that a day in hospital under anaesthetic having my tongue and any other bits biopsied.

I was beginning to feel quite important, but in among the bravado was the temptation to despair. For three days or so, all I noticed were hospitals, churches and graveyards. By God, London was infested with the bloody things.

On the way to the pub, I considered how I felt about my cancer. Nobody could answer the question, 'Why me?' Actually, I reasoned, it's probably just shitty bad luck. Nobody was out to get me and my cancer was an aberration. I thought about hating it, but I'm not good at long-term hating – I'm a momentary, flash-in-the-pan sort of chap when it comes to anger. I would say life is too short to hate cancer; I would treat my cancer as an uninvited guest and politely but firmly dismiss it from my house.

The person to act as my personal cancer bouncer was the head of radio oncology at St Bartholomew's Hospital in London. I had scans on the Monday and by Friday 19 December I was in front of Dr Amen Sibtain. I had two tumours: one, 3.5 centimetres across – golf-ball size – was the primary, located in the base of my tongue; and the other, 2.5 centimetres across, was a secondary tumour in the lymph node adjacent to the primary.

The rotten smell from my throat was necrotic cancer cells draining from the lymph node. Nice.

Cancers are staged according to their size and spread. Stage 1 means the cancer is small and contained; stage 2 is slightly larger but hasn't spread; stage 3 has spread a bit; and stage 4 means the cancer has spread further through the body.

In addition, each tumour has unique characteristics, and cells are broadly grouped as: well differentiated, moderately differentiated and poorly differentiated. Translation: well stuck together – easier to kill; moderately stuck – might go a-wandering; poorly stuck together – aggressive mavericks on a mission to wreak havoc.

Typically, 80 per cent of this type of cancer was moderately differentiated, and mine was no different. From the moment Amen spoke, softly and gently, I believed I would be cured.

At first I felt sorry for Amen. What an awful task to tell people such bad news and sometimes watch them die. As we progressed through the treatment I realised that he relished his job, and I began to speculate a bit more about what drives oncologists.

'You're a bit like a cross between a sniper and Sherlock Holmes,' I suggested. He grinned. He was also a rock fan. Not till he cured me did he confess that it was Rush, not Iron Maiden, that floated his boat.

'Do you smoke?' he asked.

'No. Why? How much difference does that make?'

'I'm 20 per cent more likely to get rid of it, and it's 20 per cent less likely to come back.'

My treatment would start on 5 January. Before that was a trip to the dentist, as there was a chance I would have to have my teeth removed. Radiation and the lower jaw are not happy bedfellows. The bone is permanently affected, whereas the soft tissue can by and large heal itself over time.

The upshot was that if any of my teeth required work or were likely to have to be removed in the future, the procedure would take place immediately.

I could not begin radiation treatment until all the healing had taken place. My salivary glands were also liable to be put out of action by the radiation, though thanks to new technology it was possible that I would get most of the functionality back. Saliva is also, of course, extremely protective for teeth.

I had recently lost a molar in the middle of the tour. A root canal had cracked, and I spent two weeks in pain as the antibiotics slowly failed and extraction was the only option. Standing at the back was one solitary molar that looked like the rock at Masada.

'Were you considering an implant?' asked my dentist.

'Well, I had considered it. Why?'

'Well, we would have to do it and wait until it had healed before ...'

'You mean delay the treatment?'

'Yes.'

'If I don't have an implant will the teeth either side look like the Leaning Tower of Pisa?'

She laughed. 'No, it doesn't work like that.'

'In which case, let's get on with it and get stuck into the cancer.'

Back to see Amen, I asked a few more questions. Actually, a lot of questions. Like was it an HPV cancer?

'Well, let's wait for all the results.'

Given a green light by the oncology dentist, I went for another scan. This time I was strapped on a gurney and a thermoplastic head and neck mould was created, which would be my home for every radiation treatment.

The only tattoo I possess looks like a small biro spot on my sternum. The nurses made it so they could align my body to within fractions of a millimetre on the radiation machinery.

Amen was playing a video game with my 3-D head, shooting radiation pulses at different angles and intensities to kill the tumours, and also to irradiate any other sites that might have been subtly infiltrated.

He warned me that I would lose a lot of weight, and that I would be very tired towards the end of the treatment and my immune system would be fried.

'I could pop a feeding tube in before Christmas.'

'You mean cut a hole in me?'

'Yes. It's very simple. Most people can't feed themselves in the latter stages and it's very important you keep up nutrition.'

'You're not cutting a hole in me. I will feed myself. If I can't, I'll let you know and you can stick a tube up my nose.'

I was not going to turn into a hospital-bed dweller.

'How long before I recover?'

Amen gave a good think to that one.

'I had an RAF fighter pilot sitting where you are now, with exactly the same tumour. It was 12 months before he was fit, fat and healthy again.'

Twelve months? That was too long. I would be bored by then.

'I'll beat that,' I declared.

I'd barely considered the question of whether I would sing again, which surprised me. I realised that I loved life above all else, and if singing was the price to pay then so be it. Amen was acutely aware of my predicament.

'I have replanned your treatment twice now. There is a natural anatomical plane, which means I will miss your larynx with the radiation.'

Hit me with your best shot, as the song goes.

Of course, my whole existence was now digging up every scrap of information on radiation therapy, survival percentages and any alternative assistance that might help. The dental issue had freaked me out. I read up on hyperbaric oxygen therapy, which was possibly a way of mitigating the damage to the bone.

'You're worried about that tooth at the back, aren't you?' He smiled.

I nodded.

'Well, don't worry. I have bent the radiation beam around it to avoid damage.'

Dr Amen Sibtain – magician.

Christmas was coming. I was determined to eat and drink like a pig and put on as much weight as I could before 5 January, when I would start chemotherapy and radiation simultaneously for nine weeks.

I had to get my house in order because I wanted to come out the other side fighting. My aviation medicals in the UK and USA would be suspended as soon as I started treatment, and getting them back would be tough. Nevertheless, while I still had a medical, I renewed my 737 and 757 licences in the simulator on 3 and 4 January.

The Iron Maiden tour was to be postponed, and Rod wanted to tell the world that I had cancer after New Year.

'You don't want this to get out there uncontrolled. Someone is sure to recognise you going into treatment. Better to announce and control it. Also, we have to tell the promoters something.'

Fortunately the tour was largely arranged but not yet announced.

'Tell them the reasons are too tumorous to mention,' I muttered darkly. 'Can we at least wait until I have finished my treatment?'

Reluctantly, he agreed.

Fighting cancer is a lonely business. I don't mean this in a maudlin sense, but it is such an intensely personal condition that it's hard for others to get close. The only people who can fight the tumour are you and the doctors and nurses supporting you.

The more research I did, the more I was convinced that any edge you could obtain was worth it to win the battle. I explored anti-tumour alternatives, and both grape-seed extract and a shiitake mushroom extract called AHCC showed promise in clinical trials. AHCC had also cleared HPV infections in six out of 12 women in a University of Texas study.

My chemotherapy drug was cisplatin, one of the first chemotherapy drugs. It shrinks tumours but is highly toxic to the rest of the body. I downloaded the government toxicology report. It contained the wonderfully obscure phrase 'the method by which this is demonstrated has not yet been fully elucidated'.

In other words, no one yet knows why this drug works, but it does. The 'platin' bit of cisplatin refers to platinum, which I was shovelling into my cells. I had plenty of platinum albums and now I was turning into one.

I sat in hospital for six hours on a drip that squirted several litres of special saline into me, then had a bag of drugs to stop me throwing up and then the cisplatin itself. I felt high as a kite.

'Nurse, what's in that bag?'

'Anti-sickness drugs.'

'Any steroids?'

'Oh, yes. Lots of steroids.'

The steroids were there to stop my kidneys going into shock when the platinum albums arrived, and I didn't go home until I was pissing out platinum like a racehorse.

The first week of treatment was like the phoney war in the Second World War. Nothing much happened except I lost my sense of taste, a side-effect that I had been warned about. Hair loss was a similar possibility and, in protest at having cancer, I grew a bushy, nasty-looking beard.

Cisplatin can be toxic to hearing and also to mental functioning – so called 'chemo brain'. I found a University of Toronto study experimenting with aspirin to alleviate the side-effects. In the UK the University of Southampton was continuing the trials. I discovered the dosages and self-medicated.

My chance of survival at diagnosis was, I learnt, 60 per cent. I wasn't terribly happy about it, but it was 10 per cent better than 50/50. If, however, my tumour was associated with the human papillomavirus (HPV), my chance of survival leapt to 70 per cent, or possibly as much as 90 per cent as a fit non-smoker.

My Christmas present was a phone call from Doctor Sibtain on Christmas Eve. I was in the supermarket.

'Good news about the bad news. It is a p16 tumour, which puts you in a whole different percentage for recovery.'

It was the best Christmas present short of being told it was all a terrible mistake.

Getting rid of cancer became a job like any other. Monday to Friday, at 11 a.m., I turned up at the hospital, and half an hour later I was on the street with two grays of radiation glowering away at my insides.

The routine was the same: turn up, say hello, take a gown, lie on the gurney, strapped down tight, barely able to breathe. The giant machine resembled a lathe that circled my head. Lying still, unable to move, an internal snapshot of where I was the previous day compared to where I was today. The metre-thick concrete doors slid shut. The noises made by the machine became familiar. When the beam was switched on, there were three pulses and I counted the seconds, 45, 45 then 30.

I was being bombarded by X-ray energy created by accelerating photons to the required speed. There was no radioactive substance in the machine. The beam was thus able to modulate the intensity of the radiation to different tissue around my head by varying the power to the photons.

Not only that, but the beam could change its shape because of a device called a collimator. Think of two sets of venetian blinds at 90 degrees to each other, which can open and shut independently. The tiny slats were less than the thickness of a pencil lead.

It was thus possible to deliver large doses to the tumours while shielding surrounding tissue, and smaller doses to other lymph nodes, all in the same 360-degree pattern.

I was receiving IMRT – intensity-modulated radiation therapy – and it was cutting-edge stuff. The nurse in charge of me,

Mandy, told me to buy an electric razor and gave me a tub of cream for my neck. As the treatment progressed, the creams became different and the redness and radiation burns more evident.

At first I didn't need painkillers, but gradually the radiation stripped my tongue of its mucous lining and my immune system fell on its face. Oral thrush appeared, a common infection, and the painkillers got stronger, until finally I was on oral morphine for the last 10 days or so.

Sleeping, eating, drinking and talking became very difficult. The pain from all the nerves in my tongue being exposed was intense. My throat was swollen. I devised a system to get to sleep for a couple of hours. I raided every local chemist for their oral topical anaesthetics and soaked kitchen roll in them and wrapped my rear teeth in the paper towel. My tongue stayed numb for just long enough to get to sleep. Bliss.

After the first two weeks, I was still pretending there was nothing wrong with me, and I would go to the pub, even though everything tasted like water. One day, my chest started to itch. I looked down.

It's the bloody cat, I'd thought. But no, the hairs were too short. It was me. My beard was falling out. There is no protocol for having your face fall off in front of your drinking companions.

I went to the loo and plucked the underside of my chin. The hair simply fell off. I got as far as looking like James Mason playing Captain Nemo in *20,000 Leagues Under the Sea*, and went back to the bar.

The next day, I went and had my radiation. Eating was still possible, so I went to a café and ordered breakfast. Scrambled eggs and smoked salmon. I could smell it, but I might as well have been eating frogspawn – it tasted of nothing.

Absentmindedly, I scratched my cheek. The opposite table regarded me with a look of horror. I looked down at my scrambled eggs; it was not black pepper, but beard bits that were tumbling from my face.

Back home, I adjusted further. Okay, not James Mason. I plucked out a nice d'Artagnan number.

Next day, that too fell out. I was left with a rather scratchy moustache and some rogue sideburns. In protest, I kept the moustache. Everyone I knew hated it, which made me more determined to keep it. I had cancer – what's your excuse?

Gradually, the side-effects built up. A mouth ulcer at first, skin breaking out and weight loss. As it became difficult to feed myself, I was ever-grateful for being a singer. One of the first things that has to be in control is the tongue, and I could therefore flatten it, open my gullet and take a huge gulp of whatever I could manage before the pain kicked in.

By the last three weeks of treatment I was on liquids only, and could not speak, simply because moving my tongue was agony.

Custard saved my life. I mixed a pint of full-fat custard from the fridge with a medical milkshake, and could manage to get it down in three or four big gulps. The whole process still took almost 40 minutes, with the odd bestial noises in lieu of being able to scream 'fucking hell, that hurts'.

At the beginning of treatment I had done 50 press-ups every day, plus long walks round Regent's Park after radiation. I had books to read through, and I would sit on the steps of Marylebone Church where there was an outdoor coffee stand. I could smell it, but no taste.

Over the years my lack of taste in matters like clothing and, in particular, trousers has never bothered me. Lack of taste with food bothered me more than I expected. Biscuits tasted like sand, chocolate like plasticine. Only aromatic foods gave any hint of flavour, and that was just because of the smell.

Slowly, my energy levels dropped. One day, I went to the supermarket, only a few hundred yards. I shuffled around and got halfway back to the house before I realised I could go no further. This was beyond exhausted. It was as if every cell in the marrow of my bones was saying, 'Lie down, right now. Give up.'

I sat on a low brick wall for a few minutes to recover. This was fatigue. I thought I had been tired in my life, but actually I'd not even been close.

Early on in treatment I planned my TV schedule – I would be watching a lot of it. Daytime TV was full of cheery adverts for cancer charities, complete with suffering victims asking for contributions. If that didn't cheer me up, there was a string of life-insurance ads, plus several offering help with funeral costs.

I had calibrated my treatment and recovery to a repeat of the classic TV series *The Avengers*. At 8 p.m. every night, after a repeat of *M*A*S*H*, all of the Diana Rigg episodes were being shown, Monday to Friday.

My thirty-third and last radiation session was on 18 February. My last three-week chemo cycle was beginning on 16 February. The radiation would actually peak in my system 10 days after the last administration of it, and would then continue to work for at least two to three months afterwards, but at a declining rate.

So my peak radiation effect and peak chemo would be on 28 February. I calculated that this would be the episode when Diana Rigg handed over to Linda Thorson. On that day I would cease to watch *The Avengers* and I would restart the process of normality, even if I had to pretend.

Oral morphine was a terrific disappointment. I was at least expecting pink elephants or literary inspiration – even a desire to cut off my ear and paint scary pictures of daffodils. No such luck. It made you drowsy, didn't seem to kill that much of the pain and, worst of all, removed the ability to have a poo.

A liquid diet of custard and milkshakes didn't help, although I emptied sachets of oatmeal into the milk in an attempt to keep at least something regular. The anti-sickness meds plus morphine put paid to any hope of normal operation.

To add to my meds, I now had a delightful substance called Movicol. I regarded it with suspicion. I was on various anti-emetic pills, occasional steroids, oral morphine plus a most-impressive substance that created a lizard-like second skin around my neck to prevent the real skin splitting open. In addition I had a bag full of antibiotics and had to take my temperature constantly in case I should spontaneously combust.

I had lost over 20 pounds (nine kilos) in weight and my head felt like it was on fire. Seeing as I had received the equivalent of 11 lethal full-body radiation doses spread over 45 days – all of it in my head and neck region – it was not surprising.

My body was eating itself. The damage to my cells put the repair teams and my metabolism in hyperdrive. The damage to the tumour was, hopefully, permanent.

None of this helped my tummy troubles. In Monty Python's *Life of Brian*, there is a girl named Incontinentia Buttocks. Chance would have been a fine thing.

My insomnia was ongoing. Two hours' sleep, plus the pain of the tongue, and I was downstairs. The awful snoring that resulted from the treatment meant that staying up all night also did the rest of the world a favour.

On TV was World Cup cricket. It was not going well for England. This, I thought, was the symbolic moment to take a shit, in concert with our batsmen. I read the instructions, mixed up a couple of sachets in water of the dreaded Movicol, drank it and waited. Nothing moved; not even the England spinners could get any movement out of me. I read further into the instructions. It had been 10 days since I had moved even a rabbit dropping: 'If this does not work, it may be caused by faecal impaction.'

Well, I didn't like the sound of that. It sounded like a Hollywood film intro about an asteroid: 'Faecal impact ...'

The thought of an asteroid coming out of my bum filled me with trepidation.

I reached for Wikipedia. I typed 'faecal impaction'. There in all its horrific glory was the awful truth. My poo had turned to concrete, and in letters that should have been brightly illuminated in red, it gave the worrying caution 'in some cases it may be necessary to manually manipulate the stool'.

I realised we were not talking about the three-legged variety. I had overdosed on Movicol and the movie still hadn't happened. I covered the floor of the loo with newspaper and set about trying to put my fingers in my bum to wiggle the bollard that was wedged inside. Had I been a chimpanzee, life would have been easier. I wandered round the kitchen looking for implements that might work better – a corkscrew, for example, but I thought it best not to.

Finally, after wiggling whatever it was while squatting, the cricket on in the background, I finally gave in, sat on the loo and made some awful noises. I can't imagine the pain of birth but, with all respect to womankind, my internal cricket ball finally exited and I feared that most of my anus had gone with it.

The body is made of sterner stuff, though, and for the next 10 minutes I basically expelled what looked like a bag of lemons. They were *Star Trek* lemons really: 'Lemons, Jim, but not as we know them.'

Three days later, I drove a car to the garage for maintenance. I caught the train home – Watford Junction to Euston. In my diary is recorded: 'Croissant and latte.' I ordered the croissant at the station and dipped it in my latte so it was soggy. Victory starts with one small step.

Three days after that, I managed noodles and a salad. It took three hours to eat, but I bloody well did it. As I finished, Mick Jagger walked past the window of the café on the King's Road. I'm nearly as skinny as you, I grinned to myself.

Next day, I ate steak and vegetables. On 15 March I ate a full meal and could actually taste some of it.

On the other hand, I looked like a semi-starved member of the Village People. Goodbye moustache. My immune system was still flat on the floor; my T cells had left the building. The rest of my blood was remarkably good.

Maiden played the album to the label – Warner – on 2 April, and I was there, to prove that I was alive and kicking. I went for a break to Lanzarote for 10 days. On 10 April I could stand it no longer and I tried to sing in the shower. It was awful. There was no vocal control; it just sounded like a cow bellowing. I tried not to panic. I was only a month out of treatment. Jan, my ENT doctor, said, 'Don't even think about singing till November.' Maybe not November, I thought – but at least the end of September.

There is an epidemic of head and neck cancers caused by HPV. The cervical cancer risk is well known and Pap screening is highly effective, but there is no equivalent test for oral cancer.

Cases of HPV oral cancer will rise by 80 to 100 per cent, and will overtake cervical cancer in the near future. It is an epidemic that is largely ignored by the press, who often prefer to pillory its victims with shame and innuendo in a way people would find outrageous were it to be inflicted on women, victims of exactly the same cancer.

Anyone from taxi drivers and musicians to pilots, diplomats, doctors and engineers – basically any male who has not lived inside a plastic bag – can be struck by this disease. There is a need for research, education and early detection. This is a highly curable cancer.

The following week, I went to speak at a dinner for Airbus lawyers. I sat next to a charming Canadian father of three in his early forties. His first question: 'How's your saliva?'

There was a look in his eye. 'You too?'

I had been seeing Dr Sibtain every two weeks post-treatment, and he was delighted by my bouncing back. When I was first diagnosed I had run up four flights of stairs rather than take the lift. I took great delight in doing it again one month after treatment. It was worth it to see the grin on his face.

He warned me that the scan to access my results could not take place for around three months.

'The radiation will still be active,' he said, 'so I might just end up with loads of red blobs.'

On 13 May I went in for the scan. Two days later, I had the most nervous day of my life.

I was clear. 'Total clinical response'. I felt dizzy with shock. I would live, I read through the report. There was a bit towards the end that I did not quite understand: 'What's this about an anatomical anomaly?'

Amen started to chuckle. 'It means ... that you used to be a fish.'

Slowly, the world came back to life in all its glory, or otherwise.

I had my airline medical reinstated after a stiff examination. The senior doctor commented, 'I can't find anything wrong with him.' (Apart from gills and a tail, of course.)

The hoops to get back in the left seat appeared: dangerous goods, security, technical refresher training, fire and smoke training, first aid and, finally, back in the simulator for a six-monthly check.

I had been flying the Fokker for the sheer joy of it. On 10 July I was back flying an airliner from Cardiff to Milan Malpensa. It was a 'proving flight' for the Maltese authorities. I was back in business.

Triplane display flying was sadly out of the question. I had to renew my display licence and practise with the team, and it was already the middle of the display season.

The US Federal Aviation Administration sent me a very nice letter asking me for my medical certificate back. Unlike the UK, which merely suspended it, the FAA took it away as soon as I notified them about the cancer treatment.

The Maiden PR machine was in full swing. I flew to the jungles of Mexico to do a photoshoot. I had a six-pack courtesy of radiation; I don't recommend it as a weight-loss programme. I reprised the 'hooligan in a loincloth with a stick' shot from the Ross Halfin Bahamas shoot years earlier, and some of the photos looked amazing.

I was chartered by the label for a Bruce Air special, taking a posse of fans and media to Paris. We flew to Guillaume Tell Studio and I talked them through the album. It was great to get behind the wheel in the sky, but also to have my feet on the ground, treading the boards and talking music.

The 747 project was back on. Air Atlanta Icelandic were now negotiating with Iron Maiden management, and we had a couple of other carriers quote for the tour. I went on a press junket to the USA and Canada. The album had been very well received and, of course, everyone wanted to know about the whys and wherefores of my cancer, all contributing to the tumour mill. Some journalists attempted some kind of responsible understanding; others just decided to take a vulgar, cheap shot.

I was flying but I still wasn't singing. Back in my kitchen, I regarded the cutlery drawer and the rattling it made with some suspicion. The house was deserted and I paced around. It was past September, and maybe, just maybe, some sound might emerge from my voice that did not mimic the cutlery drawer.

I tried 'If Eternity Should Fail'. It was originally written for a future solo album, but was decanted into Iron Maiden. It was one of the last things I had sung before I got sick; in fact, I might have been growing the tumour even as I was singing the demo.

I couldn't believe the result. The top notes were there. Actually they seemed to be purer than before. The low mid-range of my voice was unreliable, and certain vowel sounds – 'ee', for example – were quite uncontrolled in pitch. My falsetto was also under less control, although the howling banshee wail was still in evidence.

Over the next few weeks and months I tried to make sense of it all. I put myself in vocal rehab and theorised as to why things had changed around. We were due to start the tour in February, and rehearsals were only three months away. Rod had made up for a lost year by booking a 72-date world tour.

'I love your confidence in me, but what if I sing like a bag of spanners?'

There's no real answer to that, of course. I tried to analyse what I had, and what I had lost – at least temporarily. My theory was that after the tumour had gone, the remaining surface of my tongue had changed shape. Think of a thick head on a pint of Guinness. Leave it alone and the bubbles beneath the surface slowly burst, leaving the head with a bad case of subsidence. My bubbles were a golf-ball sized tumour.

The tongue is instrumental in forming complex vowel sounds, and we spend our childhood learning to speak and training it. Singing adds an extra layer of complexity. Dr Sibtain was correct about my larynx, which was seemingly unaffected. The note generator was intact, but the quality of the end product is heavily influenced by the muscle tone and spaces in the chest, head and neck cavities. I made a plan for rehearsals: I would sing a little then leave a few good days' rest in the build-up to the band practice.

The time from being given the all-clear to starting singing five days a week would be only eight months. Talk about cutting things fine.

I set about doing what I could on the other big project – learning to fly the 747. Only one big problem: we didn't have one anymore. Two months before we were about to go on tour, Air Atlanta Icelandic lost permission to use the plane allocated for us, and kindly sent back our deposit. The Maiden office was in a tailspin. I got on a plane and went to Iceland. Face to face was the only way to find out what was going on.

I met the CEO and the head of commercial. We got on very well and they explained their predicament. The only 747 they could guarantee would have to be flown to the USA to be scrapped two days after the show at Donington.

Air Atlanta Icelandic were in the process of buying two much younger ex-Air France machines, but the deal was not yet sealed. Rather than break a promise, they preferred to cancel the deal. I suggested we use the 'scrapper' only up till Donington. We would pay to ferry it to its grave, where the engines would be kept, as they were in very good shape. The CEO said he would put it to the owner of the aircraft. I left and had a very alcoholic meal with the commercial director, and flew back the next day.

When I landed, there was a text message: 'You have a deal'.

Three days later I got another one: 'Air France deal done. All back to normal'.

Breathe a big sigh of relief and get back to the rest of the planet.

I flew some disabled veterans in simulators for Help for Heroes, and I returned to Sarajevo, where the Bosnians were putting the finishing touches to a very emotional documentary they had been making about the trip I did over 20 years ago. I had missed the twentieth anniversary because of my cancer treatment, but I wanted to help them with some follow-up footage and an interview.

It was hard to recognise the place at times, then suddenly a piece would snap into place and the jigsaw of memories would return.

In order to fly the 747 I had to get a job with Air Atlanta Icelandic as a captain, so I sat at home with my laptop and the manual for the 747. I completed the groundschool course and sat the final exams – all good. The next phase was the simulator.

It was winter of 2015. I had run myself ragged. I caught a cold. Actually, I was delighted. My immune system worked as advertised. The only very strange thing was that my mucus membranes were not yet in fully working order. Having a cold without blowing your nose is quite an odd experience.

How different this Christmas was to the one a year previously. I was blessed to be here and, better than that, I felt *alive*.

Putting on a bit of weight was the name of the game, but I wouldn't be doing it by eating all my favourite puddings. While most of my taste buds were playing ball, the ones that detected sweetness had been severely impaired by the radiation. As the man who ate the Toblerone from the minibar and who loved to pig out on caramel sauce and Crunchie bars, this was, initially, a blow to morale.

After a few months the memory still remained, but the desire to eat sugar had virtually vanished. An unintended consequence was an acute awareness of how awful many of the 'foods' (or rather, products) were that I had chomped my way through in years past.

The realisation that 'flavour' was often just added sugar was a great revelation. I took solace in the fact that vegetables, meat and dairy tasted absolutely 100 per cent.

Beer was a worry. I had designed Trooper with fully operational taste buds. How would it taste, and how would I design future brews with an impaired sense of sweetness?

I took inspiration from the chef who had no sense of smell. There are many other complex flavours and aromas to experiment with in beer, not just sugar. The first test of this was the design of our new beer, Red 'N' Black, an Imperial stout/porter.

Martyn Weeks, the master brewer, and I sat down and painted the taste of the beer with a palette of existing brews. I was, I freely confess, nervous. I realised that I could detect sweetness but just couldn't taste it. Nevertheless, Martyn and I agreed on all aspects of the brew. In fact, I was inspired to take a new look at beer design, and take a more aromatic approach. The subtleties of texture, bitterness and a lingering finish in the note took on ever-greater importance. Thankfully, my old favourite, Fuller's ESB, never failed.

Drinking beer, of course, is something that should be done a long way from aircraft simulators or motor cars.

No sooner had the New Year passed than I found myself turning up to the newly built British Airways training centre on a freezing, windy 2 January.

What a rollercoaster of a year. Looking back further, what a rollercoaster of a life. From the ups and downs of school and university to the longest and fastest theme-park-ride drop ever – being in Iron Maiden.

I have often been asked, 'Would you have changed anything?' The answer is a simple no. A different and better question is, 'Have you made any mistakes?' And the answer to that one is equally easy – loads of them.

Learning to sing and perform is trial by error and fire. Training to fly can be done in a simulator. Learning to be an aviator can only be done with experience, and experience comes with mistakes built into its fabric.

So now I met one of my 747 mentors. He took me off to one side in a corner of the coffee room before my simulator partner showed up.

'How is your saliva after treatment?' he asked.

I couldn't believe it – another 'you too' moment. We spent 20 minutes discussing teeth, jawbones, saliva and his love of fine Scotch whisky and fast motor cars. His treatment was somewhat more brutal than mine because the technology was not so advanced 15 years previously as to be able to spare his parotid glands from extinction.

Here we were, though, and we soon got onto more important things – like a 400-ton flying machine with a fuel capacity of 170,000 kilograms that would soon be under the command of yours truly.

What an impossible dream for a kid from Worksop who failed physics O level and took three goes to get O level maths.

Somewhere my old grandfather Austin is drinking a beer with my godfather Flight Sergeant John Booker, and they are probably adding up the amount of money they spent on plastic aeroplanes between them. Nothing in childhood is ever wasted.

The same childlike thrill came over me when I sat in the 747 simulator for the first time. All checks complete and the first officer briefed, I turned to the instructor with a grin.

'What does this button do?'

Afterword

An autobiography is a strange beast, and an unruly one. Is it a shopping list of events in sequence? Is it a selection of in-jokes that seemed funny at the time? Is it a pointless exercise, especially if you have just finished your fifth iteration and you are only 25? My answer is that I didn't want to be any of the above. I just wanted to tell a good story. I wrote in excess of 160,000 words and there are fewer than 110,000 of them left.

Plenty of funny anecdotes never made the cut, simply because they didn't advance the narrative. Somewhere there is a book of anecdotes, but it's not a coherent tale.

Had I chosen to include airships, wives, divorces, children and entrepreneurial activities this would have been approaching 800 pages long. It would have been the type of book that people use to commit murder, or help change tyres on London buses. One thing is for sure – it would be a very unread Christmas present.

I made a personal executive decision when I started to write. No births, marriages or divorces, of me or anybody else.

There is enough here to be getting on with. Any more would be overkill, and 'overkill', as Winston Churchill observed, serves only to 'make the rubble bounce'.

Acknowledgements

Mary Henry, for translating and transcribing the Brucey Rosetta Stone, above and beyond the call of duty.

Rod Smallwood for leaving me to it, and Andy Taylor, for warding off the evil eye.

Dave Shack for leading the team, Ed Stewart-Lockhart, Sarah Philp, Helen Curl and Jake Gould for fighting the battles.

To all at HarperCollins, whoever you may be, and most notably Jack Fogg, my editor and lighthouse keeper.

Dave Daniel at CSA Agency and everybody else, you know who you are.

Trains, planes and pubs where I scribbled, and hotel pillows where I laid my head post-scriptum.

Picture Credits

All photographs are courtesy of the author, with the following exceptions:

© Associated Press/Enric Marti p13 (top); © Dimo Safari p14 (top); © Guido Karp p12 (top); © Hans-Martin Issler p12 (bottom); © Iron Maiden 1993 p12 (middle); © Iron Maiden 2003 p14 (middle, bottom); © Iron Maiden 2014 p15 (middle); © John McMurtrie pp 8 (middle left), 10 (bottom), 15 (top), 16 (bottom right); © Maiden Brews 2013 p15 (bottom); © Phil E. Neumann p3 (top, middle, bottom); © Rob Grain p4; © Ross Halfin pp 5 (top, bottom), 6 (top left, top right, bottom), 7, 8 (top middle, bottom left, bottom right), 9 (top, bottom), 10 (top), 11 (top, bottom), 16 (bottom left); © Simon Fowler p8 (top right); © Tony Mottram p8 (top left)

While every effort has been made to trace the owners of copyright material reproduced herein and secure permissions, the publishers would like to apologise for any omissions and will be pleased to incorporate missing acknowledgements in any future edition of this book.